Science Fiction, Children's Literature, and Popular Culture

**Recent Titles in Contributions to the
Study of Science Fiction and Fantasy**

Science Fiction, Children's Literature, and Popular Culture

Coming of Age in Fantasyland

Gary Westfahl

Contributions to the Study of Science Fiction and Fantasy, Number 88
Donald Palumbo, *Series Adviser*

GREENWOOD PRESS
Westport, Connecticut • London

Library of Congress Cataloging-in-Publication Data

Westfahl, Gary.
   Science fiction, children's literature, and popular culture : coming of age in fantasyland
/ Gary Westfahl.
      p. cm.—(Contributions to the study of science fiction and fantasy, ISSN 0193–6875 ;
   no. 88)
   Includes bibliographical references and index.
   ISBN 0–313–30847–0 (alk. paper)
      1. Science fiction, American—History and criticism.   2. Fantasy fiction,
American—History and criticism.   3. Children's stories, American—History and criticism.
4. Popular culture—United States—History—20th century.   5. Children—United
States—Books and reading—History—20th century.   I. Title.   II. Series.
PS374.S35W44   2000
813′.08776099282—dc21   99–045568

British Library Cataloguing in Publication Data is available.

Library of Congress Catalog Card Number: 99–045568
ISBN: 0–313–30847–0
ISSN: 0193–6875

First published in 2000

Greenwood Press, 88 Post Road West, Westport, CT 06881
An imprint of Greenwood Publishing Group, Inc.
www.greenwood.com

Printed in the United States of America

The paper used in this book complies with the
Permanent Paper Standard issued by the National
Information Standards Organization (Z39.48–1984).

10 9 8 7 6 5 4 3 2

To my late mother,
Thelma Elder Westfahl,
who gave me Charlie,
Superman, the Hardy Boys,
and other things

Contents

viiiContents

Acknowledgments

One chapter of this book has been previously published: a short, early version of "Mystery of the Amateur Detectives" appeared in the last issue of the British magazine *Million: The Magazine about Popular Fiction*. I thank its editor David Pringle for encouraging me to write on that subject and for publishing the results. Another chapter of this book, "In Defense of Stone Tablets," originated as my contribution to a panel discussion on "Beyond Cyberpunk: Science, Science Fiction, and Information Technology in the 1990s," which took place at the 16th Annual Western Humanities Conference in Riverside, California, in October, 1997; I thank conference coordinator Joseph D. Childers and moderator George Slusser for the opportunity to participate in the panel. This piece and "Giving Horatio Alger Goosebumps" were read by Andrew Sawyer, whom I thank for his helpful comments. Other people who have read, responded to, or inspired revisions in chapters of this volume include Stephen P. Brown, Susan A. George, Elyce Rae Helford, Patrick Parrinder, and George Slusser. Also of great assistance in completing this volume were my sister, Brenda Bright, who has been continually helpful in my research into the Hardy Boys, and the staff of the Interlibrary Loan Department of the Tomás Rivera Library, University of California at Riverside, who provided with amazing speed all the materials I needed to complete the chapters on the Charlie books and *This Island Earth*.

In addition, I feel continually inspired and sustained in my work by many of my other friends and colleagues, even if they are not involved with particular projects. A partial list of these people, along with some already named, who have been recently important to my career includes Gregory Benford, Michael Cassutt, John Clute, Arthur B. Evans, John Grant, Donald M. Hassler, Howard V. Hendrix, Veronica Hollinger, Edward James, Farah Mendelsohn, Kathleen Church Plummer, and Pamela D. Scoville.

I acknowledge with gratitude the work of Donald A. Palumbo, George F. Butler, Elizabeth Meagher, and the other associates and employees of Greenwood Press who helped to get this book into print. Finally, I thank my two employers,

Acknowledgments

Sarah Wall, Interim Director of the Learning Center of the University of California at Riverside, and David Werner of the University of LaVerne; my other supportive colleagues at those two institutions; Maureen Zika, an always-helpful family friend; and, as always, my wife, Lynne, and children, Allison and Jeremy, who are at this moment being ignored (on Mother's Day, no less!) while I rush to complete this final section of the manuscript—such, they have learned, is sometimes the life of a busy scholar's family.

Introduction

If I were in the mood to create a long, polemical introduction, the arguments embedded in this volume could no doubt be presented in a sufficiently contentious and controversial manner. For I believe that there is a strong and inevitable relationship among the three categories of expression in my title; that science fiction naturally seeks to appeal, and succeeds in appealing, to children and the general public; and that the resulting interactions have been beneficial to all concerned.

First, science fiction has been continually invigorated and inspired by its relationship with youthful readers—the audience that the genre has always enjoyed—and science fiction has more recently been strengthened and empowered by its relationship with the masses—the audience that the genre had to work harder to attract, or perhaps an audience that had to evolve in order to appreciate the genre. Of course, there have also been ongoing struggles to pull science fiction away from its young readers, to make the genre more mature, and to pull science fiction away from its general readers, to make the genre more a literature for an elite class, whether it is a scientific elite or a literary elite; and these efforts have proved beneficial as well, both in the noteworthy works they have engendered and in the stimulating tension they have generated.

Children's literature and popular culture have also benefitted from their connections to science fiction, for the genre can effectively serve as both a refreshing new conduit for ancient myths and time-honored truths and a device to challenge old beliefs and construct new paradigms. While one cannot be entirely pleased by the profusion of films, television programs, juvenile series books, computer games, music videos, and merchandise that draw upon the conventions and imagery of science fiction, I would argue that today's children's literature and popular culture have generally become livelier, more variegated, and more imaginative due to the successful invasions of science fiction and fantasy.

A further reason to study these three fields together is that they collectively reflect, and influence, the process of coming of age in our contemporary technological civilization. As others have noted, even science fiction stories written for adults often feature children as characters or focus on adolescents striving to achieve adult stature; and children or childlike characters are of course endemic in children's literature and popular culture as well. All these forms further demand an unintentional or deliberate aura of immaturity, of incompleteness, while projecting no pretenses of sophistication; for this reason, these are stories that characteristically appeal to young readers, whether they are marketed as such or not, and stories that can have both an immediate and lasting impact on those readers. As science fiction and fantasy increasingly permeate the entertainment of children, adolescents, and young adults, members of contemporary society are effectively growing up in a fantasyland. Thus, we must closely analyze examples of those popular forms of entertainment, no matter how inconsequential or artless they may appear, in order to discover what we are learning from these stories, and what sorts of adults we are becoming as a result.

To continue and intensify such arguments, however, might convey the impression that this is a polemical book; yet this is actually the least polemical book I have ever published. None of the works discussed herein was chosen to illustrate any thesis; in fact, two of them were chosen in part so that I could rescue them from the reductionist theses of other critics. Rather, this book considers only the works that were important to me as a child, or works that became important to me as an adult experiencing a second childhood while raising my own children. Somehow, without my realizing it, this has become a very personal book. I learned this when I attempted to complete an opening chapter on some popular stories for very young children, the collaborations of Margaret Wise Brown and Clement Hurd; after doing the research and planning the argument, I found on three separate occasions that I was simply unable to finish the piece. The problem, I concluded, was that the Brown/Hurd books, while undeniably interesting and appealing to innumerable children, had not been to my knowledge a part of my own childhood, and I had made no emotional connection to them while reading them to my children. To begin the book, then, I needed to go back to the first story that *I* could remember bonding with as a child, which led me to the adventures of Charlie and to a new opening chapter that was finished quickly and without problems.

This book, then, endeavors to convey the experience of growing up in contemporary culture by examining, in the order they are usually encountered and cherished, representative works of science fiction, children's literature, and/or popular culture: the simple picture books and comic books that appeal to small children; the formulaic adventure stories that appeal to older children; the films and television programs that appeal to children and young adolescents; the music videos and music programming that appeal to older adolescents; and the popular novels that appeal to adults. All works examined met the following criteria: either I enjoyed the work while I was growing up, or I would have enjoyed the work had it been available to me while I was growing up. "In Defense of Stone Tablets: Isaac Asimov Explains Why Science Fiction Is Skeptical about 'New Information Technologies'" may seem out of place as a general argument about science fiction and new trends in narrative forms, but I now prefer to view the chapter as a response to the singular stories of Isaac Asimov which provided its thesis, even if those stories are discussed only briefly. The final chapter, "Partial Derivatives: Popular Misinterpretations of H. G. Wells's *The Time Machine*," is an integrative exercise discussing both Wells's remarkable novel and various responses to it in novels, magazines, comic books, children's fiction, and films, employing one particular vector to traverse all the territory that the book covers in its own selective fashion.

Originally, I planned to present in this volume all of my previously published works touching upon children's literature or popular culture, along with new material; however, wishing to limit the book to a reasonable length, and finding myself with more new material than originally expected, I decided to include only one chapter that has been published before, "Mystery of the Amateur Detectives: The Early Days of the Hardy Boys," which appeared in the last issue of a dying magazine and as such has been seen by very few readers. Still, this does mean that several essays that relate to or augment the contents of this book are not available here. For the convenience of the interested reader, I will list them here, with complete publication data available in the bibliography. For a glimpse of one thread of the polemical introduction that never was, readers may consult "The Genre That Evolved: On Science Fiction as Children's Literature." "Zen and the Art of Mario Maintenance: Cycles of Death and Rebirth in Video Games and Children's Subliterature" examines another form of entertainment popular among the very young—video games—along with sidelong glances at some comic books and juvenile series fiction. "Superladies in Waiting: How the Female Hero Almost Emerges in Science Fiction" first considers science fiction stories and concludes with an extended analysis of the comic book character of Supergirl. Sufficiently conveyed by its title are the contents of an essay I co-authored with Lynne Lundquist, "Coming of Age in Fantasyland: The Self-Parenting Child in Walt Disney Animated Films." My essays addressing science fiction film and television include "The Dark Side of the Moon: Robert A. Heinlein's *Project Moonbase*," analyzing another science fiction film of the 1950s; "Extracts from *The Biographical Encyclopedia of Science Fiction Film*," consisting of fourteen brief essays from a proposed reference book on important actors, writers, directors, producers, and special effects artists (now available in revised and expanded form as part of the website of the science fiction magazine *Interzone*); "The True Frontier: Confronting and Avoiding the Realities of Space in American Science Fiction Films," surveying space films of the last half century; and two essays about *Star Trek*, "Where No Market Has Gone Before: 'The Science-Fiction Industry' and the *Star Trek* Industry" and "Janeways and Thaneways: The Better Half, and Worse Half, of Science-Fiction Television." Finally, "Point and Cringe: A Non-Innovative, Non-Interactive Column" considers other issues raised by the new forms of interactive fiction.

If the hurried explanation and justification of the chapters that follow seems insufficiently grounded in critical theory and lacking in references to the works of recognized authorities, that reflects my growing suspicions that at the heart of literary criticism as a productive activity is the interaction of an individual reader and an individual text, and that elaborate theoretical constructs erected to facilitate that interaction, while sometimes helpful, can also be irrelevant or even harmful to the process. Here, I have elected to focus my energies almost exclusively on analyzing and learning more about the representative works I have chosen; and, having found the experience to be enjoyable and enlightening, I hope that readers of this volume will feel the same way.

1

How Charlie Made Children
Hate Him: Fantasy and Reality
in Stories for Small Children

It is a matter of record in the Westfahl family that when I was very young, my very favorite story was "How Charlie Made Topsy Love Him," by Helen Hill and Violet Maxwell, featured in my cherished *Better Homes and Gardens Story Book*. I never forgot its simple narrative: a little boy named Charlie, who keeps picking up and holding his kitten, Topsy, despite its evident displeasure, learns to treat Topsy nicely after a giant girl picks him up and manhandles *him* for a while. As an adult years later, browsing through a used book store, I was happy to stumble upon a copy of a small book, *Charlie and His Kitten Topsy*, copyrighted 1922, which included my childhood favorite as the first of seven Charlie stories; and more recently, when I decided that Charlie might be an ideal focus for an exploration of the literature of small children, my research led to the discovery that this was only the first of five Charlie books, all published in the 1920s.

Since *Charlie and His Kitten Topsy* had spawned four sequels and remained in the marketplace for at least three decades—the *Better Homes and Gardens Story Book* including its first story was copyrighted 1950, and the used copy of *Charlie and His Kitten Topsy* I purchased was the twenty-first printing in 1952—one would expect to find some critical attention paid to the Charlie books. However, my searches through standard bibliographies, reference books, and the Internet turned up absolutely nothing at all except the titles of the five Charlie books, stored in the Library of Congress. The only commentaries I could locate were a few quotations in *Book Review Digest* about the last two books suggesting that the Charlie books were in fact considered a popular and successful series in their day. So, while I waited for my university's Interlibrary Loan Department to deliver copies of the other four books, I had two mysteries to ponder: why the original Charlie story had been so appealing to me, and why this once-popular series had so utterly vanished from sight.

Part of the answer to the first question, no doubt, was simply that I enjoyed reading about a small boy who owned a kitten, because I had always wanted a cat but could not have one because we were living in an apartment. However, given my lifelong interest in science fiction, one would like to suppose that I found the story's fantastic elements especially appealing. Charlie lived in a magical world where he could simply go for a walk and encounter a gigantic girl who would hold him like a doll and unceremoniously dump him in her pocket. Only a pale shadow of Jonathan Swift's *Gulliver's Travels* to an adult critic, this scenario was undoubtedly more impressive to the three-year-old boy who first heard the story in early 1955.

In two of the other stories in *Charlie and His Kitten Topsy* that I first read as an adult, the focus is unexpectedly on Topsy. In "Why Topsy Decided to Be a Kitten After All," Topsy is tired of being washed by his mother Jane and runs away to briefly join families of rabbits, squirrels, and beavers before deciding, after learning about their lives, that he would rather be a kitten after all; and in "How Topsy Climbed a Tree," Topsy climbs up a tall tree in defiance of his mother's orders, finds he is too frightened to climb down, and must be retrieved by the fire department. While following the convention of animals who think like, and in the former story talk like, human beings, these stories otherwise lack fantasy elements and come across as rather lackluster efforts. (Even in 1922, the story of a frightened cat in a tree rescued by firemen must have been a cliché.)

The other four stories, however, perfectly mirror the first story in their structure and contents: Charlie is being disobedient in some way, fantasy enters the picture to plague Charlie with a magical amplification or exaggeration of the problem, and a chastened Charlie returns to reality resolved to be better behaved in the future. In "How Charlie Became a Little Fish," Charlie keeps lingering in his bath and splashing everything, so Auntie one day wishes that he could be a fish instead of a boy; instantly transformed, Charlie the fish is washed down the drain into a river and caught by a little boy who sells him to Charlie's Mother. She puts the fish she admired in a fishbowl, which is where Charlie remains until Auntie wishes that Charlie could return; at that moment, he turns back into a little boy and never causes trouble at bathtime again. In "How Charlie Took Root," Charlie always lags behind Mother and Auntie during walks in the park and eventually finds his feet rooted to the ground; since a policeman does not allow Mother and Auntie to dig him up because digging in the park is against the law, Charlie must stay in the park, with Mother and Auntie bringing him breakfast every day, until Topsy digs up his feet and he runs home, determined to never lag behind again. In "How the Wind Changed," Charlie is always very grouchy in the morning, and one day, when the wind changes, he finds that his face is frozen in a perpetual scowl, making everyone think he is unhappy even when he is enjoying something. The next day, the wind changes again, Charlie can smile again, and he resolves to be more cheerful in the morning. In "How Charlie Grew Littler Instead of Bigger," Charlie keeps refusing to go to sleep, staying awake and demanding glass after glass of water, even though Auntie tells him that unless he goes to sleep, he will begin to grow smaller instead of bigger. The next day, Charlie actually starts to shrink; his clothes don't fit, and Mother must put him in a baby dress and walk him in a baby carriage. After a good night's sleep, Charlie starts growing bigger again and from then on always goes to sleep promptly.

To a modern reader, accustomed to children's literature that incorporates fantasy elements in generally positive ways, it is striking to observe that fantasy, in the world of Charlie, functions solely as a way to bludgeon Charlie into behaving properly when the admonishments of the real people in his life prove ineffectual. Only one story ventures to explain these events: in "How Charlie Became a Little Fish," after Auntie says, "I wish you were a little fish instead of a little boy, and then you could live in the water *always*," the narrator continues, "The Auntie's fairy godmother must have been listening—for her wish *came true*" (27; authors' italics here and in all subsequent quotations); and when Charlie turns back into a boy, this magical being is again cited as the cause (33). Yet it is surely a new, and churlish, sort of fairy godmother that enters the picture not to bestow wonderful gifts but to help adults punish children. Also, the punishments consistently appear disproportionate to the crimes: to be turned into a fish because you were playfully uncooperative in the bath? To be rooted to the ground for days because you lagged behind your parents in the park? To be shrunk to the size of a baby because you didn't go to bed promptly? Even in an era that approved of strict discipline for small children, many may have regarded the forms of discipline implemented in these stories as rather excessive.

However, children take what they want from stories, not necessarily what is given to them, and no matter how punitive and narrow-minded the magic of Charlie's world appeared to be, there was still something very appealing about it. Charlie's life was certainly more variegated and interesting than mundane reality, as he learned firsthand exactly what it felt like to be a doll, a fish, and a tree. Further, even though these experiences occurred as punishments, there remained a positive aura about them: the little girl who picked up Charlie adored her lifelike little doll, Mother and Auntie continued to care for Charlie even after he was rooted to the ground, and Topsy still recognized and loved Charlie even after he became a fish. Also, the way the stories were told, young and old readers understood that Charlie is never in any real danger, and that his encounters with the fantastic would be temporary; this made the stories delightful rather than frightening. Children could ignore the oppressive morals and vicariously enjoy Charlie's magical adventures.

While none of the other stories in *Charlie and His Kitten Topsy* quite matched the appeal of "How Charlie Made Topsy Love Him," it seemed that Helen Hill and Violet Maxwell had hit upon an interesting formula for children's stories, and I anticipated that the other Charlie books would feature similar stories about a recalcitrant Charlie being educated by means of magical intervention. However, reading the second book in the series, *Charlie and His Puppy Bingo*, I made an unsettling discovery: Charlie had turned five years old, and simultaneously all the magic had gone out of his life.

In the first story, "Bingo Comes to Live with Charlie," the cat Jane, sad because her kitten, Topsy, has grown so big, somehow finds and brings home a little puppy, which the family adopts and names Bingo—and that is as unrealistic as the book gets. In the subsequent stories, Charlie goes driving in his toy automobile and a friendly man teaches him the traffic laws; climbing up a kitchen cabinet, Bingo knocks over a bag of flour and makes himself all white; while going with his family in a train to vacation in the country, Charlie is invited to ride in the engine and learns how a train works; on the farm, Bingo is frightened by a rooster; Charlie accompanies the rural stage driver while he delivers the mail; Charlie builds a dam to make a pool where he can sail his toy boat; back in the city, Charlie and Daddy borrow some bricks from the construction workers building a house nearby so they can build their own little house in Charlie's backyard; a rambunctious Bingo gets lost, and after some boys find him and return him to Charlie, he learns to always come when he is called; and during a rainy day, Charlie's Auntie shows him how to build paper houses and make little cities to drive his toy trains through.

The next three books in the series carry on in similar fashion. In *Charlie and His Coast Guards*, Charlie and his family spend the summer on the Maine coast, where he has several interesting and enlightening encounters with some retired sailors, fishermen, and members of the local Coast Guard. In *Charlie and His Surprise House*, while Charlie's Mother is away on vacation, Charlie's Daddy buys a ramshackle house in the country and fixes it up as a surprise for Mother, with help from Charlie, while various local adults, including some gypsies, an Italian truck farmer named Tony Mamola, and a friendly Indian, Mr. Akaiyan, provide Charlie with additional instruction. In *Charlie and His Friends*, Charlie and three children who live near the surprise house have some more educational adventures in their school and with Mamola, Akaiyan, and a storekeeper and former cowboy named Mr. Gummidge. The only magical transformation mentioned is in *Charlie and His Surprise House*, when Akaiyan tells Charlie an Indian legend about a warrior who, dying from a rattlesnake bite, wishes that the Great Spirit could provide something to help his people combat rattlesnakes; in response, the Great Spirit changes the man into an ash tree that will provide Indians with useful wood to make bows and arrows to kill rattlesnakes and to build barricades to keep them away. After hearing this story, Charlie oddly fails to mention the time that he himself was rooted to the ground. Indeed, while the later books do sometimes refer back to events in previous volumes, none of Charlie's fantastic experiences are ever mentioned; it is as if, in his new, realistic world, those events never happened at all.

What replaces magic in Charlie's world, and what he professes to find perfectly enchanting in its own way, is knowledge of, and access to, the adult world. His developing fondness for reality is communicated in *Charlie and His Coast Guards* by his reaction to Captain Zeph's stories about sailing around the world: "He used to bring home much more splendid cargoes than he had taken over—silk and ivory and ginger and spices and wonderful carpets and rugs—beautiful things that one reads of in fairy tales. But this was all true" (20-21). This is the typical pattern of his new adventures: Charlie first has an encounter with his father or another adult male who is unfailingly kind, attentive, and respectful to Charlie. In response to the situation at hand, the adult male then conveys information, or demonstrates a skill, that usually is only the province of adults. After Charlie diligently masters the knowledge or skill that has been presented to him, the adult male or another adult male, by means of some statement or gesture, effectively bestows upon him the status of an honorary adult. His first experience of this sort occurred in "Charlie Learns the Traffic Laws," the second story of *Charlie and His Puppy Bingo*. Because Charlie carelessly zigzags across the sidewalk while driving his toy automobile, he runs into an "old gentleman" (17). Upon hearing that Charlie "does not know the traffic laws," the man, Mr. Armstrong, says to Charlie, "I would be very glad to take you for a drive this afternoon and teach you every traffic law there is" (18). After this enlightening experience, Charlie carefully obeys all the laws on his little drives, which leads the policeman in the park to tell him, "As soon as you are sixteen years old, you can come to me, and I will see that you get a license to drive a *real* automobile. If everybody obeyed the traffic laws as well as you do, there would never be any accidents at all" (27).

So it continues: Later on in *Charlie and His Puppy Bingo*, Charlie learns how to be a railroad engineer, how to deliver mail, how to build dams, and how to build little houses. In *Charlie and His Coast Guards*, Charlie learns how buoys and signal flags are used by sailors to communicate and how to tie knots like a real sailor; he puts little buoys up to keep travelers on a nearby creek safe just like Coast Guard buoys protect ocean travelers, learns to row his own little boat, and keeps the coast near his vacation home neat and clean as part of his duties as a honorary member of the Coast Guards. In *Charlie and His Surprise House*, Charlie's Daddy trains him in all aspects of home repair and improvement while Akaiyan teaches Charlie various authentic Indian skills; and in *Charlie and His Friends*, Charlie gets more instructions about Indian furniture and agriculture from Akaiyan, learns how to put out a brush fire, and applies his lessons from school when he gets to run Gummidge's store all by himself. Overall, the dreary utilitarianism of these books is well conveyed by this comment on *Charlie and His Surprise House* from the *Saturday Review of Literature*: "This book will answer many questions, and will show that work can be made as easy and delightful as play" (cited in *Book Review Digest* 1927).

Contrasting the four later books, which are clearly not fantasies, with *Charlie and His Kitten Topsy*, which is clearly a fantasy, one observes the following dichotomies which, to many contemporary readers, will be disheartening.

Fantasy is feminizing, reality is masculinizing. In the first book, the governing adults in Charlie's life are Mother and Auntie: they are always around him, they take him to the park every day, and they bathe him every night. In contrast, Charlie's Daddy only appears occasionally, and his Uncle Jim only makes one brief visit. The controlling spirit behind Charlie's fantasy adventures is, apparently, Auntie's fairy godmother. It is further worth noting that Charlie is picked up by a giant girl, who coos over him like a doll, shows him to her mother, and plans to take him to her friend Sophia, thoroughly immersing him in a woman's world. Later, when he shrinks to the size of a baby, the only piece of clothing his Mother can find at the store that fits him is a baby *dress*, which he is then obliged to wear—surely, the ultimate act of emasculation.

In contrast, once fantasy is removed from Charlie's life, his Mother and Auntie retreat to the background—in *Charlie and His Surprise House*, the Mother is entirely removed from the scene—and his Daddy becomes the major adult in Charlie's life, teaching him various skills and frequently taking time off work to spend more time with his son. When his father is not around, Charlie is instructed by, or accompanied by, other male mentors: Mr. Armstrong, the railroad engineer, the mail carrier, and the construction workers in *Charlie and His Puppy Bingo*; the Captain of the steamer, former sailors Captain Zeph and Mr. Chick, an unnamed fisherman, an unnamed boat owner, and current members of the Coast Guard in *Charlie and His Coast Guards*; Mr. Pidgely, his son Jim, Akaiyan, and Mamola in *Charlie and His Surprise House*; and Akaiyan, Mamola, and Gummidge in *Charlie and His Friends*. Although Charlie keeps his cats from *Charlie and His Kitten Topsy*—pets often associated with girls—he gains a dog for his later adventures—the pet associated more with boys. In *Charlie and His Coast Guards*, the sleeping arrangements for the boat trip to Maine are that Charlie sleeps in a room with his Daddy, while Charlie's Mother and Auntie stay in the other room; Charlie stays with the men, and the women are exiled. While one of the three friends in *Charlie and His Friends* is a girl, she is left behind on the book's major adventure, an overnight camping trip with Akaiyan, which allows the boys to engage in some manly skinny-dipping. As additional signifiers of his masculinity, Charlie gets a "C" on his jersey to make it his uniform as an honorary member of the Coast Guards in *Charlie and His Coast Guards*, and he gets to wear the costume of a real Indian warrior in *Charlie and His Surprise House* and *Charlie and His Friends*.

Fantasy is enervating, reality is empowering. In *Charlie and His Kitten Topsy*, the fantasy experiences all tend to make Charlie helpless in some way, as he becomes a doll for a giant girl, a little fish in a fishbowl, a boy rooted to the ground unable to move, a boy who cannot change his facial expression, and finally, and literally, a little baby. Further, the intent of all these transformations is to teach Charlie to be a well-behaved little boy; he is being trained to always listen to his parents and to do everything he is told.

When Charlie begins to learn the ways of the world, in contrast, he becomes more powerful; as he gains the knowledge and skills of the adults, he earns their respect and enjoys greater privileges. He can build his own house, anchor his own little buoys, paint his room a color of his own choice, construct his own wigwam, run a store all by himself, and plant and raise his own crops. The geographical scope of his adventures expands: while Charlie was restricted to his city home and its immediate surroundings in the fantasy *Charlie and His Kitten Topsy*, the other, realistic books take Charlie to a farm, the coast of Maine, and a house in the country, and Charlie is sometimes allowed to travel on short adventures all by himself—on foot, in his toy automobile, or in his little boat. Thus, while fantasy mastered Charlie, reality enables Charlie to become the master of his own environment.

Fantasy is juvenilizing, reality is maturating. Even more so than his parents, fantasy treats Charlie like a child; it puts him into the hands of a giant girl and makes him into a tiny little fish. In "How Charlie Grew Littler Instead of Bigger," the principle is enacted most clearly, as disobedience makes Charlie littler, and even turns him into a baby. Implicitly, then, obedience will allow Charlie to keep growing and become bigger.

The four later books show this process occurring: at the beginning of *Charlie and His Puppy Bingo*, Charlie has his fifth birthday, in *Charlie and His Coast Guards* he is six years old and learning to read, and by the time of *Charlie and His Friends* he is identified as seven years old and already finishing his first year of school. Charlie is also not only gaining the acceptance and admiration of adults, but increasingly thinking in terms of his coming adulthood: after riding with the railroad engineer and fireman in *Charlie and His Puppy Bingo*, he announces that he wants to become a fireman when he grows up, and in *Charlie and His Coast Guards*, he is determined to first become a sea captain and then to join the Coast Guards as soon as he reaches the age of eighteen. In short, having abandoned fantasy, Charlie starts growing up, is provisionally admitted into various adult worlds, and begins thinking seriously about the day when he will become an adult.

As another indication of the maturing effects of reality, the later books are significantly longer, and represent more advanced reading, than *Charlie and His Kitten Topsy*, indicating that the later books are designed for older readers. This is eventually announced in an untitled and unattributed afterword at the end of *Charlie and His Friends*: "Little boys and girls who have liked to have this read aloud to them, or are just learning to read themselves, will enjoy the stories in 'Charlie and His Kitten Topsy,' another Little Library Book. Then for older boys and girls, over six, there are more Charlie stories by Miss Hill and Miss Maxwell: 'Charlie and His Puppy Bingo,' 'Charlie and the Coastguards' [*sic*], 'Charlie and the Surprise House,' all published by the Macmillan Company" (169). The comment also provides one possible explanation for the authors' decision to wrest Charlie away from fantasy and direct him toward reality: Hill and Maxwell were advised, or decided, to orient the later books in the Charlie series toward older children, requiring that the childish imaginativeness of *Charlie and His Kitten Topsy* be abandoned in favor of practical education. When children reach the age of six, after all, they start to go to school.

Of course, few commentators will be surprised to see, in stories from the 1920s, the traits of femininity, weakness, and juvenility linked together in contrast to the linked traits of masculinity, strength, and maturity, though it is interesting that the dichotomy is here attributed to, and most prominently marked by, the presence or absence of fantasy. Still, there is one overriding similarity between all the Charlie books that might be a matter of additional concern: both Charlie's world of fantasy, and Charlie's world of reality, are entirely *adult* worlds.

In the first three books of the series, Charlie appears to spend almost no time with other children; he plays by himself, with family members, or with other adults. Other children are glimpsed only rarely: in *Charlie and His Kitten Topsy*, there are only the giant girl and her unseen friend Sophia, and the boys who rescue the fish Charlie from the river and sell it to his Mother. In *Charlie and His Puppy Bingo*, there are only the neighborhood boy who finds the lost Bingo and the other boys who return him to Charlie. And in *Charlie and His Coast Guards*, there are absolutely no children at all. Instead, up to this point in the series, it is the adults who are the dominating figures: in the first book, Charlie's parents watch over Charlie while a fairy godmother enforces their wishes; and in the next two books, Charlie's parents and other adults teach Charlie and praise him for learning his lessons so well. Brutalized by the adult world of fantasy, nurtured by the adult world of reality, Charlie seems in either case alienated from the world of children, as he is entirely intent upon obeying, emulating, and pleasing adults. Even in an era when children's admiration for parents and adults was considered normal (unlike today, when such attitudes are often regarded as strange), it is easy to see how Charlie might have been despised by other children, both those in his neighborhood and those obliged to read about his exploits. After all, the boys in *Charlie and His Puppy Bingo* recognize Bingo as Charlie's puppy and know where to return it; they all know who Charlie is; but there is no indication that they ever play with him, or want to play with him. Indeed, what child, then or now, would really want to play with a boy who keeps boasting about how he learned all the traffic laws, how he learned to build a real house, how he became an honorary member of the Coast Guards, and so on?

Although Charlie continues to spend most of his time with, and trying to be just like, adults, the final two books in the series do suggest that Charlie's life is moving in a new direction. Mr. Akaiyan, while in many respects simply another adult dispensing lessons, can be viewed as a liberating figure, since the sorts of skills he is teaching—how to build a wigwam, how to start a fire without matches, how to make Indian furniture—are interesting to a little boy but utterly impractical; Charlie is not going to be an Indian when he grows up. In the fourth book, children begin to make appearances again: the teenage carpenter Jim, Mamola's older and younger children, and a little Gypsy girl rescued by Bingo. And when Charlie discovers the 1851 toy box of a boy named Ezra Burril, and hears stories about the long-departed man from an elderly local woman, he makes a spiritual connection with a boy from the past and is able to recognize that adults were once children who spent much of their time playing, and not simply preparing to become adults.

However, it is in the final book of the series, *Charlie and His Friends*, that other children finally and prominently enter Charlie's life, perhaps because readers had noted their incongruous absence in previous books. During a summer at his new house in the country, Charlie makes three friends: a red-haired boy named Dick spending the summer with his aunt, Jo (short for Giovanni) Mamola, and his sister Bianca Mamola. He attends their one-room schoolhouse for three weeks, and he regularly plays with them. And, while an ongoing impulse to achieve adulthood still motivates Charlie in matters such as learning to run a store and growing food in his own Indian garden, one chapter suggests that Charlie is beginning to break free of the adult world.

"Charlie and Dick Seek Adventure" begins: "One day, Dick came over directly after breakfast, and, the moment he arrived, of course he wanted to play Indian and work in the Indian garden" (137). Based on his past experiences, a day of productive Indian agriculture would seem to be just the sort of thing that Charlie would love to do. Instead, surprisingly,

Charlie had a different idea. He said, "The Indian garden is coming on nicely. I pulled up all the weeds last night and I watered all the plants with three watering cans full of water—so *I* don't think that we need to work in the garden to-day. But I tell you what! Let's go forth and explore the unknown territory beyond the stone wall at the top of our garden."

Dick thought that was a good idea, especially when Charlie went on, "It will probably be a very dangerous expedition. We don't know what savage tribes may live up there in the forest, so I have decided that we'll leave Bingo at home, but we'll take Topsy because he is a useful scout." (137-38)

So they proceed: "every now and then they passed huge rocks with caves underneath and they pretended that each cave was the home of a bear or a mountain lion, though they knew from Jim that no such large wild animals lived so near them" (140). They run away from a frightening "extraordinary animal" (143), which they later discover was a porcupine. They pick what they believe to be two wild pumpkins, but they turn out to belong a farmer, who is angry at them until they offer to pick a lot of wild raspberries for him; surprised and gratified that the boys are "conscious of their obligations" (151), the man carves their pumpkins into jack-o'-lanterns, which they bring home so that Charlie's Auntie can place candles in them.

Years of adult training and indoctrination, it turns out, have not entirely dulled Charlie's imagination. Once again, he is leaving his home in search of fantasy adventures with "savage tribes" and "wild animals." Even if his Auntie's fairy godmother is not there to provide real magic, Charlie can still enjoy "pretending" some magic is there. The re-emergence of Topsy, and the temporary exile of Bingo, further suggests a return to the spirit of the first book. And, during this carefree day of playful adventure, Charlie also *disobeys an adult*—albeit unknowingly—for the first time since *Charlie and His Kitten Topsy*, engaging in what is an act of petty theft even if it is promptly forgiven. In this chapter, for the first time since the first book, Charlie seems to be acting like a real little boy, not an adult in training.

After this adventure, Charlie and his friends return to drudgery—harvesting their crops, grinding corn meal, and cooking fish to provide their adult companions with a final "Indian feast." But they also prepare some entertainment for the event, with Bianca as a hungry Indian maiden who is helped by a bean mouse, played by Dick, who provides beans; a squirrel, played by Jo, who provides nuts; and a bear, played by Charlie, who provides honey. This culminating celebration suggests a synthesis of sorts, with Charlie still prepared to labor as a miniature adult but now also able to engage in frivolous, creative play. Further, even if games of make-believe and dressing-up are not entirely equivalent to the unambiguously magical experiences of the very young Charlie, they at least represent a return to the spirit of fantasy, and, since Charlie is now exercising control over what he does, these scenes do represent a degree of liberation from his previously adult-dominated world.

Unfortunately, it is also at this precise point that Charlie ceases to be interesting to his readers. What Charlie has so far given them is access to realms beyond ordinary childhood. In the first book, Charlie encounters fascinating magical happenings; in the later books, Charlie learns adult skills and knowledge which, while less fascinating, still might be appealing to children curious to know how a train engine works or how to build a house. When Charlie simply starts to play the sorts of childish games that all children play, there is no longer any reason to read about him; what is the point of reading about Charlie and his friends pretending to be Indians when you can go outside and pretend to be Indians with your own friends? While still something of a goody two-shoes, Charlie could now be disliked also because he was becoming so ordinary, no longer someone who could open interesting doors to either fantastic or realistic other worlds.

By adding children to Charlie's world, and by allowing him to escape from both vindictively magical adults and invitingly educational adults, then, Hill and Maxwell made their young protagonist not only more normal, but more boring as well; so it is not surprising to find that *Charlie and His Friends* brought the series to a close. Perhaps adult and young readers grew tired of the Charlie books and stopped purchasing them, leading to the publisher's decision to stop producing them; perhaps Hill and Maxwell themselves grew tired of their own character, or felt that they had exhausted all possible directions for his development, and abandoned him to work on other projects. So, while Hill and Maxwell continued to produce children's books in the 1920s and 1930s, they never wrote about Charlie again.

More so than other genres, children's literature is regularly examined in the context of marketing considerations, and from that perspective, the decline and disappearance of the Charlie books can be attributed to two poor decisions by their authors. First, by eliminating the element of fantasy from the Charlie books, they reduced his appeal to future readers who would be more amenable to fantasy. Second, by reducing the element of adult-provided education to focus on interactions with other children, they reduced his appeal to readers of their own era with an interest in learning about the real world.

To be kinder to Hill and Maxwell, however, one could also say that their Charlie books deserve attention because, intentionally or not, they sequentially epitomize the process of a child's socialization. As very young children become aware of the world and their position in it, they initially rebel against the lowly status of childhood. They first seek to escape from the mundane world of childhood into a world of fantasy, by imagining magical transformations of themselves or their environment; then, they seek to escape into the world of adulthood, by learning from and imitating the adults around them. Finally, now reconciled to the status of childhood, they make friends with other children and happily live in a child's world, alternately drawing upon their memories of excursions into fantasy and memories of lessons about reality, sometimes pretending to be explorers in a wilderness filled with wild animals, sometimes pretending to be real, adult sailors in the Coast Guards. From this perspective, the Charlie books represent not a poorly planned series crippled by abrupt changes in direction and finally terminated as a result, but rather a well-conceived, carefully executed, and satisfyingly complete work of literature.

Today, there is no need to argue that developing children need both large doses of fantasy and large doses of reality to mature into stable, well-rounded individuals. Contemporary commentators can readily criticize the children's literature of the past because it so often endeavored to downplay the importance of fantasy, to relegate it exclusively to literature for very small children (the stance of the Charlie books), or in some cases to eliminate it altogether from children's reading material. Yet today's children's literature may be open to criticism because it emphasizes fantasy too much: while works of nonfiction that mirror the earnest didacticism of the later Charlie books can still be found in bookstores, they may go unnoticed amidst masses of Goosebumps books, Animorphs books, and other fantastic adventures. When one factors in the other common experiences of today's children—children's films and television programs, video games, and computer games, the vast majority of which involve science fiction or fantasy—it is easy to conclude that the child of today grows up drenched in fantasy, bombarded with celebrations of magical escape from reality and only infrequently urged to take life seriously and to begin mastering some of the important crafts and lore of adulthood. Since the busy parents of today often have little time for their children, perhaps it is only natural that the literature now written for children often lacks an adult presence or perspective, but it is also lamentable.

Thus, if the Charlie books erred in abandoning fantasy, today's children books may frequently err in abandoning reality. If we accept that the desire for fantasy and the desire for adult reality are both important to children, then, it is possible that a child of the new millennium, surrounded by more than enough stories of giant children and children transformed into animals, just might enjoy the quaint story of a boy whose father takes the day off to build a little house with him in their backyard. To many modern children, neglected by adults and left to spend their time exclusively with children or involved in fantastic adventures, such a story might inspire some envy, or seem like the greatest fantasy of them all.

2

The Three Lives
of Superman—
And Everybody Else

To fully understand the complex character of Superman, one must first realize that *Superman is a person with three separate identities*. He is Kal-El, one of the few survivors of the destroyed civilization of the planet Krypton. He is Superman, an internationally famous super-being who fights crime and rescues people from natural disasters. And he is Clark Kent, a respected journalist in the city of Metropolis.

In the comic book chronicles of Superman, these three identities emerged at various times. In the 1930s and 1940s, Superman was mainly Superman; Clark Kent was an occasional interruption to his heroic adventures; and Kal-El did not exist, since early stories depict Superman as totally unaware of his past until the appearance of kryptonite prompts some investigation and the eventual discovery of his true heritage.

In the 1950s and 1960s, Kal-El came to the forefront. Editor Mort Weisinger, former editor of the science fiction magazine *Thrilling Wonder Stories*, pushed the stories in the direction of science fiction by emphasizing Superman's alien background. During this time, Superman made at least two visits back in time to visit Krypton; in a series of Superboy adventures (since Superman was now depicted as aware of his origins, and actively engaged in fighting evil, while still a teenager), Superboy employed a special machine to bring back vivid memories of his early childhood experiences on Krypton; and, most significantly, a number of other survivors of Krypton started arriving on Earth. Some of these were minor or one-time visitors, including various Kryptonian criminals exiled into space or into the Phantom Zone; Kal-El's robot teacher; a scientist accidentally transformed into a gorilla; and a super-monkey who was a stowaway on Kal-El's rocket to Earth. More prominent Kryptonian companions were Krypto the super-dog, Superboy's pet; Supergirl, Superman's cousin who grew up in a Kryptonian city that survived the explosion of Krypton intact and briefly flourished; and the entire city of Kandor, miniaturized and stored in a bottle by the villainous Brainiac before the destruction of Krypton, then rescued by Superman and kept in his Fortress of Solitude. In this era, then, Superman could temporarily shrink himself and experience life in an actual Kryptonian city, and he could regularly communicate with a close relative—Supergirl—who was a fellow Kryptonian; indeed, she became the only person who regularly addressed him as "Kal."

During this time, Clark Kent was slowly developing as a character in his own right, but he truly achieved this status in the 1970s. When Denny O'Neill and other writers refashioned the Superman series at that time, Clark was finally divested of his uniform-like blue suit, and he now dressed in a more variegated and fashionable manner. He was shifted to a new, more glamorous job as a television news anchor, a visible sign of his growing prominence. New colleagues—irascible boss Morgan Edge and egotistic sportscaster Steve Lombard—made Clark's work experiences more lively and involving. And a new series of stories, "The Private Life of Clark Kent," presented vignettes about Clark Kent solving problems as Clark Kent, without ever stripping down to his Superman suit. Responding to this new substance in his character, Supergirl started calling Superman "cousin Clark," not "Kal," and Lois Lane, previously enamored of Superman, developed an extended crush on Clark Kent. The title of the most recent Superman television series, *Lois and Clark: The New Adventures of Superman*, in a way validates and celebrates this growing emphasis on the Clark Kent character.

As Clark came to the forefront in the 1970s and 1980s, Kal-El receded into the background: all forms of kryptonite were purportedly destroyed (though the element later crept back into some stories), the city of Kandor flew away into space and never returned, Supergirl was killed, and the other visitors from Krypton appeared more and more rarely. (This shift can also be observed in the Christopher Reeve films: while the original *Superman* [1978] featured an extended opening sequence on the planet Krypton, and while the ghostly presences of his parents Jor-El and La-Ra regularly appear to guide Superman in that film and its immediate sequel *Superman II* [1980], the later films *Superman III* [1983] and *Superman IV: The Quest for Peace* [1989] make no references to Superman's Kryptonian past.)

While different stories and different eras pay differing amounts of attention to Superman's three identities, it is important to stress that all three of these identities are *real*. When Jules Feiffer's "Introduction" to *The Great Comic Book Heroes* described Clark Kent as a "put-on" (19), he was speaking only of a handful of early stories. In later decades, Clark definitely becomes a real person: he spends most of his time as Clark Kent, relates to most of his friends and colleagues as Clark Kent, and, in the stories of "The Private Life of Clark Kent," develops a distinct personality as Clark Kent. It is also significant that Clark Kent is the only persona of Superman who has a birth certificate and a legal identity; without his status as Clark Kent, Superman would in effect be an illegal alien.

Kal-El is also *real*: that is the name and the character that Superman was born with, and an identity he can never entirely escape. Superman's diary in the Fortress of Solitude is written in Kryptonian, which remains the language Superman uses to express his innermost feelings. And Superman's most extreme emotional reactions have involved regret over the destruction of Krypton or anger over attacks on surviving representatives of its culture.

Superman, of course, is also *real*, since only in that identity does he unveil the full extent of his abilities, and since that identity is best known to the world. Still, one can argue, this is Superman's *least* important role, at least in his own eyes: his true emotional commitments are to his lost planet Krypton and his friends at the Daily Planet, while the other people he rescues as Superman are usually strangers to him.

It is easy to recognize Superman's three identities as one aspect of his enduring popularity, since he can appeal to three different dreams of childhood: to be revealed as the child of royal parents (Kal-El), to be recognized for amazing successes (Superman), and to be accepted as an ordinary person (Clark Kent). But there is something more striking and innovative in Superman that one does not observe in other characters with two or more identities, and this is the second essential realization about Superman: *having three identities suits him just fine.*

When Superman is required to be Clark Kent, he enjoys being Clark Kent; when he is required to be Superman, he enjoys being Superman; and when he is required to be Kal-El, he enjoys being Kal-El. While working at the *Daily Planet* or his television station, he does not spend his time longing for some emergency to arise so that he can become Superman; while doing heroic deeds as Superman, he does not daydream about talking to Supergirl or visiting Kandor; and while visiting the bottled city, he does not count the days until he can return to his journalist career. Superman embraces, and delights in, all facets of his tripartite identity.

And in this respect, Superman stands in stark contrast to the general attitude of Western culture and literature that human identity should be unitary: A person should always be the same person, regardless of the circumstances she is in. The common phrase "leading a double life" has a strong negative connotation, and characters in literature who maintain two identities are typically depicted as deceitful, psychologically unstable, or filled with inner turmoil. Robert Louis Stevenson's *The Strange Case of Dr. Jekyll and Mr. Hyde* is an obvious example, but many other, less extreme cases could be cited, including Superman's most famous cohort in crime-fighting, the Batman.

Noting Superman's refusal to be bothered by his multiple identities, critics might say that this simply reflects the simple-minded, juvenile nature of comic books, which invariably avoid any explorations of complex personal problems. Yet such critics have hardly been keeping up with comic books, which have markedly matured in recent decades and today are aimed almost exclusively at an adult audience. Chroniclers of the Batman, for example, have effectively recast the character as a tormented, divided figure, almost deranged and destroyed by his vengeful drive to oppose evil, a revisionist view that is evident in Tim Burton's 1989 film *Batman* and in graphic novels like Frank Miller's *The Dark Knight Returns* (1985). However, sporadic attempts to develop similar tensions in the character of Superman have failed miserably; he has suffered, he has died, and he has been reborn, but he still seems essentially the same person. In overt defiance of both ancient attitudes and contemporary comic book trends, Superman remains doggedly cheerful about a situation that conventional wisdom suggests should be driving him crazy.

In this way, I suggest, the comic book adventures of Superman reflect an insight into the modern human condition which has largely escaped other astute observers.

During most of humanity's history, personal identity has necessarily been unitary. By and large, people lived their entire lives in the region or village they were born in, remaining in touch with all those who knew them while they were growing up. The men and the women who needed to work would take over the family farm, or become apprentices to local artisans, and their customers would largely be the same people they had always known. Men would marry women in their village and settle down to a social life that continued to involve familiar people. Travel and migrations might occur in response to changing conditions or desperate need, but people would characteristically move in groups, effectively bringing their societies with them instead of facing the obligation to join new groups. And, when you are always around the same people, you tend to always act the same way. Hence, the feeling developed that this was the proper way to live one's life—as one person, and always as the same person.

Modern people—in Western societies at least—lead quite different lives. Living in an increasingly mobile culture, few people remain in the place they grew up: their families move to another state, they go away to college and stay in that area, or they accept job offers on the opposite side of the country. They thus become separated from their original homes, and their original identities, although by writing letters to relatives and old friends, and by making occasional visits to their home towns, they can sporadically re-connect with their previous existence.

Once settled into their adult lives, most people then develop a bifurcated lifestyle. Their workplaces may be an hour's commute away from their homes, or in other ways completely separated from their home lives; they inevitably build friendships and relationships with colleagues and co-workers who know them only as fellow employees; and by means of office parties and informal gatherings, they maintain an intermittent social life with those people. Then, when they get home to their neighborhoods, they interact with their family members and with an entirely different set of friends—neighbors, people they meet at church or bridge clubs, and parents of their children's friends.

Therefore, a modern American citizen is essentially three separate people: She is the person she grew up as, the person who works at her job, and the person she is at home. Each identity involves totally different people and therefore demands significantly different behaviors.

Not incidentally, this is exactly the situation that Superman represents. Kal-El is the person he was born and grew up as. Clark Kent, working journalist, is his job. And while Superman's altruistic activities constitute another career of sorts, Superman is also his leisure time, the time when he can break away from the daily demands of reporting and exercise his mental and physical abilities to the fullest. Superman has adjusted to this situation without any problems; similarly, modern Americans have adjusted to their own tripartite identities without any problems.

To me, this is the most powerful and most profound message embodied in the character of Superman. I doubt that I found him appealing as a child because he was pandering to my juvenile power fantasies, and I doubt that he taught me very much about respecting Truth, Justice, and the American Way. The fact that he overtly represented such conventional and respectable values was perhaps a necessary disguise for the underlying subversive lesson he was really conveying: namely, that it's okay to be more than one person. You can live with that. You can even enjoy it.

As an army brat who moved four times—once to Germany—during the six years that I most regularly read Superman comic books, I could relate to that. Today, as someone who grew up in several different places and now works forty miles from my house, I can still relate to that. In short, Superman's divided life is the life that most of us are living today, and it is important, even exhilarating, to discover a literary character who validates what traditional attitudes would regard as our perverse lifestyles.

Beyond Superman's veneer of patriotism and his commitment to democratic and altruistic ideals, then, it is his calm and quietly blissful acceptance of his multiple identities that, in my opinion, qualifies Superman as the true all-American hero.

3

Mystery of the Amateur
Detectives: The Early Days
of the Hardy Boys

The first literary ambition that I can recall was to someday become an author of Hardy Boys books. Even as a nine-year-old, I could examine the list of the forty or so Hardy Boys books written by Franklin W. Dixon, some with copyright dates in the 1920s, and deduce that Mr. Dixon was getting to be a pretty old man. Soon, I concluded, he was sure to die or retire, so that there would arise the need for a talented new writer like me to carry on the adventures of the Hardy Boys.

At the time, I would have been greatly disillusioned to learn that "Franklin W. Dixon" was merely a pseudonym employed by various anonymous writers following outlines developed by a man named Edward Stratemeyer (1862-1930) and his successors in a company called the Stratemeyer Syndicate. Even as an adult, Canadian writer Leslie McFarlane experienced a similar shock regarding his favorite boyhood author, "Roy Rockwood." After answering a 1926 advertisement, he was hired to write a Dave Fearless novel from a Stratemeyer outline, to be credited to Roy Rockwood: "Discovery of the truth about Roy Rockwood left me a little stunned. . . . He was just as fictitious as Bomba the Jungle Boy" (13).

After some success with the Dave Fearless books, McFarlane was then sent Stratemeyer's outlines for a new series—the Hardy Boys—and, unlike other Syndicate writers, he later wrote an autobiography describing his experiences, *Ghost of the Hardy Boys*. Armed with this information from the flesh-and-blood author who first assumed the name of Franklin W. Dixon, we can begin to examine the mystery of this unending series—still going strong today with over two hundred volumes published—and its enduring popularity. The first eight books, all by McFarlane, are especially noteworthy, since they can be knowledgeably examined as the products of a stimulating collaboration between a mechanical generator of plot lines and a creative author desperately trying to add some wit and style to the stories.

One issue that must be mentioned first is whether all the claims in McFarlane's autobiography are true. Undoubtedly, he did write many of the early Hardy Boys

adventures, but his book seems to be based entirely on his memory and is sometimes inaccurate: on two occasions he speaks of *The House on the Cliff* when he
clearly means *The Missing Chums*, and he slightly misspells the title of *The Sinister
Sign Post* as *A Sinister Signpost*. There is also a fascinating lacuna in his book: in
listing his books, McFarlane names 19 of the first 26 Hardy Boys books (#1-11;
15-17; 22-26) and says, after finishing #4, that he wrote "sixteen more volumes"
(189). If McFarlane only wrote 19 or 20 of those early books, then who wrote the
other six or seven? Possible explanations are that McFarlane simply forgot about
those other books, that he forgot to mention them, that the Stratemeyer Syndicate
sometimes gave Hardy Boys books to other authors, or that McFarlane occasionally
declined an assignment. In the latter cases, though, one would think that hearing
about another Hardy Boys author or turning down a project would be something
McFarlane would remember and discuss in his autobiography. The issue is worth
examining someday because the seven "unclaimed" volumes include some of the
strangest and most disturbing adventures in the series, such as the Hardy Boys' far-
ranging pirate adventure, *The Twisted Claw*, and their one science fiction horror
story, *The Disappearing Floor*.

On another authorship issue, it does not seem right to attribute these books primarily to Stratemeyer, as is the practice of some librarians. McFarlane says the
outlines "ran for three pages of single-spaced typescript" and quotes the outlines
for the first two of twenty-five chapters of a Dave Fearless book, two series of
sentence fragments each about fifty words long (22). Surely, the person who turns
a 1,300-word outline into a 55,000-word manuscript should be credited as the
principal author.

To justify an intensive look at the Hardy Boys, we can employ the evidence
provided by McFarlane to answer a traditional objection to these books from
librarians and literary scholars—that books in these series are written by "commit-
tees" and lack the inspiration and true creativity of the works of a single author.
Here, we know who the major author was, and we can observe some moments
when he was inspired and creative. There remains another objection: that by
whatever aesthetic standards one establishes, these books are not very well written.
Yet the early Hardy Boys are an exception to that rule as well. True, the prose style
of those books will never be admired in creative writing classes, but McFarlane was
a more careful writer than other Stratemeyer employees, and the embellishments
and incidents he added to the outlines do make his Hardy Boys books superior to
works in other series. McFarlane described his reactions to receiving the first Hardy
Boys outline:

The sensible course would have been to hammer out the thing at breakneck speed, regardless
of style, spelling or grammar, and let the Stratemeyer editors tidy it up. . . . It seemed to me
that the Hardy Boys deserved something better than the slapdash treatment Dave Fearless
had been getting. . . . I opted for Quality. (63-64)

To be sure, one cannot make great claims for the "Quality" of the Hardy Boys
books, and McFarlane's own description of his works acknowledges that they were
written "within the limits of the medium which was in this case mass-produced,

assembly-line fiction for boys" (187). Still, even while working on the assembly line, McFarlane managed to slip some interesting tensions into the formulaic outlines he was obliged to follow.

In the early Hardy Boys books (and I am speaking only of the original versions, not the modernized and homogenized "revisions" that surfaced decades later), one finds Frank and Joe Hardy apparently in the typically confined world of the 1920s teenager. Their mother wants them to become a doctor and a lawyer. Their father, famous detective Fenton Hardy, is more encouraging about their desire to become detectives, but gives them no real work or training that would prepare them for that career. In an early passage in *The Tower Treasure* (#1), Joe complains that their father "laughs at us" when they talk about becoming detectives, and "Tells us to wait until we're through school" (3). The policemen of Bayport see the Hardy Boys as nuisances and troublemakers: At one point, patrolman Con Riley calls the Hardys and their friends "his natural and hereditary enemies" (*The Secret of the Old Mill* [#3] 105). To their friends, the Hardy Boys are just everyday chums, fit targets for their practical jokes and good companions for typical teenage outings.

Everything changes, however, as soon as the Hardy Boys get out of Bayport. There, they find excitement, adventure, and mystery. There, they can act as independent agents and confront major criminals. There, they can begin to become detectives.

This pattern is enacted three times in the first Hardy Boys book, *The Tower Treasure*. At the start, Frank and Joe are motorcycling through the countryside, doing an errand for their father, and they happen to encounter a maniacal red-haired driver who almost runs them off the road. Later, they locate his wrecked car and learn that he has stolen Chet Morton's car and, possibly, the treasure of eccentric millionaire Hurd Applegate.

When there are no new developments in the case, the Hardy Boys and their friends decide to spend one Saturday hiking through the woods. Joe happens to see some unusual tire tracks, which lead them to Chet's car and the discovery of the thief's red wig. Stepping in to do some real detective work, Fenton Hardy tracks down the thief, now dying in a hospital, and extracts the deathbed confession that the treasure is hidden in "the old tower." However, the Hardy Boys' search of the old tower of the Applegate Mansion yields nothing.

Frustrated and disappointed, the Hardy Boys decide to go for a motorcycle excursion to make them feel better. They happen to come upon railroad tracks with a new water tower next to an old, abandoned water tower. They have a sudden idea: Since the thief used to be a railroad worker, perhaps he was referring to that "old tower." They search it and, of course, find the treasure.

Other early adventures follow the same formula: Get out of town, stumble into some exciting discovery. In *The House on the Cliff* (#2), the Hardy Boys and friends decide to take a look at a deserted house that is reputed to be haunted; they hear strange noises and their tools are stolen. Subsequent investigations reveal that the house has new residents: the leaders of a smuggling ring. In *The Secret of the Old Mill*, a hike through a forest includes a chance encounter with a farmer, who suggests that the boys take a look at a nearby old mill where some suspicious people have recently moved in. Eventually, they learn that the mill houses a massive counterfeiting operation. In *The Mystery of Cabin Island* (#8), a brief winter visit to a deserted island leads to a confrontation with a hostile stranger determined to keep them off the island; a later, more extended trip leads to the discovery of a stolen stamp collection in a cabin on the island.

As these descriptions suggest, the key element in most of the early Hardy Boys' successes is amazing coincidences and dumb luck. The most egregious example is surely *The Secret of the Caves* (#7). Randomly pondering places for possible vacations, the boys decide to travel to some deserted caves along the shore. The day before they depart, a woman comes to Fenton Hardy for help in locating her missing brother, a professor who is apparently suffering from amnesia and wandering around the country. Then, just before they leave, they find out that one of the Shore Road car thieves has just escaped. When they arrive at their destination, they quickly discover that the supposedly uninhabited caves actually have two residents. Guess who they are.

Furthermore, finding these men involves no great mental feats either. The professor, calling himself a sea captain, introduces himself to the boys, helpfully sprinkling his conversation with "By Jings" and walking with his shoelaces untied, the professor's two distinctive traits mentioned by his sister. The car thief obligingly gets drunk and passes out on the shore, so that the Hardy Boys can literally trip over him.

At times, the Hardy Boys themselves and their friends show some awareness of the incredible fortuitousness of many events in their adventures. In *Hunting for Hidden Gold* (#5), the Hardy Boys go ice-skating on a remote lake and happen to run into an old miner (his house almost falls on them) with a sad tale to tell about losing four bags of gold near the Montana town of Lucky Bottom. At that moment, Fenton Hardy is in Lucky Bottom, looking for some missing gold. "Isn't that a strange coincidence?" comments Mrs. Hardy (51), and later Frank says, "isn't it strange how Jadbury Wilson, away back in Bayport, should be connected with this case, away out here in Montana?" "It's a coincidence, all right," responds Joe (151). When the Hardy Boys go to Montana, they randomly choose to go searching down a trail; it turns out to lead directly to the outlaws' hideout. "This was a stroke of luck," the narrator points out (144). While exploring a cave, the Hardy Boys escape from a pack of wolves by accidentally falling into a mine shaft that is deep enough to keep the wolves from following them, but not deep enough to cause serious injury when they fall; "We're lucky," says Frank (185). Since these asides and tidbits of conversation were surely not included in Stratemeyer's terse outlines, they can be attributed entirely to McFarlane, an author speaking through his narrator and characters to comment on the absurdities of the plot he had been given.

It is also apparent that one very important factor in the Hardy Boys' lives is transportation: They need a way to get out of Bayport so that their adventures can begin. As Carol Billman notes, they are "Quintessentially mobile" (80). From the very first page of their first book, the Hardy Boys have motorcycles; in the third book, they get a boat; in the sixth book, they purchase a car; and the eighth book unveils their special ice-boat. (In later books, the Hardy family also gets their own airplane.) And much of the nefarious goings-on around the Hardys involve some assault on their means of transportation: As noted, a thief almost crashes into their motorcycles in *The Tower Treasure*; their boat is stolen in *The Secret of the Old Mill* and almost suffers a ruinous collision in *The Missing Chums* (#4); two scruffy youths attempt to run into their ice-boat in *The Mystery of Cabin Island*; a drunken pilot almost crashes his airplane into their car in *The Great Airport Mystery* (#9); and the villains in *The Shore Road Mystery* (#6) are a ring of car thieves who eventually steal their car.

Three early books present interesting variations on the basic pattern. *The Missing Chums* begins with what appears to be a role reversal: The Hardy Boys are forced to stay home with their mother while Fenton Hardy busies himself with a far-off mystery, and it is their friends Chet Morton and Biff Hooper who are going out of town on an extended boat trip. Clearly, Chet and Biff are trying the Hardy formula for successful adventure: Leave Bayport, find adventure. That they are in some ways stand-ins for the Hardy Boys is reinforced by what happens to them on their trip: They are kidnapped by foes of Fenton Hardy who think that they *are* the Hardy Boys. Their trip, needless to say, turns out to be no fun at all, as they spend all their time at the gangsters' hideout, with their hands tied around their back, until Frank and Joe apply their amazing detective skills to the task of finding them. (A friend of Biff's mentions to Frank that Biff was talking about going to Blacksnake Island, so they go there and find their friends and the criminals.)

The Missing Chums might be read, then, as a message to Chet, Biff, or any other young lad: Do not imitate the Hardy Boys, because the wonderful things that happen to them on their perilous journeys will not happen to you. It is possible that Edward Stratemeyer was receiving letters from hostile parents, complaining that the peripatetic escapades of the Hardy Boys were encouraging America's youth to engage in dangerous outings far from home, so he decided to structure the next mystery as an explicit warning against such activities.

The next mystery, *Hunting for Hidden Gold*, begins in a typical fashion: A trip away from Bayport leads to a chance encounter with a man who tells them about a mystery. This time, however, instead of remaining in the vicinity of Bayport to investigate it further, the Hardy Boys get a message from an injured Fenton Hardy in Montana, asking them to come help him look for missing gold, which, of course, turns out to be the old miner's original find. This book anticipates the formula of later books, when an initial excursion beyond Bayport would only be the prelude to some grander adventure, an investigatory expedition to England, the Sahara Desert, or the Arctic Circle.

Finally, there is *The Shore Road Mystery* (#6), undoubtedly the most important of the early Hardy Boys books. This is the only mystery that spawned a sequel of sorts (in the subplot to *The Secret of the Caves*), the one mystery that is repeatedly referred to in later volumes as the Hardy Boys' "first big case," and the first time they solved a mystery "that had baffled even the great Fenton Hardy." On the face of it, there is little reason to regard the case as especially important. At this time, the boys had already broken up a major smuggling ring and a huge counterfeiting operation, so capturing a bunch of car thieves does not seem like an appreciably greater task. And Fenton Hardy had also been unsuccessful tracking down the counterfeiters until his sons stumbled into their hideaway.

What makes *The Shore Road Mystery* special is the way the Hardy Boys solved it. For once, they did not rely on an unlikely coincidence: They did not go for a hike and run into a fisherman who told them about seeing headlights coming from a nearby cave; they did not happen to see a suspicious-looking man driving about in a stolen car. Instead, they took deliberate and purposeful action to track down the criminals. Straining their intellects to the utmost, the Hardy Boys reasoned that if you want to find a car thief, the best way to do it is to disguise yourself as a car. That is exactly what they did: They purchased an attractive but unreliable "lemon," parked it where most of the other car thefts took place, hid in the trunk, and waited to be stolen. It worked; and after being discovered and escaping, the Hardy Boys lead the authorities to the caves being used to hide the cars and round up the entire gang. Compared to the methodology in other early adventures, this was a brilliant masterstroke; and the story thus anticipates future books where the Hardy Boys would actually do something resembling detective work.

I have noted that the Hardy Boys feel confined while in Bayport but liberated outside of Bayport; but the exact opposite was true for author McFarlane. When the boys were on their adventurous outings, he was obliged to follow Stratemeyer's outline; but while they were at home between adventures, he had some freedom to improvise. And he took advantage of it.

In *Ghost of the Hardy Boys*, McFarlane describes some of the additions he made to his depictions of the Hardys at home. For one thing, he placed special emphasis on food: "From my boyhood reading I recalled enjoying any scenes that involved eating. . . . I decided that the Hardy boys and their chums would eat frequently. . . . the provender would be described in detail" (64). Arguably, eating is the sensory pleasure that most closely approximates sex for the prepubescent male, so McFarlane was in a way embellishing his mysteries with a kind of culinary pornography. He was also determined to add humor: "Why not inject a few rib ticklers into *The Tower Treasure*?" (64). Early books are filled with funny scenes involving the elaborate practical jokes of Chet Morton and the lazy, pompous, and stupid policemen of Bayport; in *The Tower Treasure*, for example, the Hardy Boys keep them occupied with a "bomb" that turns out to be an alarm clock in a box. He also added references to their lives as students in *The Secret of the Old Mill*: "The Hardy boys, hitherto existing only on weekends, were actually seen at school. . . . just for the hell of it I tossed in an episode about the lads hitting the books and undergoing the torments of cramming for exams" (179).

One can discount, perhaps, the words of praise that McFarlane cites regarding these embellishments: "Dozens of small boys have told me that the Bomb Hoax has always been high on their private list of Select Comic Readings of All Time" (70); and a reporter told him "Those old books were well written" (209). Still, it was undoubtedly these depictions of the Hardy Boys' everyday life that most contributed to making the Hardy Boys seem real, something that their improbable escapades on the road could never accomplish.

While there are many moments like these to notice and celebrate in the early Hardy Boys book, only one of McFarlane's creations is overwhelmingly important: the introduction of Aunt Gertrude in *The Missing Chums*. Not only would she prove an absolutely indispensable addition to the Hardy family, but she would also emerge as the most complex and well-rounded of all the characters in the books.

Stratemeyer first suggested a maiden aunt as a solution to an emerging story problem: It had been established that Fenton Hardy was frequently out of town for weeks at a time working on important cases, and the Hardy Boys of course also needed to get away from Bayport in order to be involved in their own mysteries. This, however, would leave poor Laura Hardy at home by herself, and it was clear that this naive, frail, and feeble-minded woman could not function on her own.

Consider what McFarlane describes as "probably the only time Laura was ever allowed to get in on any of the action" (177), in *The Secret of the Old Mill*: The whole town is talking about, and her husband and sons are investigating, a flood of counterfeit money; Laura Hardy is well aware of these crimes and even says, "I'm sure I don't know what the world's coming to when men will make bad money and know that poor people are going to lose by it" (32). Yet she later accepts $800 in cash as payment for an expensive rug from a door-to-door rug salesman. Anyone with half a brain would suspect the money was counterfeit, as it was; but Laura Hardy "had forgotten all about this scare about counterfeit money and hadn't given the matter a thought" (157). It seems that Fenton, Frank, and Joe do all the thinking in the Hardy family.

Thus, since Fenton Hardy's work was paying the bills, the adventures of Frank and Joe would apparently have to be curtailed, so they could remain at home and protect their poor mother from unscrupulous rug salesmen and the other vicissitudes of everyday life. In fact, that is exactly the situation at the beginning of *The Missing Chums*: The boys cannot go with Chet and Biff on their trip because their father is out of town, so they must stay home with their mother. However, with the arrival of an elderly relative to stay with Laura, the boys would be free to go. That is all Stratemeyer had in mind: "Because Fenton Hardy and sons were scheduled to be away from home for long stretches of Volume Four, he suggested that a maiden aunt should come a-visiting to keep Mrs. Hardy company" (184).

However, it was McFarlane who decided to give Aunt Gertrude a personality: "I doubt if Stratemeyer intended her to be amusing" (184). The character he created had "a small fortune and a sharp tongue" (*The Missing Chums* 51), and her outspoken, dictatorial, and explosive personality immediately added an entirely new element of amusement to the series.

Aunt Gertrude offered more than occasional comic relief, though. To understand her full significance, one should realize that the Hardy Boys were living in what would now be called a dysfunctional family. Their father seems qualified to provide strong and solid guidance, but he is rarely around to do it. Their mother is either unwilling or, more likely, unable to provide any guidance at all, so she consents to whatever outlandish scheme her sons propose. In effect, the Hardy Boys had no parents: They were living with a friendly but distant older brother, and an acquiescent and nurturing older sister.

As one example of their essential freedom from parental control, consider this scene from *The Shore Road Mystery.* When the Hardy Boys decide that they need a car as bait for the car thieves, they take some money out of their savings, buy a car, and drive it home, surprising their parents considerably. It simply does not occur to them to ask their parents' permission to buy a car, or even to inform them that they were buying a car.

Aunt Gertrude thus fills an important gap in the Hardys' family life. Although the texts describe her as domineering and unreasonable, all Aunt Gertrude says to the boys is what any normal parent would say. You want to hike out to some remote lake and go ice-skating on a day when there might be a blizzard? Ridiculous—much too dangerous! You want to get in your boat and go searching for your missing friends on an island infested with poisonous snakes? "Blacksnake Island! Frank Hardy, have you gone completely off your head?" (*The Missing Chums* 84).

The fun, of course, was that Aunt Gertrude talked like a parent, but lacked the authority of a parent. With the quiet support of Fenton and Laura, the Hardy Boys could thumb their noses at all of her commands and dictates and continue to do whatever they wanted. Acts of rebellion have no impact unless there is someone to rebel against; and with Aunt Gertrude obstinately objecting to their every adventure, the Hardy Boys for the first time could play the role of youthful rebels.

Also, if feminist scholars feel that they have exhaustively studied the more familiar female characters in literature, they might consider a long, hard look at Aunt Gertrude, perhaps in an essay entitled "If Fenton Hardy Was a Woman." For despite her protestations against detective work, there is ample reason to believe that Aunt Gertrude was in fact interested in and capable of excellent detective work. As evidence of her potential abilities, consider this incident from her first adventure, *The Missing Chums.* A letter arrives for Fenton Hardy while he was out of town, and Aunt Gertrude insists upon opening it. In the note, anonymous criminals announce that they have kidnapped the Hardy Boys and are holding them for ransom. Since the Hardy Boys are there at home when the letter arrives, it seems puzzling, to say the least; but Aunt Gertrude has an explanation:

> "It must be a practical joke of some kind," said Mrs. Hardy, in perplexity [as always].
> "Practical joke, nothing!" scoffed Aunt Gertrude shrewdly. "Did Fenton Hardy go to Chicago after some criminal?"
> "He went to arrest Baldy Turk," replied Frank.
> "There!" Aunt Gertrude pounded the table. "That explains the whole thing. The companions of this Baldy person sent that letter in the hope that it would bring Fenton Hardy back from Chicago by the next train."
> "But the letter is addressed to Bayport."
> "Certainly! Why not? They wouldn't know where to reach him in Chicago, so they sent the letter here and trusted that it would be forwarded to him. And if *I* hadn't been here," said Aunt Gertrude, "it very probably *would* have been forwarded to him. Am I right?"
> "I usually forward his personal mail," admitted Mrs. Hardy.
> "There! Didn't I know it?" (72-73)

As it happens, Aunt Gertrude is wrong. Also as it happens, that is the only act of intelligent deduction in the entire book; and the moment anticipates later books when Aunt Gertrude, while maintaining her outward disapproval of the Hardy Boys' detective work, would occasionally contribute a useful idea or shrewd suggestion, actually helping them solve a mystery.

The reason Aunt Gertrude could not participate openly in mystery-solving, of course, was that she grew up in a time when intelligent women, and working women, were frowned up; and so, unlike her brother, she was unable to achieve her proper avocation and instead settled into the social acceptable roles of old maid and old battleaxe. Aunt Gertrude, in fact, illustrates that in pre-liberated America, the only way for women to gain power was to remain unmarried and amass "a small fortune." Otherwise, they are perpetually doomed to powerlessness and invisibility. Surprisingly, Callie Shaw and Iola Morton, the pallid and generally vacuous girl friends of Frank and Joe Hardy, once offered a proto-feminist protest regarding their second-class status:

"I wish I were a boy," sighed Callie Shaw.
Iola Morton looked up from her ice-cream soda. "Me too."
"It's tough luck that you're not," said Joe Hardy. "We'd like to have you along on the trip with us."
"Boys have all the luck. Girls have to stay at home." (*The Secret of the Caves* 43)

Later books change the character of Aunt Gertrude in another way, perhaps to soften her a bit: She became a wonderful cook, always baking some cookies or a pie to be stuffed into the gaping mouth of the obese, perpetually hungry, food-obsessed Chet Morton, who is also the only other regular character in the early books worth an extended glance. From the start, he is the first among equals in the Hardy Boys' circle of friends, and, following the stereotype of the fat boy, he is pictured as a fun-loving practical joker (though the way he humiliates his friends Frank and Joe after they unknowingly accept a counterfeit five-dollar bill in *The Secret of the Old Mill* borders on the sadistic). *The Mystery of Cabin Island* first presents Chet in what would become his most important role: perpetual bumbler. When he asks to steer an ice-boat, his ineptitude almost causes a crash and provides some moments of excitement, and when he and the other boys go on a fox hunt, Chet cannot help much because he forgot to load his rifle. In later books, Chet would perform the same function as Nigel Bruce's Dr. Watson in Basil Rathbone's Sherlock Holmes films: the capable detective's incompetent companion, whose constant mistakes keep the plot in motion long after the detective acting alone would have ended it.

There is quiet, ongoing competition between muscular Biff Hooper (his real first name is Allen, but only the very first book provides that information), and Italian immigrant Tony Prito (about as daringly ethnic as the early books could get) for the status of second-best friend: Tony surges to the forefront in *The House on the Cliff*, but Biff seems entrenched as the major character as early as *The Missing Chums*. In later books, Tony would take his place as the fourth member of the Hardy team; then Biff starts to creep back into prominence. It is hard to see why Stratemeyer, McFarlane, or the other writers could never make up their minds about which character to emphasize, because except for Biff's fondness for athletics, and Tony's occasionally useful boat, there is virtually no difference between the characters.

Other barely distinguishable friends drift in and out of the series for cameo appearances: Phil Cohen, the fourth-best friend, seems to be there solely to prove that yes, some of the Hardy Boys' best friends *were* Jewish, and Perry "Slim" Robinson has a major role in *The Tower Treasure* but afterwards only appears rarely and briefly. There is an interesting tale to tell about the changing fortunes of the fifth-best Hardy friend, Jerry Gilroy. In *The Tower Treasure*, he is simply listed, along with Frank, Joe, Chet, Biff, Tony, and Phil, as a member of "the gang" (130). However, at the start of *The House on the Cliff*, he accompanies Frank, Joe, Chet, and Biff on their excursion to the deserted house, suggesting he might become a regular member of their entourage. However, he is so frightened by the strange noises they hear at the house that he declines to accompany the Hardys on their second investigation; in his place, Tony and Phil come along. Poor Jerry never recovered after this unforgivable lapse: Gluttons, simpletons, and robots are acceptable company for the Hardy Boys, but cowards cannot be tolerated. In *The Secret of the Old Mill*, Jerry tries to recover some visibility by imitating the stock characteristics of other Hardy friends: He is suddenly described as "an ardent ball fan" (22), although athletics was Biff's established obsession, and as someone "who could never resist anything in the nature of food" (34), although gluttony was Chet's established obsession. Poor Jerry, it seems, could not think up a colorful eccentricity of his own, and in later volumes he reverts to being just another name on the list of friends. (It might be amusing to rewrite a Hardy Boys adventure in the manner of Tom Stoppard, from the perspective of its most invisible characters: *Robinson and Gilroy Are Dead.*)

Because other commentators have usually not bothered to read each and every one of the Hardy Boys books (my own reading stopped at #66), they sometimes offer inaccurate and hasty generalizations about the books, which can be qualified or refuted by careful reading of first eight Hardy Boys books. One of these comes from Leslie McFarlane himself: "As for booze and tobacco, if a Hardy Boys' villain every took a snort or broke open a pack of fags he did it on the sly between chapters" (178). Yet I have already mentioned the drunken criminal found in *The Secret of the Caves* and the drunken pilot of *The Great Airport Mystery*; and in *The Shore Road Mystery*, one car thief "was lazy and he drank a lot" (24). It was perfectly acceptable for villains to have vices like drinking; the Hardy Boys and their friends, of course, would never think of touching the stuff. As for tobacco, I cannot recall a cigarette, but miners Jadbury Wilson and Bart Dawson do puff on their pipes in *Hunting for Hidden Gold*, and the amnesiac professor in *The Secret of the Caves* uses chewing tobacco. It might also be mentioned that the major criminal activity the Hardy Boys combat in *The House on the Cliff* is an opium smuggling ring. Their world, in short, was not nearly as sanitized as some would suggest.

In *The Secret of the Stratemeyer Syndicate*, Billman comments that Nancy Drew "thinks rings around the sometimes dimwitted Hardys" (100), and while their mental acumen goes up a few notches in later adventures, "sometimes dimwitted" is a reasonably accurate description of the early Hardy Boys. More tactfully, Carole Kismaric and Marvin Heiferman say that the boys "make the most of their common sense" (46). This much can be said in their favor, however: the Hardy Boys never make the same mistake three times.

On some occasions, the Hardy Boys did make the same mistake twice. In *The Tower Treasure*, the Hardy Boys first see a wrecked car, but after stopping to make sure no one was inside, they go away without thinking about it. When they later realize that it might be the car that almost ran them over, they return to the car, look at it intently, and establish it is the same car. But only when the man emerges as a suspect in the tower robbery does it occur to the Hardy Boys to return to the car a third time and *look for clues*. In *Hunting for Hidden Gold*, the Hardy Boys, making their first cross-country trip, meet a friendly stranger who guides them to the right train. It turns out to be the wrong train. Stranded in a remote town, they meet a friendly stranger who offers to drive them back to their station. He starts driving in the wrong direction. Only after this second incident do the Hardy Boys finally learn "to beware of strangers from now on," as Frank says. "Evidently one lesson isn't enough" (79).

At least one Hardy Boys commentator, Arthur Prager, proffers an explicitly Freudian reading of the books, and others similarly emphasize their proclivities for exploring caves and tunnels, tiptoeing through decaying old buildings, and digging up buried treasure and other objects. The implications need not be elaborated here because this is, after all, well-mined territory. However, this is an interpretation of the Hardy Boys that seems based more on reading the titles of their books than on reading the books themselves. Yes, the Hardy Boys do spend a lot of time in dark old houses and caves, but they also go ice-skating, hike through forests, swim in rivers, and motorcycle through the countryside, and many of their most important clues and exciting adventures are in broad daylight. Kismaric and Heiferman recognize that "The Hardy Boys spend more time out of doors than Nancy does, and it's the fearsome and dynamic power of nature that permeates the atmosphere that they breath" (53).

Speaking of the Jerry Todd books, Prager comments, "Jerry and his gang did something else that was considered rather daring in the modest 1930s too. It was nude swimming. There was never a bathing suit in the crowd, and the boys were always stripping down for a cooling dip in the lake. Stratemeyer and Percy Keese Fitzhugh boys always wore bathing suits" (257-58). However, there are several times in their early adventures when the Hardy Boys and their friends do go skinny-dipping; for example, in *The Secret of the Caves*, "It was one of the finest natural swimming places they had ever seen and the boys lost no time flinging off their clothes and splashing out into the cool water. For about half an hour they enjoyed themselves as only boys can, swimming and diving, until at last, refreshed, they came up onto the beach and donned their garments again" (48). And later in the book, the boys' clothes are drenched by the rain, so they again remove their clothes and dry themselves by a campfire wearing only some blankets.

The thought of the naked Hardy Boys frolicking in the water with other naked young males, of course, will inevitably strike people in some circles as suggestive.

Followers of critic Leslie Fiedler, who intensively studied odd pairings between light-skinned and dark-skinned males in American literature (Natty Bumppo and Chingachook, Ishmael and Queequeg, Huck and Jim), might wish to inquire into the Hardy Boys' strange fondness for the olive-skinned Tony Prito. Joe's alleged affection for Iola Morton might be viewed as a displacement of his actual affection for her brother Chet. And eyebrows might be raised at scenes when the Hardy Boys and their chums work out in their backyard gymnasium, working up a sweat and displaying their young, muscular bodies.

I sketch this homoerotic interpretation of the Hardy Boys only to ridicule it. Like other characters in children's literature, the Hardy Boys' mental age is vastly different from their chronological age: They are said to be seventeen- and eighteen-year-olds, but they think like nine- and ten-year-olds. They are not homosexual or heterosexual, but asexual: the only sensual pleasures they seek are good food and daring adventures.

For the determined homoerotic critic, only one character in the Hardy Boys books might warrant extended analysis: Chet Morton. In *The Mystery of Cabin Island*, he is chosen to prepare the boys' first dinner, so he put on "an apron" to prepare a delicious stew and later "beamed with satisfaction when the others complimented him on the meal" (67), suggesting perhaps a desire to assume a nurturing, feminine role towards his friends (Kismaric and Heiferman call Chet "the feminine foil for the Hardy Boys" [86]). Later, when Frank offers to climb up the cabin chimney to search for the missing stamp collection, Chet volunteers, "You will certainly need a bath when you come out"; when Joe is actually chosen for the job, Chet "consoled him": "We'll all take turns at scrubbing you when you come out." And after all four boys are accidentally covered with soot, Chet said, "I vote we all take a bath" (155, 156, 161). Since young boys are typically indifferent or hostile to cleanliness, Chet's evident eagerness to have his friends remove their clothing and take baths—and even to help scrub them off—does seem a bit queer.

If the charge that the Hardy Boys were subtly undermining the masculinity of American boys can be easily refuted, there remains the fact that in other ways, the early books in the series have subversive elements. In this respect, Billman's comments about the world of the Hardy Boys seem particularly inappropriate. Largely based, it seems, on her reading of one later novel in the series—*The Mystery of the Chinese Junk* (#39)—she concludes that the city of Bayport is a "fantasy island": "it's there for characters to live in, it is secure, it throws up no real dilemmas. . . . It is a frozen and fixed world where mysteries come and go, but there is no change or human complexity," a place with a "halcyon moral climate and golden rules operative" (93, 92). In the revised versions of older books and in the newer books, largely drained of interesting textures and sanitized to remove almost anything "which could possibly discomfit anyone" (Murphy 18), this picture of Bayport as a simple-minded utopia might be defended; but the world of the early Hardy Boys books is an altogether darker and more divided place.

Many of these undertones should be attributed to Leslie McFarlane, an underpaid, struggling writer in Canada who clearly had more than enough reason to lack sympathy with the American power structure, and not to Edward Stratemeyer, a self-made millionaire with a sunny disposition and an undoubtedly unalloyed faith in the American Dream. Without straying from the outlines, McFarlane manages to incorporate hints of social commentary, protests against the existing order.

First, the Hardy Boys books sometimes offer some rather cynical comments about human nature. In *The Tower Treasure*, after Perry Robinson's father is arrested for stealing the Applegate treasure, "There was a great deal of public sympathy for the family, but little for the accused, as most people seemed to take it for granted that he would not have been arrested if he had not had something to do with the crime"; later, after he is cleared, "People said that they knew all along that Mr. Robinson was innocent of the theft, and went as far out of their way to be nice to him as they had gone out of their way to be unkind to him and ignore him when he was accused of theft." Little wonder that when the Hardy Boys are then loudly praised for solving the case, "the boys took [it] with a grain of salt, as the saying is, for they knew that the public is fickle and as quick to condemn failure as it is to praise success" (69, 208). Indeed, their sterling reputation for solving eight important crimes did not prevent the Bayport police from throwing them in jail for mail theft in *The Great Airport Mystery*, on the flimsy basis of a sweater found at the scene of the crime.

Also, the social and financial status of the Hardy family, compared to that of other Stratemeyer heroes, does not seem that high. To be sure, the Hardys are not poor: Fenton Hardy's work as a detective was once described as "more lucrative" than police work (*The Secret of the Old Mill* 13), and the family is capable of occasional extravagances like motorcycles for their sons and an eight-hundred-dollar rug for the living room. However, their home, to the extent that it is de-scribed at all, does not seem particularly luxurious, although it does have a garage and an old barn in the back. *The Tower Treasure* has one cryptic reference to "a servant" in the Hardy house (116), but no servants ever appear, and, as noted, the coming of Aunt Gertrude was specifically designed to make sure that Laura Hardy would not be alone in the house. One must assume that reference was a slip of the pen and that the Hardy family, in fact, cannot afford servants—distinguishing them from earlier series heroes like the well-to-do Rover Boys or the self-made million-aire Tom Swift. It is with genuine enthusiasm, if not downright greed, that Frank and Joe accept large cash rewards for the first cases that they solve, and their parents are pleased to get the money as a way to pay for their college education, something they would apparently be unable to finance on their own. Although Aunt Gertrude is hardly pleasant company, the Hardys are obliged to be nice to her because "she was possessed of a small fortune . . . [so] none dared offend her" (*The Missing Chums* 51). Evidently, all of the Hardys are hoping that Aunt Gertrude will remember them in her will.

Other friends of the Hardys are in even worse financial straits. *The Tower Treasure* reveals that friend Perry Robinson is the son of a servant in the Hurd Applegate mansion, and when the man is falsely accused of stealing the treasure, he is immediately fired, so his family must move into a shabby house "in one of the poorest sections of the city" (109) and Perry must quit school and get a job in a grocery store. In *The Secret of the Old Mill*, we are told that Callie Shaw, Frank's girl friend, lives with an unmarried cousin of modest means, Miss Pollie Shaw, and when the woman innocently accepts fifty dollars in counterfeit money, the loss "left her pretty short of cash" (28). And in *The Shore Road Mystery*, one reason the Hardy Boys get involved is that the father of friend Jack Dodd is thrown in jail for possible car theft, and until the Hardy Boys and Fenton Hardy help out, the family cannot afford to pay bail: "Five thousand! They'll never be able to raise that much money!" (31).

There is also one peculiar moment of affinity between the Hardy Boys and the most wretched and despised subclass of American society in the 1920s: African-Americans. In *Hunting for Hidden Gold*, when the boys are about to be captured by the nefarious thugs who are trying to keep them away from Montana, they are rescued by a group of poor rural blacks who are chasing the criminals because they ran over some of their chickens:

> "Ef dey runs oveh any moah of mah chickens, Ah'll folley 'em fum heah till Dooms-day," declared the big negro.
> "You certainly showed up in the nick of time," said Joe, brushing off his coat. "They had us beaten two to one."
> "White trash!" declared the other colored man. "Ah knows 'em. Dey jes' pool room toughs." (78)

To be sure, their accents and attitudes are purely stereotypical, but their hearts are in the right place; and because of this scene, perhaps, one might forgive the rather less complimentary picture of a "shuffling" black porter earlier in the novel (87), and one might also forgive Frank Hardy for once using the expression "there's a nigger in the woodpile" (*The House on the Cliff* 77).

In contrast, the rich people of the early Hardy Boys books come off rather poorly. Hurd Applegate, as noted, cruelly fires a loyal and capable servant based on unwarranted suspicions, and until he and his unmarried sister are mollified by the return of his treasure, they are positively unfriendly to the Hardy Boys who are trying to help them find it. When they later help another millionaire, Elroy Jefferson, recover his lost stamp collection, a discussion of the man's life implies that he married a woman only to obtain her valuable stamps. While their later gratitude does transform the men into friendly benefactors for the Hardy Boys—in *The Great Airport Mystery*, they post the bail when the Hardy Boys are thrown in jail—they have also revealed themselves as not particularly pleasant people.

Figures of authority are similarly cast in a negative light. There is genuine contempt in McFarlane's early depictions of the Bayport police force: In *The House on the Cliff*, Chief Collig and Detective Smuff sit at the station idly playing checkers and seem too frightened to go investigate the haunted house until Frank mentions the possibility of negative publicity. And in *The Secret of the Old Mill*, patrolman Con Riley is extensively depicted as a simple-minded, egotistical, and lazy officer who falls asleep on the job. After Stratemeyer wrote McFarlane a letter complaining that he was showing "a grievous lack of respect for officers of the law" (182), the policemen became more altruistic and dedicated, but they never became particularly bright, or particularly helpful.

There are grounds, then, for a Marxist reading of the early Hardy Boys: Members of the proletariat, they work on behalf of their fellow workers against the interests of an obtuse and oppressive ruling class. After all, one of their major motives in *The Tower Treasure* and *The Shore Road Mystery* is to help two classmates whose fathers are in jail; in *The Secret of the Old Mill*, their investigations will help a poor lad named Lester living with the counterfeiters; in *The Missing Chums*, they are trying to find and rescue friends Chet and Biff; in *The House on the Cliff*, they want to save their father; and in *Hunting for Hidden Gold*, they wish to help down-and-out miner Jadbury Wilson. While their perpetual mobility and personal freedom in themselves made the Hardy Boys threatening role models for America's youth, their frequent inclination to side with the poor and against the rich and powerful could be seen as even more subversive.

The odd thing is that the Hardy Boys have no reason to remain in, or stay sympathetic to, the working class. The cash rewards from their early cases made them far wealthier than any of their friends—in the first three adventures alone, they earned \$4500, a fabulous sum in 1927. Free from true parental control, they could have quit school, moved into an apartment, purchased fabulous luxuries, and enjoyed the lifestyle of the rich and famous. With wise investments and continuing luck in solving crimes, they might have become like Tom Swift, independently wealthy by the age of twenty. In light of these possibilities, it seems almost incredible that the Hardy Boys end their adventures by dutifully returning home, meekly stashing all their money away in a savings account, and starting to study for their finals, just like all of the other little people.

There is thus a resemblance between the Hardy Boys and another modern American hero—Superman—who strangely chooses to spend most of his time in the guise of humdrum, ordinary Clark Kent. Superman catches a falling airplane and saves its passengers, then he puts on his blue suit and pretends to be a mild-mannered reporter; the Hardy Boys help the police smash a major smuggling ring, and collect a five thousand dollar reward, then they return home and pretend to be Frank and Joe, typical American teenagers. Jules Feiffer has wondered why Superman would want to live this way, and even speculates about Superman's "masochism," but part of the answer is surely this: Both Superman and the Hardy Boys want to be renowned as world-famous heroes, but they also want to be accepted as ordinary people, hence demanding their two identities. And certainly, it is the everyday lives of Superman and the Hardy Boys that provide the impetus for their heroic lives: Clark Kent becomes Superman in order to help people like Clark Kent, and the Hardy Boys become masterful detectives in order to help people like the Hardy Boys. Feiffer also explains the initial reason for Clark Kent's creation: "The truth may be that Kent existed not for the purposes of the story but for the reader. . . . His fake identity was our real one. That's why we loved him so" ("Introduction" 19). Similarly, the young male readers targeted by Stratemeyer could easily identify with the ordinary daily lives of Frank and Joe, even if they were not able to emulate the daring adventures of the Hardy Boys.

Because the Hardy Boys predate Superman by at least a decade, it is only an interesting coincidence, though, that in *Hunting for Hidden Gold*, when the Hardy Boys must disguise themselves from evil-doers, they both decide to put on glasses, which works as well for them as it did for Superman.

Eventually, however, like many other young upstarts, the Hardy Boys would be sedately co-opted into the power structure. Significantly, the last two of their early adventures—*The Secret of the Caves* and *The Mystery of Cabin Island*—lack the element of helping the young and downtrodden: The Hardy Boys are simply working for clients, the sister of the professor and Elroy Jefferson, people who are not in desperate straits. *The Secret of the Caves* offers a surprising conclusion: The Hardy Boys refuse to accept the reward for finding the missing professor. Apparently, they don't need the money anymore.

The most striking signal of a change in their status, however, occurred in the ninth book in the series, *The Great Airport Mystery*. The title in itself announced a new aura of importance surrounding their activities—this was their first "great" case—and their perilous trip hidden in the storage area of a small airplane, in pursuit of a gang of ruthless mail thieves, did seem to be an adventure on a higher plane, so to speak, than some of their previous exploits. In the book, the Hardy Boys would actually graduate from high school, forcing them to soon make a difficult decision: Should they go to college, or join father Fenton Hardy as professional detectives? (As it turns out, they never had to make that decision, since subsequent books quietly returned them to high school, although they later seemed to never spend any time in school.) They would also be accused of mail theft and find themselves thrown in jail, another sign that the world was now taking them more seriously. There are ample grounds, then, for viewing *The Great Airport Mystery* as marking the end of the Hardy Boys' adolescence, and the beginning of their maturation.

Over the years, other changes in their situation and priorities would occur. Gradually, the Hardy family would become significantly affluent as Fenton Hardy hires an assistant, Sam Radley, purchases a private airplane, and focuses almost exclusively on international cases. Instead of solving mysteries in Bayport to help their friends, the Hardy Boys would be accepting out-of-town assignments from billionaires, businesses, or the government. Poor Perry Robinson would vanish from the scene, the fragile finances of Callie Shaw's cousins would never be mentioned again, and the Hardys' other friends would somehow seem to gain more spending money. The Hardy Boys and Chet Morton would start to live the lives of true jet-setters, forever catching a flight to investigate some far-off mystery. In contrast, their existence as ordinary teenagers in Bayport would be reduced to a vestigial page or two before they received a telegram summoning them to Central America or Bombay. No longer content to play the roles of Frank and Joe, they would become full-time Hardy Boys, making them about as interesting as a Superman who never became Clark Kent.

In fact, while there are other valid criticisms to make about the later Hardy Boys books—their blandness, breakneck pace, simplistic prose, and humorlessness—the major problem in them is that the Hardy Boys have risen above any ability to identify with people like the typical boys who read their books. They are members and agents of the adult ruling class, acting on behalf of that ruling class. And while there would be occasional gestures of friendship and support toward impoverished or lowly guest stars, like a young Arab in *The Mysterious Caravan* (#54), these would seem to stem not from genuine empathy, but from a sense of *noblesse oblige*.

It is no mystery, therefore, why the more recent Hardy Boys books often seem so pale and lifeless: the Hardy Boys sold out. They joined the system. And all of the undercurrents of tension introduced by McFarlane—between the rich and the poor, between the powerful and the powerless—are gone, leaving nothing but a meaningless blur of plane trips and car chases and fist fights, what Murphy called "pure plot" (18), as the Hardy Boys mechanically advance through what is truly a global "fantasy island" from which all unpleasantness, and all hints of social inequities, have been removed.

Undoubtedly, many trends and developments contributed to this homogenization of the Hardy Boys: One notices, for example, an increasing and evident desire to avoid being objectionable at all costs, and Billman notes that the projected age of Hardy Boys readers has steadily shifted downward from "early to mid-teens" to "10 to 14" to "eight to twelve" (95), which would in itself account for certain simplifications in the texts. However, one important factor is surely that McFarlane stopped writing the books after *The Phantom Freighter* (#26), so that the later adventures were produced by writers who were less talented and less sensitive. Throughout the McFarlane books, one sees a conscious effort to darken the picture a bit, to add a knowing remark or two to his generally innocent-minded narrative, to make the Hardy Boys and their friends a little more poor and oppressed than they needed to be, to make the rich and powerful a little more unreasonable and stupid than they needed to be. In one passage from *Ghost of the Hardy Boys*, McFarlane acknowledged such a subversive intent: "I had my own thoughts about teaching youngsters that obedience to authority is somehow sacred. . . . Would civilization crumble if kids got the notion that the people who ran the world were sometimes stupid, occasionally wrong and even corrupt at times?" (183).

In sum, to follow in the footsteps of Franklin W. Dixon was my foolish childhood dream, because Franklin W. Dixon did not exist and never had existed. But Leslie McFarlane did exist; and to follow in his footsteps strikes me today as an appropriate and admirable aspiration.

4

Giving Horatio Alger Goosebumps, Or, From Hardy Boys to Hapless Boys: The Changing Ethos of Juvenile Series Fiction

While there have been studies of science fiction, fantasy, and horror written for children and adolescents, scholars often fail to discuss the stories that are both read by and requested by youthful readers: namely, juvenile series fiction. To be sure, the classics of children's literature, such as the Newbery Award winners, are meritorious and genuinely enjoyable for their intended audience, but these remain books that children typically must be led to; they do not ask for them. What they ask for—often to the dismay of parents, teachers, and librarians—are iterative, mass-produced books, of little apparent literary value, which provide familiar recurring characters, settings, and plots.

While the origins of such fiction might expansively be traced back to ancient myths and legends, in which popular heroes like Hercules and Roland figured repeatedly, a calmer literary historian would probably begin with American children's literature of the nineteenth century, especially the genre of dime novels, for which authors like Horatio Alger, Jr., and Luis Senarens churned out innumerable adventures featuring youthful heroes. Alger's characters had different names but were always variations on one type, the poor but virtuous lad who makes it to the top with pluck and determination, and Senarens was noted for stories about resourceful young inventors like Frank Reade, Jr., and Jack Wright.

However, while the fiction of Alger and Senarens soon faded from view, one of their younger colleagues, Edward Stratemeyer, would in the twentieth century establish a more lasting tradition of hardcover book series. Setting up his Stratemeyer Syndicate, and hiring writers to produce novels based on his outlines, Stratemeyer launched dozen of series with various sorts of leading characters, allowing the most successful ones to continue on with new titles as long as the sales were good. Noting the popularity of Stratemeyer stars like the Rover Boys, Tom Swift, and the Bobbsey Twins, other publishers followed his example, and series fiction has endured as a major area of children's literature, with new series like the Animorphs and the Baby-Sitters Club now competing with surviving icons like Stratemeyer's Nancy Drew and the Hardy Boys.

Though Stratemeyer, like Alger, usually placed his heroes in realistic modern settings—with implausible coincidences as their only fantastic element—a few series strayed into more imaginative territory. The Tom Swift books were a mild sort of science fiction, since Tom's less-than-spectacular inventions were usually at least a few years ahead of their time, while the Hardy Boys drifted as close to horror fiction as the conventions of the day would allow, with titles like *What Happened at Midnight* and *While the Clock Ticked* that promised terrifying events and with one adventure, *The Disappearing Floor*, that was a pure horror story, as Frank and Joe Hardy visit a haunted house inhabited by a mad scientist whose diabolical inventions include a machine that projects the image of a ghost. However (to mention at least one non-Stratemeyer series, even though he did dominate the form), the most successful fantasy series was L. Frank Baum's Oz books, which were first written intermittently but later became an annual event, a tradition carried on for decades after his death by other writers. All these series have long been popular. The first Tom Swift series lasted until the 1940s and has been followed by three successor series launched in the 1950s, 1980s, and 1990s; the Hardy Boys have appeared continually since their debut in 1926; and new Oz books were published until the 1950s and were revived in the 1980s and 1990s by Baum's great-grandson Roger Baum.

While the reasons behind the powerful appeal of these series might be epitomized in different ways, there are arguably three basic qualities that explain their success.

The first quality, most often noted by critics, is their *continuity*. All books in a series feature a familiar environment—Tom Swift's home town Shopton, the Hardy Boys' home town Bayport, and the Emerald City of Oz—that is the locale, or at least the starting point or endpoint, of every adventure. All books feature a familiar set of characters: Tom Swift is accompanied by father Barton Swift, housekeeper Mrs. Baggert, friend Ned Newton, girlfriend Mary Nestor, and his embarrassingly stereotypical African-American assistant Eradicate Sampson; the Hardy Boys interact with parents Fenton and Laura Hardy, friends Chet Morton, Biff Hooper, and Tony Prito, girlfriends Callie Shaw and Iola Morton, and "peppery" Aunt Gertrude; and the regularly observed inhabitants of Oz include Dorothy, the Wizard, the Scarecrow, Glinda the Good, and Princess Ozma. And all books feature a familiar sort of plot: Tom Swift perfects his latest invention while battling crooked entrepreneurs seeking to steal or thwart his work; the Hardy Boys confront and solve a mystery; and an Oz character embarks upon a quest through Oz or its environs to achieve an important goal. To be sure, the books in these series were never as predictable as their dime-novel predecessors, and each series includes some books that depart from the pattern in some significant way; but there is some truth in Selma Lanes's comment that "Like the vacationer who returns to a beloved summer house year after year, the addicted reader opens book three or four or eleven in a given series and is thoroughly at home in the locale—its by now familiar native characters, the verbal shrubbery and the narrative floorboards that occasionally creak" (cited in Billman 13).

The second quality could be epitomized as *assertiveness*. While children in classic books like Johann David Wyss's *The Swiss Family Robinson* and P. L. Travers's *Mary Poppins* were often content to follow the dictates of parents or parental figures, the young protagonists of series fiction urgently wish to take charge of their own lives; they chafe under the restrictions imposed by older authorities, respectfully request more freedom, and seek to solve mysteries or achieve success entirely by themselves. And it is their own independent actions, not mere luck or the helpful intervention of others, that lead to the triumphant conclusion of their adventure. As one potent emblem of assertive freedom and individual initiative, *travel* is a central motif in these series: Tom Swift's inventions include an array of impressive vehicles for land, sea, and air travel; the Hardy Boys progress from motorcycles to their own boat, car, and airplane; and characters in Oz often move about in extravagant ways, such as flying through the air by means of magic slippers, flying monkeys, or the Gump. And boys and girls surely find it gratifying to read about youngsters not unlike themselves who take matters into their own hands to rescue victims and foil evildoers.

The third quality, emerging from the interaction of the continuity that series impose upon protagonists and their assertive desire to achieve change, is *gradual maturation.* Characters do not remain exactly the same; in overt or covert ways, they grow older, become more mature, enhance their reputation, and expand their range of operations. Tom Swift grows to adulthood, becomes an independent businessman with several employees, and even marries Mary Nestor. Since this aging process, not unusual in other series of its day, was thought to be a factor in Tom Swift's diminishing popularity, the Hardy Boys were not allowed to mature to this extent and remained perpetual high school seniors, but characters in such series inevitably develop, regardless of their overseers' dictates: thus, the Hardy Boys moved steadily from local mysteries involving haunted houses to globe-trotting exploits against international conspiracies, and progressed from being ridiculed "boys playing detectives" to the status of widely known and respected sleuths whose assistance is eagerly sought by people all over the world. And Oz, at first an unsettling realm with menacing adults opposed by benevolent adults, evolves into a land literally governed by children, with Princess Ozma, assisted by her friend Dorothy, serving as the benevolent and all-powerful protector of its inhabitants while Glinda, who first played the role, recedes into the background. Thus, for youths who read the consecutively numbered books in a series, there is a slow but visible success story about young, belittled, and unimportant young people who by means of hard work and achievements eventually become more mature, more respected, and more significant figures in their worlds.

This is, of course, a familiar story, an extended version of the rags-to-riches story made famous by Alger, a writer Stratemeyer admired who left several unfinished manuscripts that were completed posthumously by Stratemeyer. It also happens to be the story of Edward Stratemeyer himself, a young man who found something he did well—writing fiction for children—kept working hard at it, and made himself successful step by step: He began his career in 1883, was soon publishing dime novels, moved to book publication in 1894, achieved great popularity with his novel *Under Dewey at Manila* in 1898 and his first Rover Boys book in 1899, and by 1905 had set up the Syndicate that would ensure lifelong prosperity for him and his heirs. Clearly, Stratemeyer had every reason to personally believe in the stories he presented, and to this day the success of his various series demonstrates the appeal of the Horatio Alger story he revered and enacted.

However, despite the continuing popularity of the old and new series following the Stratemeyer pattern, there has now emerged another variety of juvenile series fiction conveying a rather different philosophy of life; and the development and evolution of this new form demands extended examination.

The story begins in 1979 with the introduction of a new series from Bantam Books entitled the Choose Your Own Adventure books. The man who created the series and wrote several of its early books, Edward Packard, was (according to a blurb in his first book, *The Cave of Time*) "A graduate of Princeton University and Columbia Law School," now "a practicing lawyer and an officer of Vermont Crossroads Press," who "conceived the idea for the Choose Your Own Adventure books in the course of telling his children stories at bedtime" (117). This was their pattern: A story begins, unusually related in the second person, and proceeds for a page or two before stopping at a decision point; the reader is offered two (sometimes three or four) choices, each requiring that the reader turn to a different page; after the reader goes to the selected page, the narrative continues until another decision point is reached, with a new choice; and the process continues until the narrative comes to one of numerous different conclusions, some favorable, some unfavorable. By changing decisions, a reader may go through the same book any number of times and experience a different story each time. An agreed-upon term for such books has not yet emerged: One lofty term offered by Bantam Books was "reader participation fiction"; others call them "gamebooks," though the term also takes in other sorts of interactive books; and the Library of Congress tends to call them "multiple-ending books," though there is also multiplicity in their beginnings and middles. What they definitely are, by any name, is a new form of juvenile series fiction, since the logo "Choose Your Own Adventure" is prominently displayed on every cover, and since the books are serially numbered 1, 2, 3, and so on, as a way to guide young readers who may be eager to collect every book in the series.

Yet the Choose Your Own Adventure books were unlike previous series fiction. First, there was no continuity: Volumes involved no shared setting, recurring characters, or characteristic story line; indeed, books varied even in their basic genre, alternately venturing into science fiction, fantasy, horror, mysteries, westerns, and other types of popular fiction, and the fact that a given journey through a book could lead to either a happy or tragic ending further undermined any sense of unity. And with different authors credited by name, there was no overarching pseudonym like Tom Swift's Victor Appleton or the Hardy Boys' Franklin W. Dixon to suggest stylistic uniformity; only the format of the books—reader choices leading to "multiple endings"—provided a feeling of connectedness between volumes.

Second, the books did not offer readers acting as protagonists any meaningful opportunities for assertiveness, despite appearances to the contrary. To be sure, one might argue that these books were "empowering": Instead of listening passively to an authorial voice dictating everything that happens in the story, young readers are actively involved in the process of story-telling, making key decisions and driving the plot in certain directions. But it is difficult to valorize this format as a forum for assertiveness. First, the choices given readers are carefully regulated and distributed: One reads for a while in the usual dutiful manner, then one is abruptly presented with a choice to be made. Readers are not truly assertive, only *reactive*; they are "empowered" only at moments chosen for their temporary empowerment by the authority controlling the story. The broader objection is that books often require readers to make decisions on the basis of insufficient information, and the wisdom or stupidity of any particular decision bears no discernible relationship to the felicity of its results. What does the cave-exploring reader in *The Cave of Time* do when the choice is "If you enter the left-hand passageway, turn to page 24" and "If you enter the right-hand passageway, turn to page 25" (16)? One way may lead to salvation, the other to a hasty death, and there is no way of knowing which way is best. Thus, though I elsewhere note that choosing boldness and altruism will most likely lead to desirable results (in "Zen and the Art of Mario Maintenance"), there are no guarantees in these books, and success or failure is essentially a result not of intelligence or proper choice, but luck: If you are lucky, the cave you choose leads to a treasure; if you are unlucky, it leads to a man-eating monster. You might as well flip a coin to decide, and that boils down to an argument in favor of passivity, not assertiveness.

Finally, there is no overall sense of maturation in these books. Each book begins anew, with new characters stumbling into new predicaments, and characters in the hundredth volume are no older or wiser than the characters in the first volume. Thus, the series provides no grounds for any belief in progress; instead, there is only the stasis resulting from a continuing series of randomly presented decisions leading to unpredictable results.

However, a denunciation of these books for these reasons—which some might suspect is my purpose—would rest upon a debatable proposition: that the message of Alger and his successors is essentially *true*, and thus should be imparted to young minds, while the contradictory message here is essentially *false*, and thus should be condemned. But the immediate and enormous popularity of the Choose Your Own Adventure books suggests that they, at least for some, conveyed a truth of their own: Just as Alger struck a chord in the 1880s and 1890s, these books undeniably struck a chord in the 1980s and 1990s. Many youngsters loved the books, calling them "full of surprises," "very adventurous," and "great fun" (cited in Packard, *The Mystery of Chimney Rock*). The series did advance to a hundredth volume and beyond, and spawned both a spinoff series for younger readers and many imitations from other publishers. Even the stalwarts of the Stratemeyer Syndicate, the Hardy Boys and Nancy Drew, jumped on the bandwagon with a brief series of "Be a Detective Mystery Stories." At some level, then, many young readers found these discontinuous paeans to a randomized universe more persuasive than the earnest success stories of Tom Swift or the Hardy Boys.

If Alger figures as chief developer of the original philosophy of juvenile series fiction—celebrating continuity, assertiveness, and gradual maturation—with Stratemeyer as Alger's most visible disciple, then Packard may someday be regarded as the chief developer of a new philosophy of juvenile series fiction—celebrating incoherence, passivity, and stasis—with another writer, R. L. Stine, currently functioning as his most prominent and influential successor.

Based on the data presented in his autobiography, *It Came from Ohio!: My Life as a Writer*, and my own desperate efforts to compile a complete and accurate bibliography of his works for a reference book, one can begin to understand the remarkable and intriguing career of R. L. Stine. As he tells the story, he graduated from college in the mid-1960s, taught junior high school for one year, then moved to New York to become a writer. And what a writer he became! In the two decades that followed, he basically wrote anything that anyone would pay him to write: phony "interviews" with celebrities for obscure teen magazines; articles for a magazine called *Soft Drink Industry*; vignettes for children's magazines like *Junior Scholastic* and *Bananas*; captions for Mighty Mouse and Bullwinkle coloring books; a series of bubblegum cards entitled *Zero Heroes*; scripts for the puppets on the Nickelodeon show *Eureeka's Castle*; and, increasingly, books for children of every conceivable sort—advice books, how-to books, joke books, and movie novelizations, sometimes under the name Jovial Bob Stine. By the 1980s, one of his major avocations had become—appropriately, as we shall see—multiple-ending books. As R. L. Stine or as Eric Affabee, he wrote over two dozen books of this kind in three series—Twistaplot; Find Your Fate; Wizards, Warriors, and You—featuring Indiana Jones, G.I. Joe, and other heroes. Surveying his formative career, one searches in vain for any pattern, any sign of meaningful progress or direction towards a goal, and Stine himself never communicates having any ambition at the time other than making a living as a writer, which he certainly did, albeit unimpressively. Thus, while the first two decades of Stratemeyer's New York career fit the Alger pattern of hard work and steady progress toward a goal, the first two decades of Stine's New York career fit the pattern of a Choose Your Own Adventure book: Stine was asked to write something, he agreed, he kept at it until the work was finished, he was asked to write something else, he agreed, and so on for years of unassertive labor interrupted by arbitrary decision points.

Further, Stine's period of success apparently proceeded in a similarly directionless fashion: First, a publisher friend asked him to write a young-adult horror novel, to which he responded, "A young-adult horror novel? I didn't really know what she was talking about. But I never said no to anyone in those days!" (*It Came from Ohio!* 107-8). After that book and other similar ones proved popular, his fan mail inspired another thought: "maybe I should try writing a *series* of scary books" (110). When the resulting Fear Street books were well-received, an editor gave him a new suggestion: "Maybe younger kids would like to be scared too. . . . Maybe you could write a series of scary books that are also funny" (114). The publishing phenomenon that followed, the Goosebumps books, engendered another project: "The idea for the *Goosebumps* TV show came from . . . letters from kids asking to see the stories on TV" (121). And though Stine does not provide details, one must assume that random brainstorms or others' proposals then led to everything else: Give Yourself Goosebumps books, Goosebumps anthologies and omnibuses, Goosebumps merchandise, his adult horror novel *Superstitious*, and three series of books displaying his name but surreptitiously acknowledging other authors on the copyright page: the Ghosts of Fear Street, the Fear Street Sagas, and the Goosebumps TV Specials.

Observing this frenetic activity, one might regard Stine as the modern equivalent of Stratemeyer, another New Yorker building a publishing empire with children's literature. But Stratemeyer had a plan, and proceeded thoughtfully and methodically, which does not seem the case with Stine. Since *Under Dewey at Manila* as by Stratemeyer was so popular, Stratemeyer might have achieved some quick sales by publishing many other books by himself and by others under that name; but the series books he later wrote or outlined for other writers were attributed to pseudonyms, sacrificing short-term success to achieve the long-term viability of names like Franklin W. Dixon and Nancy Drew's Carolyn Keene that still attract readers long after Stratemeyer's death. Stine willingly presents himself as the author of every book emerging from his company, resultingly selling a fair number of books now, but virtually guaranteeing that the Stine empire will collapse when he dies and can no longer be plausibly presented as the author of new books. To ensure ongoing success while genres waxed and waned in popularity, Stratemeyer strived to diversify his output, launching variegated series with diverse protagonists like students, inventors, jungle adventurers, detectives, sports stars, airplane pilots, deep-sea divers, soldiers, moviemakers, and cowboys. Stine produces only horror stories, placing all of his eggs in one basket and leaving himself open to disaster should the popularity of horror fiction dramatically decline. Stratemeyer expanded cautiously, beginning with three books as "breeders" for potential series and continuing them only if they were popular, so that his company eventually specialized in a limited number of series with steady sales. Stine seems intent upon flooding the market with his products, some of them ill-conceived and apparently likely to eventually have undesirable results: Why produce Ghosts of Fear Street titles by other authors to directly compete with your own Goosebumps books? Why publish Goosebumps TV Specials that repeat in simplified form the plots of your most popular Goosebumps novels? However, one must surmise, somebody had a notion, or somebody approached Stine with a proposal, and he decided to go along with the idea.

If, therefore, Stine's own life consistently reflects the incohesiveness, unassertiveness, and directionlessness of the multiple-ending books he once produced so prodigiously, one might expect that his horror novels would reflect and project a similar philosophy. And, increasingly, they do exactly that.

His first series, Fear Street, represents a transitional effort, in some ways resembling traditional juvenile series fiction while in other ways reflecting the incoherence of the multiple-ending book. In the beginning, Fear Street novels displayed some of the characteristics of the Stratemeyer books, especially continuity. They shared a common setting; a town with a notorious neighborhood, Fear Street, where there were spooky old houses, a cemetery, and a dark forest in which teenagers taking a shortcut were likely to end up murdered. There were occasional common characters; the heroine of one novel might briefly appear at a party in a later novel. The books displayed a general sort of pattern: There were unsettling events, like several murders, seemingly involving the supernatural, but finally given a rational explanation. Also, teenagers in the novels were often capable of meaningful activity in confronting evil people and aggressively investigating strange goings-on, and with a few recurring characters, there was the possibility of development and maturation in the series.

However, the connective tissue in Fear Street novels soon faded from view as the series progressed: Fear Street became less important as a focus of attention, and entire novels might take place out of town without a single visit to the epynomous locale; the device of characters returning from previous novels was gradually abandoned; stories became more varied, at times involving truly supernatural events; and the teenagers began to act more like helpless victims than competent opponents of evil, with survival or death more a matter of chance than anything else (in the Cataluna Chronicles series, for example, thoughtless young men repeatedly drive a haunted car and allow themselves to be threatened by its vengeful spirit). And as characters became a bit denser and more inept than their predecessors, the series reflected no sense of progress, and even a degree of devolution. In sum, what first resembled a Stratemeyer series took on the aura of the Choose Your Own Adventure books.

For the Goosebumps books, which would directly compete with the Hardy Boys and their compatriots, Stine from the start eschewed connectedness: These books would have no shared setting, continuing characters, or standard plot. Protagonists would usually be around twelve years old, perhaps with a bratty kid brother or sister, and essentially incapable of independence or significant action. While they would attempt to deal with the supernatural or scientific menaces entering their lives, they would only dimly understand what they were confronting, and their victories would be due to luck more than anything else and might be only temporary, as the last sentence might hint about the eventual return of the monster.

Thus, while overt differences in the genres of these series—Stratemeyer's realistic stories sprinkled with science fiction versus Stine's outright horror—might be viewed as a shift from powerful to powerless protagonists, it is the ambience of Stine's fiction, more than its genre, that represents the major change. After all, in the 1960s and 1970s, the Hardy Boys themselves moved forcefully in the direction of horror, as reflected in titles like *The Haunted Fort, Danger on Vampire Trail, The Witchmaster's Key*, and *Night of the Werewolf*, but they lost none of their courage and self-confidence; Stine chooses young, inexperienced and unassertive protagonists who are bewildered and rendered helpless by the horror they confront. They usually survive, but like readers who happen to emerge from a multiple-ending book with a bag of gold and happy future, their final survival is more a matter of luck than anything else.

To see how juvenile series fiction has changed, consider the tales of two werewolves: the fifty-ninth Hardy Boys book, *Night of the Werewolf*, and the fourteenth Goosebumps book, *The Werewolf of Fever Swamp*. When the Hardy Boys apparently see a werewolf, they research the subject at a library and talk to the author of a book about werewolves. They are asked to travel to upstate New York to investigate the possibility that an architect's son is a werewolf, getting a tranquilizer gun for protection. While spying on the suspect, they interview several people, gradually discerning schemes to protect a crooked architect, discover a valuable silver tomahawk, and discredit the son so he will not receive a large inheritance. After other adventures, they confront the werewolf, stop it with the tranquilizer gun, and discover that it is only a Doberman pinscher wearing a spooky disguise. Finally, they fight with and capture the criminals, also finding the silver tomahawk in the process.

In contrast, Stine's Grady Tucker is forced to move to Florida with his parents. He and his older sister get lost in Fever Swamp and flee from a strange hermit. He hears howling noises and is told by a new friend about a werewolf lurking in the swamp; he occasionally ventures into the swamp but runs away at the first sign of danger. In his one moment of decisive action, he sets his dog free when his father, blaming the dog for some slaughtered animals, wants to get rid of him. Grady is finally attacked and bitten by the werewolf (who is the friend), though the dog kills the beast. In the end, Grady becomes a werewolf himself. In sum, the first book is a story of heroism, the second a story of victimization. And one cannot protest that Stine is aiming at younger readers (Hardy Boys books are next to Goosebumps books in bookstores), or that his novels have younger protagonists (that is Stine's choice, not a generic requirement). Even stories for and about young children can depict meaningful action, and even the young children in the Stratemeyer series for young readers, the Bobbsey Twins, regularly displayed more courage and initiative than Stine's hapless hero.

I have suggested that Stine may have absorbed this approach to writing not only from his own background, but from his experience in writing multiple-ending books; as evidence for the connection, one might examine the Goosebumps book that first gave me the idea: *The Beast from the East*. Ginger and her twin brothers wander away from their parents into a forest, where they get lost (a regular Stine plot device). They see, and try to avoid, large, menacing-looking beasts; finally, a beast approaches, hits her, and screams "You're it!" (28). The creatures are playing a version of tag in which the person who is "It" is named "The Beast from the East," but the game has many bizarre rules which the children do not know, as they keep protesting: "We can't play a game without knowing what it is" (32), and "You have to tell us the rules. All of them" (35). But after a few vague comments, the children must start playing, even without knowing the rules, in order to avoid being eaten. At one point, they fearfully find themselves covered with snakes, but that turns out to be a good move—"Double Snake Eyes" (48). One brother touches a rock, which explodes and forces him to be put in a cage; it was a "Penalty Rock" (66). Once, when they are about to be captured, a cloud covers the sun; "Made in the Shade," a beast exclaims, explaining they are temporarily free to go (80). Ginger sneaks up and tags a monster, making him "the Beast from the East"— except that she didn't tag him from the direction of the east, so it didn't count (89). So the story proceeds, the children unknowingly making good moves or unknowingly making bad moves, thus exactly paralleling the experience of reading making bad moves, exactly paralleling the experience of reading through a multi-ple-ending book, constantly making decisions without any knowledgeable grounds for doing so. Though Ginger does engage in purposeful and effective action exactly two times—freeing one brother from a living tree by tickling its branches, and tricking a monster into making itself dizzy so she can tag it—her temporary triumphs are ultimately futile, as the book ends with Ginger and her brothers about to be eaten; but when the beasts see the twins together for the first time, they announce, "You did a Classic Clone!" (115), identifying the children as "Level Three" players, who should not be playing with Level One monsters, and thus effecting their freedom—until they meet a Level Three player while returning to their parents. In this awful novel, then, the children—like readers of a multiple-ending book—are trapped in a game without knowing what to do, they randomly make decisions, they get lucky, and they avoid an unfavorable outcome.

One must also consider another series launched by Stine, Give Yourself Goosebumps, featuring scary stories in the Goosebumps mold adapted to the multiple-ending format. Generally the two types of books are remarkably similar: Both offer the same bland prose, both present a series of random horrific events demanding arbitrary decisions, and both proceed to resolutions that are not logi-cally related to those decisions; other than the absence of variety when rereading Goosebumps books, the atmosphere and affect in each type of book are surpris-ingly congruent. Interestingly, Stine shifts the approach of the multiple-ending book towards fewer, and less meaningful, choices. In Packard's *The Mystery of Chimney Rock*, there are choices to make on 47 of its 106 pages of text, or about 39% of the pages; in Stine's Give Yourself Goosebumps book, *Beware of the Purple Peanut Butter*, there are choices on only 31 out of 105 pages of text, or about 23% of the pages. In addition, only two of Packard's 47 choices are essen-tially arbitrary, deciding which room of a mysterious house to venture into; the others involve choices that might involve or reward serious thought. In Stine's book, 11 of the 31 choices are compromised. His most startling innovation is to have two choices that aren't really choices at all, since *the book only allows you to choose one option*: On page 108, if you want to avoid going into the basement, the page you are sent to chides you for cowardice and sends you back to page 108 to make the correct choice; on page 129, if you wish to avoid a bully, the page you are sent to criticizes your decision and sends you to the page you just rejected to confront him anyway. Five other choices are arbitrary, a matter of guesswork, such as choosing the blue liquid or purple liquid on page 21. And five "choices" are predetermined by circumstances; at one point (98), readers with an even number of letters in their first name are dispatched to their deaths, while readers with an odd number of letters survive, and other "choices" hinge upon what day of the week it is or what month the reader was born in. Giving away the game, another "choice" begins, "You might as well leave it to chance. Flip a coin three times" (52) to decide which page to go to; yes, to determine whether they live or die in the worlds of Goosebumps, readers necessarily must "leave it to chance."

Though the publication dates are wrong, one could thus portray the Give Your-self Goosebumps books as an imaginative re-creation of the evolutionary process that took Stine from writing Find Your Fate books to writing Goosebumps books. First, you write in the multiple-ending format. Then, you reduce the number and meaningfulness of choices to create a more directive narrative while maintaining the semblance of choice—which would result in a book like *Beware of the Purple Peanut Butter*. Finally, you remove the element of choice entirely and write a multiple-ending book in which the author makes all the choices—which would result in a book like *The Beast from the East*. In all cases, readers experience a narrative which presents life as a series of choices imposed upon people, who must make decisions arbitrarily and without sufficient knowledge, and who then suffer the unpredictable consequences of their actions. We have moved from Alger's Social Darwinism to chaos theory.

In arguing that a sea change in juvenile series fiction has occurred, I do not wish to make judgments or offer recommendations. It would be naive, for example, to praise Stratemeyer's books as wholesome, uplifting entertainment while denouncing Stine's books as insidious bad influences. But it is interesting to speculate about why juvenile fiction of this kind is emerging and finding a wide audience today. Perhaps, as already suggested, it reflects changing lifestyles. In an era when people like Stratemeyer typically lived in one place and held one job for their entire lifetimes, they might naturally view life as a purposeful struggle towards a single goal and write or seek fiction reflecting their own stability. Today, in an era when people like Stine typically live in many places and hold many jobs, they might naturally view life as a series of random events with unpredictable consequences and write or seek fiction reflecting their own instability.

More stridently, one might ask Andrew Ross's question—whose interests are being served by these philosophies?—to see in Stratemeyer and Stine the messages that the elite classes of two eras wished to communicate to the masses. First, when an industrial civilization is in the process of being constructed, and is in need of submissive and energetic workers, it is expedient to tell young people that success emerges from grit and ambition. However, when that civilization is already constructed—with many gritty, ambitious workers who somehow never advanced into the elite—and is in need only of those workers' complacent acceptance of their lot in life, it is expedient to tell young people that success is, after all, a matter of luck, so that one's lowly status is nothing to get angry about but merely something that might be corrected by, say, a parent's visit to a casino or the purchase of a winning lottery ticket.

Conversely, one could see both philosophies as benign and complementary. Since even Alger and Stratemeyer acknowledge that success sometimes involves luck, and since even Packard and Stine acknowledge that success sometimes involves purposeful action, the two sorts of books differ only in their emphases, and, with both types now available to them, young people can obtain a balanced view of life, learning both the importance of purposeful labor (from Stratemeyer books) and the reality of random chance (from Goosebumps books).

Finally, one might interestingly compare my analysis of a growing disempowerment of children in juvenile series fiction with Gary Kern's analysis (in "The Triumph of Teen Prop") of a growing empowerment of children in films, suggesting perhaps that the different media are appealing to different groups of children: Those who wish to feel powerful go to the movies, while those who wish to feel powerless read books.

In the end, of course, all readers must Choose Their Own Adventures, and I cannot conceal my own preferences. As a child, I read the Hardy Boys books, along with several Tom Swift, Jr., and Oz books. As an adult, I returned to them with genuine pleasure, reading the original versions of the Hardy Boys books, books in the first and third Tom Swift series, and the later Oz books. I emerged believing that such books, for all their manifest flaws, still represented valuable experiences for the children who read them and intriguing documents for the adults who looked over their shoulders. Due either to my critical acumen or blinding nostalgia, I cannot react this way to the multiple-ending books or the Goosebumps novels; and today, when I see the Hardy Boys and Nancy Drew in bookstores, still holding their own next to all the Stine books, I hope that they will emerge triumphant in the competition, just as they have overcome many previous challenges. Indeed, to young heroes and heroines schooled by Horatio Alger, Jr., a few goosebumps should be nothing to worry about.

5

From the Back of the Head to
Beyond the Moon: The Novel
and Film *This Island Earth*

Though I have read several discussions of science fiction films derived from science fiction novels, I can recall no mention of the film *This Island Earth* (1955), based on Raymond F. Jones's novel of that name. Some scholars may be unaware of the novel's existence or may have been unable to obtain a copy, since it quickly went out of print after appearing in 1952 and did not resurface until its inclusion in a 1994 anthology, *Reel Future*, edited by Forrest J. Ackerman and Jean Stine. Other scholars may have recognized, or surmised, that Jones's novel was not exactly a science fiction classic on a par with other, more prominent novels turned into films, like *Dune* or *The Martian Chronicles*, and decided that it did not merit much attention. For whatever reason, neglect of the novel *This Island Earth* is unfortunate, for examination of its contents helps to explain why the film is so distinctive, so haunting, and so difficult for critics to approach.

The textual history of Jones's novel is not particularly complicated, but it has never to my knowledge been explained in detail. First, in the June 1949 issue of *Thrilling Wonder Stories*, then a bimonthly science fiction magazine, there appeared Jones's story "The Alien Machine," divided into four chapters, which with minor changes became the first four chapters of the novel. The first story describes how radio engineer Cal Meacham of the Ryberg Instrument Corporation receives an astounding piece of electronic equipment, followed by a catalog, from a mysterious company; he orders the materials to build a device called an interocitor; after days of painstaking labor involving thousands of parts, he successfully assembles the device, and a man appears on its television screen to explain that Cal has passed the test and is now being offered the opportunity to work for the organization; then, at the designated time, Cal arrives at a runway to be met by a pilotless plane, ready to fly him to his unknown destination.

Since the next Meacham story did not appear until three issues later, it is reasonable to suppose that Jones finished "The Alien Machine" not entirely sure how, or even whether, the adventure would continue, and one can appreciate the story as a complete work. As such, it can be defended as a masterpiece. Unique, intriguing, and evocative, the story is unsurprisingly the one sequence from the novel that the film duplicated almost exactly, and it surely accounts for much of the film's enduring appeal. When I first watched *This Island Earth* on television in the early 1960s, I was utterly fascinated by its opening scenes, for I had never experienced a science fiction story that unfolded in precisely this way and gripped me so powerfully from the very start (which made it all the more frustrating when my parents insisted that we had to leave the house after the first thirty minutes, forcing me to wait a few more years until I could watch the entire film). If Jones had never written another word about Cal Meacham, "The Alien Machine" might have been enshrined as a classic science fiction story, frequently anthologized and analyzed, like Tom Godwin's "The Cold Equations," as representative of the genre's special qualities. Indeed, whatever description of effective science fiction one prefers— whether it be Hugo Gernsback's "charming romance interwoven with scientific fact and prophetic vision," the 1930s' "sense of wonder," Brian W. Aldiss's "search for a definition of man," Darko Suvin's "literature of cognitive estrangement," or Alexei and Cory Panshin's "search for transcendence"—the story has something to offer; it speaks weirdly and wonderfully, with its own sort of halting eloquence, about the reasons why people love to build machines, the allure of imagined technology, the thrill of scientific triumphs, and the sense that mastering advanced science constitutes a sort of initiation ritual allowing access to higher levels of reality.

As a side issue, it is interesting to explore why Jones created the term "interocitor"—or, to enter the conceptual realm of the narrative, why the aliens chose to invent this English term for their machine. While one might detect in the latter half of the word the root "occident," meaning "west," and regard the communication device as the aliens' way to unite the good—in the geopolitical mindset of the era, western—worlds in their alliance against the evil— eastern—worlds, the political allegory seems strained. Though it may be an equally fanciful reading, I would prefer to discern the root "occip," meaning "the back of the head," making the interocitor a machine that connects the backs of heads. This would anticipate the revelation, in the next two stories, that the interocitor is really a device for telepathic communication. Later, in the novel, when Cal employs the interocitor to perceive a malignant alien mentality, he "felt the back of his neck turn cold" (171). Further, since the back of the head is the location of the more primitive parts of the brain, the medulla and cerebellum, this reading suggests that the interocitor, for all its mechanistic and technological trappings, in some way stirs our primal emotions (in Carl Sagan's scheme, our "reptilian brain"), not our intellects (our "mammalian brain").

In any event, while Cal Meacham's saga might have been most memorable as an enchanting fragment, Jones did elect to continue the narrative. The next two stories, "The Shroud of Secrecy" and "The Greater Conflict," are best regarded as a single, two-part novella despite their separate titles. Clearly, they were conceived and written around the same time, they appeared in consecutive issues of *Thrilling Wonder Stories* (December 1949 and February 1950), and "The Shroud of Secrecy" concluded with a blurb advertising its immediate sequel:

Cal Meacham and his aides battle to end warfare forever, and finally learn the strange truth about their Phoenix plant in the next adventure of the Peace Engineers—

THIS GREATER CONFLICT
A Dynamic Complete Novelet
by
Raymond F. Jones (79)

(And in the original title for the third story, "This Greater Conflict," we find one source for the novel's title.) The four chapters of "The Shroud of Secrecy" became with minor changes chapters 5 through 8 of the novel, while the six chapters of "The Greater Conflict" became with minor changes chapters 9 through 14.

(To explain what all these "minor changes" amounted to: while I did not undertake a line-by-line comparison of the two texts, an examination of the beginning and ending passages of each chapter, and an overview of the other material, indicated that the versions were essentially identical except for the removal of some incidental conversation, removal of some language recapitulating previous developments, and removal of the chapter titles.)

In "The Shroud of Secrecy," Cal is flown to a plant near Phoenix, where he meets and talks with several people: another recruited scientist, a psychiatrist named Ruth Adams; an administrator, Dr. Warner, who informs Cal that he will be asked to oversee a factory that manufactures interocitors; a former college roommate and scientific colleague, Ole Swenberg, who is vocally suspicious of the strange organization he works for and soon quits; and the head of the entire project, Jorgasnovara, who describes his Peace Engineers as a centuries-old secret society dedicated to pursuing scientific research and preserving humanity from harm. After all this conversation, Cal and Ruth concentrate on their work for several months before suddenly making two discoveries: that interocitors are devices for telepathic communication, and that the interocitors made on Earth are being shipped into outer space.

In "The Greater Conflict," Cal and Ruth re-establish contact with Ole, still working for the Peace Engineers in Los Angeles despite his continuing misgivings; he has figured out, as Cal and Ruth soon learn from overhearing more of Jorgasnovara's mental messages, that the Peace Engineers are enmeshed in an interstellar war. When Cal attempts to flee from them in an airplane, he is pulled into a spaceship and flown to the Moon, where he meets Ruth and Ole and gets the whole story from Jorgasnovara. The Peace Engineers are really extraterrestrials, engaged in a vast, ancient conflict against implacably evil aliens, and they surreptitiously recruit humans and other less advanced races to assist in whatever ways they can. In the passage that is the other source of the novel's title, he explains the humans' situation:

"You have had experience during your own recent World War. . . . You saw these primitive peoples sometimes employed or pressed into service by one side or the other. On the islands of your seas they built airfields for you; they sometimes cleared jungles and helped lay airstrips. They had no comprehension of the vast purpose to which they were contributing a meager part, but they helped in a conflict which was ultimately resolved in their favor."

Cal's face had gone white. He half-rose from his seat. "You mean—"

Jorgasnovara waved him down. "This greater conflict of which I have spoken has existed for hundreds of generations. Your people were barely out of caves when it began. It will not be ended in your generation or mine. . . . But we need your help."

"To build an airstrip?"

Jorgasnovara smiled. "These interocitors which you find so interesting are a small item of communication equipment which is used in some of our larger vessels. . . . They are simple devices, comparable, say, to your pushbuttons. We need you to make some pushbuttons for us." (127-28)

Once returned to Earth, Cal resigns himself to the realities of his situation, telling Ruth, "Let's go. It's getting late, and tomorrow we've got to make a lot of—pushbuttons" (133). And the title of the final chapter, "A Lifetime of Service," suggests that this may have been where Jones once intended to conclude the story.

In contrast to the excitement and promise of "The Alien Machine," the revelations in these two stories are devastatingly depressing to Cal and to humanity. He had been invited to become not a colleague of wise and powerful beings, but only an underling. His achievement in single-handedly assembling an interocitor was a trivial matter to his alien masters, who regard Cal and his civilization as "primitive" and the machine as a "pushbutton." The work that Cal must now devote himself to, while not entirely without value, will have little effect on the galactic war. The title of the first chapter of "The Shroud of Secrecy," "End of a Dream," seems poignantly appropriate as a description of what Cal will discover while in Arizona.

In keeping with his greatly reduced stature in this new context, Cal also becomes essentially powerless. Previously a confident and independent scientist in his own domain, Cal now spends most of his time listening to other people tell him what is going on, or what he is obliged to do. Cal's minimal efforts to investigate his suspicious situation, primarily his trip to Los Angeles to interview Ole, yield no definite answers, and when he attempts to escape, he is immediately and easily captured. Even his one apparently effective action—modifying one interocitor so that he can "overhear" the telepathic projections of Jorgasnovara—was, it turns out, deliberately arranged by the alien as a way to investigate Cal's motives and to gently provide him with clues about his true circumstances.

This abrupt shift of mood in the second and third stories, to be sure, is not entirely uncharacteristic of science fiction; while sometimes derided for its unwavering celebrations of adolescent hubris, the genre also at times chillingly presents humanity as a tiny, insignificant race devoted to futile activities within a vast and uncaring universe, as in certain works of Olaf Stapledon and Arthur C. Clarke. Still, Jones's stories also present a reassuring picture of the alien Jorgasnovara and his colleagues—mature, knowledgeable, and capable—to suggest that the cosmos could in fact be mastered and controlled. When Jones later struggled to extend Cal's saga to the length of a novel, however, there came a new and disturbing revelation: Not only were Cal and the human race incompetent, but their alien overseers were pitiful and powerless as well.

This turn of events is signalled almost immediately in the novel's first new chapter, Chapter 15, when Jorgasnovara's benevolent alliance is named as the Llannan Council, formed to oppose the evil alien alliance known as the Guarra. Even readers who do not consult an etymological dictionary may discern that the Sheep ("lan" = wool, with the double "l" to further suggest "llama") are waiting to be butchered by the Warriors ("guerr" = warrior). While endeavoring to increase Earth's production of interocitors, Cal is baffled by the aliens' stubbornness and ignorance; they do not understand why the workers at the interocitor plant are disgruntled and likely to strike, and they do not see the logic in, and repeatedly oppose, his plans to decentralize the operations. Cal now refers to the aliens as "Supermen—who didn't have sense enough to come in out of the rain" (167). Evidence of Llannan ineptitude mounts: They allow the strike to occur, halting the production of interocitors; the aliens do not recognize that subsequent vandalism at the plant is the work of Guarra saboteurs and not union thugs; and they have also failed to figure out that Ole is really the "chief Guarra agent for Earth" (188), assigned to sabotage Earth's production of interocitors, which are now, incongruously, described as a key contribution to the galactic war.

A disconsolate Jorgasnovara then informs Cal and Ruth that the Llannan Council has decided to retreat in response to an unexpected Guarra thrust in the direction of Earth, cruelly abandoning Earth and ensuring that the planet is doomed. Soon, the alien has needlessly sacrificed his own life in a fierce telepathic battle, via the interocitor, with Ole. It is left to Cal to notice and to inform the Llannan Council that they have been relying too much on their computers to make decisions, making their actions overly predictable to the Guarra with their own superior computers and leading to deliberately random Guarra actions—like their offensive toward Earth—that leave the Llannan Council with no alternative but to continue retreating. Cal sums things up by noting, mildly, that "The Llanna had made foolish blunders" (219). Finally, after listening to Cal's arguments, the Council decides to reverse course and defend Earth, possibly saving humanity from destruction.

As an inspired rhetorical flourish, Cal's speech to the Council provides a new and contrasting context for Jorgasnovara's earlier metaphorical reference to the Llanna as advanced beings amidst savages. "We've seen it happen on Earth," he tells them, referring to Llannan vulnerability to the Guarra attacks. "Troops trained and drilled and marched through forests to be slaughtered by random attacking aborigines" (217). While Jorgasnovara referred disparagingly to the ignorant natives of the Pacific islands during World War II assisting the Americans, Cal recalls the Indians of eighteenth-century North America, who showed themselves fully capable of resisting British soldiers (as did the American colonists who learned to imitate Indian fighting techniques); in some situations, "primitive peoples" can be superior to more civilized peoples. Previously likened positively to the skillful American soldiers of the twentieth century, the Llanna are now being less positively likened to the arrogant British soldiers of the eighteenth century, unable to adapt to and learn from the fighting styles of inferior opponents and thus doomed to defeat. Further, after his speech, the novel refers to Cal's "introduction

of guerrilla fighting techniques in space war" (219), explaining even more clearly why Jones devised the term "Guarra." More importantly, though Cal is discussing the Guarra, he is implicitly referring to other "aborigines" like humanity, suggesting that the capabilities of advanced species like the Llanna may really be equivalent to those of humbler beings like Cal, who is after all now assuming the role of their adviser.

As the added chapters increasingly present the Llanna as dull and decadent, one might expect Cal to re-emerge as the intelligent and efficient scientist of the original story. Surprisingly, this does not occur: Cal remains as passive and incompetent as he was in the second and third stories. He never does anything at all to improve or increase the production of interocitors, and, like the Llanna, he does not realize that the Guarra are sabotaging the plant or that Ole is conspiring against them. Interestingly, Ruth (now Cal's wife) does suspect that persons other than union thugs are behind the damage, and that Ole is not to be trusted, and both her suspicions are proven correct. Cal's failure to be wiser than the only female character in the novel thus adds an element of emasculation to his diminished stature. Stupidly allowing himself and Ruth to be captured by the sinister Ole, Cal is saved only because Ole, stupidly, decides to lock them in a closet instead of killing them. While Cal and Ruth do contrive to escape from the closet and then lend their mental powers to Jorgasnovara's telepathic contest with Ole, they are largely helpless bystanders to the life-or-death struggle. Reduced in the end to the position of begging for Earth's survival, Cal achieves a victory of sorts only because he turns out to be slightly less obtuse than the Llannan Council in realizing that their string of defeats is due primarily to an over-reliance on predictable computer decisions.

Viewed in its entirety, then, the novel is a saga of degeneration and regression: In the first part, both Cal and the unseen aliens appear to be capable, intelligent beings; in the second part, Cal is revealed to be incompetent and slow-witted; and in the final part, the aliens are similarly unveiled as inept and obtuse. (Interestingly, contemporary reviewer P. Schuyler Miller, though unfamiliar with its publication history, discerned an incohesive tripartite structure as the novel's major problem: "It's hard to explain why 'This Island Earth' seems to thin out after a promising start. . . . Perhaps it's because three quite different—though smoothly related— *kinds* of problems for our hero to solve destroy the unity a novel needs" [151].) Furthermore, as the aliens manipulating events on Earth emerge as less and less capable, the other overarching manipulative figure in the novel—the author— emerges in parallel fashion as less and less capable as well. The adventures that appeared in *Thrilling Wonder Stories* were logical and cohesive, but as Jones tries to keep his story going in the chapters added for book publication, he is visibly losing control of events, and there are several developments other than the increasingly obvious Llannan stupidity that simply do not make sense. Given that Ole was Cal's old college roommate, and that Ole had the habit of complaining about Jorgasnovara and his crew at every opportunity, it makes no sense to abruptly transform him into an enemy agent, and his final actions as an enemy agent—allowing the foul smell of his alien cohorts to let Cal and Ruth learn his secret, then locking them in a closet instead of killing them—make no sense as well. Given new revelations that the interocitor, far from being a mere "pushbutton," is actually a critically important weapon to the Llannan struggle, it makes no sense for the aliens to relegate its production to a backwards planet and to make no effort to defend its factories against saboteurs. Further, if successful use of the interocitor inevitably results in the user's death—which is more or less what the dying Jorgasnovara acknowledges—it makes no sense to celebrate the device as a valuable weapon.

As a final signal of his own increasing incompetence, Jones ends *This Island Earth* without really completing the story: Earth is still threatened by imminent destruction that can only be prevented by the Llanna, who are now revealed to be somewhat dense and on a long losing streak in their war with the Guarra. While it would appear potentially helpful if Cal could rush back to Earth and build a few more interocitors for the Llanna, he instead bizarrely expresses the desire to opt out of the struggle to defend his own planet. In the book's final paragraph, Cal says that he "Must be getting old for that sort of thing," referring to space travel, and continues: "I think I'm ready for the little house with a lawn around it—and kids riding tricycles on the sidewalk" (220). Not only does the image of children on tricycles underline Cal's regression to powerlessness in the novel, but his impulse to abandon the story and tend his garden surely reflects Jones's own decision to abandon the story, send in the manuscript, and get to work on something else.

One can understand the trap that Jones fell into as the result of one of the inherent contradictions in the evolving aesthetics of science fiction. On the one hand, science fiction writers were urged to write in an exploratory manner, following ideas wherever they led to generate innovative stories that would be unpredictable to both authors and readers. As John W. Campbell, Jr., the editor who purchased several of Jones's early stories, put it,

the fun of science-fiction writing [is that] the plotting is as nearly 100% uninhibited as anything imaginable. . . . In this field, the reader can never be sure just how the author may wind up—and because the author feels that freedom, he can led the story have its head, let it develop in any direction that the logic of the developing situation may dictate. Many times a story actually winds up entirely different from the idea with which the author started. And, very rarely, an author can simply start a story, and let it work its own way out to a conclusion! ("Introduction," *Who Goes There?* 5)

And that is, according Jones's own report, pretty much how he created *This Island Earth*: "The story was not really planned as a trilogy, a novel, or anything else. It just kind of grew" (cited in Skotak 19). On the other hand, commentators agree that science fiction stories should manifest logical and consistent development to avoid disturbing readers: Campbell also said that a science fiction writer must have a "carefully mapped outline in mind to get consistency of minor details" ("The Old Navy Game" 6), and Darko Suvin agreed that "If the suggested alternative world, or the alternative formal framework, is not suggested *consistently*—if, that is, the discrete syntagmatic novelties are not sufficiently numerous and sufficiently compatible to induce a coherent 'absent paradigm' . . . then the reader's specific SF pleasure will be mutilated or destroyed" (*Positions and Presuppositions in*

Science Fiction 67). The question is: What happens when the recommended process of free, uninhibited science fiction writing begins to generate inconsistencies? A. E. van Vogt was one noted writer who often had problems of this kind, creating novels like *Slan* and *The World of Null-A* that first engrossed readers with their feverish inventiveness but eventually alienated them with conspicuous illogic. His subsequent fall into relative obscurity suggests that for all his obvious gifts, van Vogt may have lacked the talent to produce science fiction that met his readers' expectations.

Still, while one can readily, and with some justice, label writers like Jones and van Vogt who allow their stories to fall into chaos as incompetent, there are a few types of stories where this sort of incompetence may be paradoxically productive, and *This Island Earth* may be one of them. Just as I suggest elsewhere in this volume that Jacqueline Susann's inability to bring *Valley of the Dolls* to a satisfying conclusion strangely functions to persuasively convey the novel's own message about the helplessness of women in Hollywood, one can argue that the developing inconsistencies of *This Island Earth*, caused by the author's own ineptitude, serve to persuasively convey the novel's own message about humanity's weakness and insignificance in the face of a vast and incomprehensible cosmos, perhaps even more powerfully than the reasoned and controlled visions of more gifted authors like Clarke and Stapledon. They carefully crafted narratives of human insignificance in the cosmos; Jones accidentally drifts into writing such a narrative. The only trouble is that Jones aborts the process by ending his story prematurely, failing to allow its flaws and discrepancies to blossom into complete absurdity. Such a performance, of course, would have violated the conventions of the science fiction genre and possibly exposed the author to ridicule, so Jones's reluctance to continue his story in that manner is entirely understandable.

Hollywood, however, would feel no such reluctance.

It will be my contention that the film version of *This Island Earth*, despite numerous changes in the novel's story, is entirely faithful to the novel in spirit, and that the film is especially fascinating because it not only adapts but also continues, amplifies, and completes Jones's narrative. Unlike other film adaptations, *This Island Earth* does not simplify or coarsen its source novel; rather, it fulfills the novel. The fact that this almost certainly occurred unintentionally does not tarnish the singular success of the film.

Before explaining how the film adheres to and enhances the novel, I must first discuss how the film's story differs from the novel's story. My analysis will often employ the useful "MagicImage Filmbook" *This Island Earth*, edited by Philip J. Riley, which includes brief remembrances from star Jeff Morrow and screenwriter Franklin Coen; Robert Skotak's essay "Production Background" describing the making of the film; and a copy of the film's final script, which records (with a few changes, as I will occasionally mention) what ended up on the screen. While the numerous alterations in the story might be categorized in various ways, one could classify them as aspects of three broad changes: First, the Llanna are significantly diminished in stature and ultimately destroyed; second, the story line is embellished with colorful and superfluous action; and third, the stupidity of everyone involved in the story, and of the entire story itself, is visible more quickly and immeasurably increased.

In the film, the Llanna are no longer the leaders of a huge alliance waging a space war that stretches across the galaxies, but merely the residents of a single planet, Metaluna, struggling to defend themselves against a race of aliens called the Zahgons who are hurtling meteors at their world. The name "Metaluna," meaning "beyond the Moon," etymologically places the aliens closer to Earth, even though the film identifies their planet as beyond the solar system. In addition, the Metalunans are in far more desperate straits than the Llanna, and they have correspondingly grown not only decadent but even, in some cases, evil. Now, they are not only willing to abandon Earth if that proves expedient, but they are prepared to mentally enslave humans, kill humans, and even immigrate to and dominate the Earth if that serves their purposes. Further, reflecting the concerns of the early 1950s, original screenwriter Edward G. O'Callaghan apparently turned the Metalunans into communists of a sort, adding an atmosphere of sinisterness to all their activities that revisions to eliminate the film's political subtext did not entirely remove. (According to Robert Skotak, the first script had "a big anti-communist theme which [producer William Alland] felt didn't belong in a fantasy film" [Skotak 19], one reason why he hired Franklin Coen to do an extensive revision.)

One small change in the film suggests a heightened perception of the aliens as a doomed, decadent aristocracy—the move of their headquarters from the Arizona desert to a Georgia plantation. As critic Cyndy Hendershot (to be further discussed later) would have it, this signals the anti-communist theme that Alland attempted to remove from the film, "since Georgia is the one state name that is common to both to U.S. and the U.S.S.R." (36). However, this reading demands a greater awareness of European geography than the filmmakers may have had, certainly a greater awareness than anyone might reasonably attribute to film audiences in the 1950s.

From the perspective of persons immersed in the film community, however, a story portraying these aliens as a decaying elite class might have recalled Hollywood's most famous film about the destruction of a decaying elite class, *Gone with the Wind* (1939), the other movie one immediately thinks of that largely takes place at a Georgia plantation. In fact, there is substantive textual support in the film for interpreting the aliens as the equivalent of Southern slaveholders. Ruth refers to the scientists' laboratories as "Exeter's slave quarters" (35), and Exeter later tells Ruth, "Why don't you?. . . Show him the grounds. We won't start cracking the whip on Meacham until tomorrow" (45). At an elegant formal dinner, we briefly observe the one African-American performer in the film—a maid, serving everyone dinner. The Metalunans also employ a device to control the minds of most of their scientists, making them their slaves, and while on Metaluna, Cal and Ruth are abruptly confronted by a monstrous "Mutant," a race of subhuman insect-like creatures that, Exeter tells them, the Metalunans "have been breeding" to perform "manual work" (90—in the film, actor Jeff Morrow actually says "menial work"), making them the alien's slave labor force. Film critic Raymond Durgnat even refers to the Mutant as the "guard-slave" (258). Following this line of reasoning, one suddenly notices in the facial features of the Mutant a grotesque exaggeration of stereotypical African-American features—including huge eyes and huge lips—with the shuffling walk of the wounded Mutant, and its seemingly erotic pursuit of the beautiful Ruth in its dying moments, further recalling racist film portrayals of indolent and sexually aggressive African-Americans. Finally, the numerous scenes of fiery explosions on Metaluna, and the ultimate transformation of the constantly-bombarded planet into a sun, could be viewed as the burning of Atlanta writ very large.

As additional evidence that the filmmakers may have had Hollywood more than world politics on their minds, one notes that while the Jorgasnovara character in the film was originally called Warner, borrowing the name of his subordinate in the novel, the name was changed at the last minute to Exeter—probably to avoid any perception that Universal Pictures was offering any commentary on their rival studio, Warner Brothers, though the vaguely-remembered name of a noted private school may have also been preferred as a suggestion of an effete patrician class.

If the Metalunans suggest in the indicated ways the fading aristocracy of the antebellum South, Durgnat detects additional resonances with the fading aristocracy of Britain: Exeter and his assistant Brack "have high, bulbous foreheads, and the stiffness of their hair faintly suggests the wig of English judges. . . . The wigs, the very English name 'Exeter,' his expression, his scruples, suggest a certain gentlemanliness. His situation of a weak Father, too obedient to hierarchic loyalties is England's" (257, 261). He would no doubt have been delighted to learn that the script's original name for Exeter's assistant Brack was "Britt"—discarded, perhaps, as a too-obvious reference to British aristocracy.

The second set of changes in the story reflects O'Callaghan's understandable complaint, after reading the novel, that "there was no action!" (cited in Skotak 20). As a result, the film certainly offers more in the way of colorful action. The intriguing but slowly unfolding story of the building of the interocitor is now preceded by a sequence in which pilot Meacham finds the controls of his plane mysteriously frozen, though a strange green ray—later revealed as the work of the Metalunans—brings his plane to a safe landing. When Cal, Ruth, and Dr. Steve Carlson (the renamed Ole) decide to drive out and investigate an unusual excavation near the mansion, they are pursued by powerful energy beams directed by the malevolent Brack, and after driver Steve altruistically urges Cal and Ruth to seek safety in a nearby river, he is directly hit by one beam and completely destroyed, as is the entire mansion filled with the other scientists (since they are no longer important to the fleeing Metalunans, who want only Cal and Ruth to accompany them). When Cal and Ruth then attempt to escape in an airplane, they are pulled into a Metalunan spaceship and taken into space, which is what happened more sedately in the novel. Whereas in the novel this led to the first of two trips into space—one to the Moon where Jorgasnovara explains their situation to them, the other to Jorgasnovara's home planet, where Cal makes two speeches to the Llannan Council—the film condenses these into one eventful trip to Metaluna during which there is little time for conversation. Cal and Ruth dodge numerous meteor impacts, causing colorful explosions and the gradual destruction of Metaluna; Cal hits Exeter in the jaw to avoid being sent to the dreaded "Thought Transference Room" (87-88); he then allows Exeter to fight off the horrific Mutant during their escape attempt; and on the journey back to Earth, Cal and Ruth are threatened again by the dying Mutant.

All these escapades are striking primarily because they are so visibly extraneous to the central story, so obviously added on to provide the film with some extra color and excitement. Even a critic who had never read the novel, Raymond Durgnat, deduced that the initial sequence with the green ray had been added on to the film as an extra opening thrill: "I suspect that the original novel began" with the arrival of the alien technology at Cal's office, he says, "but that the film opened on the premonitory green light to reassure a public less familiar with *s.f.* than its addicts that eerie marvels are to come" (256; author's italics). And virtually everyone who worked on the film, prominently including Jeff Morrow and screenwriter Franklin Coen, despised the Mutant as irrelevant and absurd and fought to remove it from the film.

The third major change in the film is that the fundamental stupidity of the aliens, and of the creators behind the screen, emerges much earlier than in Jones's novel. The film does reflect, and does accentuate by means of its settings, the three-part structure of the novel that resulted from Jones's writing the story at three separate times. While the second and third parts of Jones's story shifted back and forth from Earth to space, the film's second part—Cal and the aliens in Georgia—is set entirely on Earth, and the film's third part is set entirely in space. However, the film's second part does not unveil only Cal's ineptitude while reserving similar reservations about the aliens and the author until the third part. Instead, virtually from the moment that Cal arrives in Georgia to begin the second part, he, the aliens, and the film's creators all start to seem inept. Indeed, so many absurdities emerge in the story from this point on that one scarcely knows how to sort them all out.

Some problems stem from the ill-advised efforts to shoehorn the trendy subject of nuclear energy into the plot. No longer just a talented radio engineer, the Cal Meacham of the film, though incongruously still employed at "Ryberg Electronics," is now cast as one of America's leading nuclear scientists. The project he is about to complete, we learn, and the real reason why the Metalunans covet his services, involves "the conversion of lead into uranium" (39). However, this procedure defies the laws of physics. In the first place, the only known ways to transmute heavy elements into other heavy elements are the slow process of radioactive decay and the explosive process of nuclear fission. Both processes must begin with radioactive elements, yet there are no radioactive isotopes of lead. In addition, these processes which remove particles from nuclei necessarily create elements with lower atomic numbers than the original elements, but the atomic number of uranium (92) is higher than the atomic number of lead (82). In the second place, even granting that such a procedure might be possible, scientists in the 1950s already knew that the process of nuclear fusion, employing deuterium or heavy hydrogen, produced far more energy than the process of nuclear fission, employing uranium; and some preliminary work on developing methods to control fusion had already begun. It is impossible to imagine that an advanced civilization like Metaluna, which has mastered faster-than-light travel and anti-gravity, would still depend on a relatively weak and crude energy source like nuclear fission.

Still, while these scientific objections might be apparent only to some viewers, anyone can see how this addition to the story shatters its narrative logic. If the Metalunans are aware of Cal's efforts to convert lead into uranium, and if that is why they want him, then why go through all the rigmarole of having Cal assemble an interocitor? As a way to determine whether a person is qualified to supervise an interocitor factory (which it was in the novel), the test makes perfect sense; as a device to arouse Cal's curiosity about the Metalunans and to increase his desire to join them (which is all it is in the film), the test seems pointless and needlessly time-consuming, particularly given the Metalunans' increasingly dire plight. When they had his plane in the grip of their green light in the film's opening sequence, why didn't the Metalunans immediately pull him into their spaceship, which presumably would have been sufficiently impressive to interest him in joining their project?

Other aspects of the Metalunans' behavior in Georgia are also inexplicable. If they are trying to pass as normal humans on Earth, why don't they dye their bright white hair and trim it to more typical dimensions? When Brack is trying to prevent the apparent escape of Cal and Ruth, the only two scientists who might be able to save his planet from destruction, why does he try to kill them with energy beams? If the Metalunans wish to spy on Cal and his colleagues, why don't they employ a device that is less conspicuous than the huge interocitor in his laboratory?

As the story moves into outer space, the suicidal obtuseness of the Metalunans becomes even more difficult to ignore. If the Metalunans have advanced spaceships armed with what we would now call tractor beams, why don't they attempt to stop the Zahgons in space instead of staying at home, huddled behind an energy-wasting, planet-wide force field? And with such abilities, why do they claim that they cannot duplicate, or even understand, the rather crude Zahgon ability to hurl meteors at planets? If their backup plan in case of impending annihilation is to emigrate to Earth, wouldn't they begin by moving, say, a few hundred volunteers to the new planet as a pilot program, and as a way to ensure that their race will survive no matter what? The final extinction of the Metalunans may be tragic, but in light of their obvious short-sightedness and just plain stupidity, it is hardly undeserved.

The film's scenes of space travel are also noteworthy because they display, even flaunt, the screenwriters' astounding ignorance of basic astronomy. In the script, the "Stellarscope" of the departing Metalunan spaceship first shows the Earth as a rapidly receding ball; then, the pilot reports that they are "leaving Earth's stratosphere" (69), which would put them only a mile or so above the surface. Someone on the set noticed that problem, and the line actually delivered was the more sensible "leaving Earth's orbit." Other, equally obvious problems, however, were not corrected. The spaceship's passage through a "thermal barrier" that temporarily raises the temperature of its interior is both uninvolving and completely lacking in scientific logic. Since "meteors" are the tiny space rocks that burn up in the atmosphere before hitting the surface, the larger rocks that are hitting Metaluna should have been called "meteorites" or even "asteroids." Exeter calls Zahgon "a planet that was once a comet" (80), but even in the 1950s scientists understood that comets are tiny objects, generally no more than ten miles in diameter and largely consisting of water, making it nonsensical to think of one somehow turning into a planet, which is a rocky ball at least a thousand miles in diameter. Finally, the constant bombardment of "meteors" turns the planet Metaluna into a new sun, yet, even if Metaluna were a massive, Jupiter-sized planet, it would need to increase its mass tenfold, demanding impossibly huge numbers of impacting "meteors," in order to ignite the process of nuclear fusion and become a star. True, this final transformation can be defended as a moment of great poetic power, as conveyed by Exeter's description: "The intense heat is turning Metaluna into a radio-active sun. The temperature must be thousands of degrees by now. A lifeless planet. And still, its existence is useful to someone. As a sun, its heat is, I hope, warming the surface of some other world, giving light and warmth to those who may need it" (102). And Arthur C. Clarke was surely thinking of this film when he concluded his novel *2010: Odyssey Two* by having his unseen aliens similarly transform Jupiter into a star, as was also depicted in the later film adaptation. Yet Clarke contrived to achieve this transformation in a manner that did not defy common sense.

All of these gross scientific absurdities serve to confirm what research reveals: that neither screenwriters Edward G. O'Callaghan and Franklin Coen nor director Joseph M. Newman had much familiarity with science fiction. Yet, even though their blunders make one wince, their inexperience felicitously led to the film's faithfulness to the contents and spirit of the novel in one crucial respect: the ineptitude and impotence of Cal Meacham, which is even more conspicuous in the film, where Cal accomplishes the task of assembling an interocitor, but absolutely nothing else. Confronted with such an ineffectual hero in the source material, a writer or director who knew more about science fiction might have had the confidence or the background to alter the story line to increase his significance or efficacy, to cast Cal as the determined investigator who single-handedly uncovers the aliens' true origins or, perhaps, as the pilot of a spaceship that leads an attack against the Zahgons. Lacking such knowledge, the film's creators left the essence of Jones's story intact while adding colorful incidents and effects that provided entertainment but did nothing to make Cal seem more capable or more important.

The added opening sequence signals Cal's ineffectiveness. He cannot prevent alien forces from disabling his airplane, and he cannot do anything to rescue himself once his plane is disabled. Arriving at the Georgia mansion, Cal is inclined to trust the Metalunans; it is left to the cat Neutrino to detect their spying, and it is left to the suspicious Ruth and Steve to actually uncover some useful information about the aliens. During his stay in Georgia, Cal makes no progress in his scientific research, though there is a brief scene where Exeter provides him with a helpful formula, emphasizing his lack of necessary knowledge. In her suspicions of the Metalunans and her fruitful investigations into their nature and activities, Ruth

again emerges as more capable than Cal. Her elevation in the film, from a psychiatrist to a nuclear scientist almost equal to Cal, recalls the novel's theme of
emasculation. When Cal joins his colleagues in their attempt to investigate a nearby
excavation, they are immediately threatened by Brack's energy beams, and, unable
to save himself or Ruth, Cal must be told by Steve to get out of the car and into the
water with Ruth, so that Steve can drive away, divert the alien's attention to
himself, and sacrifice himself to save them. When they get to an airplane and try
to fly away, Cal and Ruth are instantly captured and pulled into the Metalunans'
spaceship. Once on Metaluna, Cal's only achievement is to suddenly hit an unsus-
pecting Exeter in the jaw and make a brief, useless escape attempt. Moments later,
he takes Exeter's hand and allows the alien to lead him and Ruth to safety. When
the Mutant attacks, Exeter waves Cal and Ruth away and confronts the monster
himself, protecting them from the monster while getting wounded in the process.
When Exeter gets them back on a spaceship to Earth, the injured Mutant suddenly
appears to attack Ruth, and Cal waits desperately to be freed from the "converter
tube" he is in so he can rush to Ruth's side and, perhaps, fend off the Mutant and
finally accomplish at least one heroic deed. But the Mutant collapses, dies, and
disintegrates before he gets there, leaving Cal with nothing to do but to embrace
and comfort the frightened woman. All that Cal does in the film, then, is to obtain
information from others and to be rescued from danger by others. He otherwise
contributes in no meaningful way to the film's key events, and he does nothing to
either impede or hasten the destruction of the Metalunans.

Since everything in the preceding paragraph should be obvious to anyone who
has watched the film, it is with considerable bewilderment that one turns to Cyndy
Hendershot's analysis of the film in her essay "The Atomic Scientist, Science
Fiction Films, and Paranoia: *The Day the Earth Stood Still*, *This Island Earth*, and
Killers from Space." Her thesis is that in the 1950s, an era of "paranoia," science
fiction films characteristically conveyed the "delusion of the atomic scientist as
messianic figure" (31). However, while I am far from persuaded that this thesis
applies particularly well to *The Day the Earth Stood Still* and *Killers from Space*,
it is positively ludicrous when applied to *This Island Earth*, as Hendershot's own
analysis persuasively demonstrates. Indeed, the essay might be offered to graduate
students as a model of what critics should not do: Hendershot has constructed her
Procrustean bed, and she proceeds to fit *This Island Earth* into it, even as the facts
keep getting in the way.

One first notices that, desperate to find some way to portray the film's Cal
Meacham as an heroic figure, Hendershot on four occasions stops talking about
events in the film and instead describes the rather different events in Jones's novel,
which she persistently and incorrectly describes as a "novella" (36-38). In the first
place, since Hendershot's announced intent is to offer an argument about science
fiction films, what a critic finds only in a given film's source material cannot
provide significant support for such an argument. In the second place, discussion
of Jones's novel in the context of Hendershot's thesis is particularly irrelevant
because, as Hendershot conveniently fails to mention, the Cal Meacham of the
novel *is not an atomic scientist*. So, to epitomize the grave critical flaws in Hender-

shot's methodology: This scholar is attempting to prove that science fiction films of the 1950s valorized the atomic scientist by describing what happened in a science fiction novel about a radio engineer.

When Hendershot deigns to actually comment on the film, her statements range from dubious assertions to out-and-out lies, as these examples will demonstrate. Her statement: "In *This Island Earth* and *Killers from Space*, the scientists Cal Meacham and Doug Martin literally hold the fate of America and the entire world in their hands as they uncover alien takeover schemes. . . . Cal Meacham and Doug Martin serve as detective-scientists who uncover plots on the part of alien cultures to take over America" (32-33). The facts: Meacham, as previously indicated, accomplishes nothing in the way of meaningful detective work; everything he learns about the Metalunans is what they tell him; and the Metalunans are not actively plotting to take over Earth, but rather to obtain enough energy to defend their own planet—their settling on Earth is only an option they are keeping in mind should their efforts fail. Her statement: "In *This Island Earth*, Cal Meacham can find support for his suspicions about Exeter only in the other good American scientists, Ruth Adams and Steve Carlson, who, unlike their international colleagues, resist co-option into the Metalunan plan to colonize the Earth. Further, Neutron the cat becomes part of Meacham's pseudo-community of friends as it alerts him to the monitoring function of the interocitor" (34). The facts: Ruth and Steve are suspicious of the Metalunans before, and to a greater extent than, Cal; they find support for their suspicions in Cal, not the other way around; the Metalunans are, as noted, not really planning to colonize the Earth; the other scientists, the script stipulates, have been turned into mental slaves by Metalunan technology and hence should hardly be chastised for failing to "resist co-option"; and to appeal to Ruth's cat as evidence of Meacham's ability to form communities is clear evidence of sheer desperation. Her statement: "Cal's celebrity status results in the Metalunans saving him when his jet goes out of control and sending him an interocitor to assemble as a kind of entrance exam. . . . Interestingly, the Metalunans put Cal's jet out of control in the first place: thus, not knowing this, he is trapped into working for them out of a sense of gratitude" (36). The facts: Before reaching Georgia, Cal has no idea either that the Metalunans paralyzed his plane or that they saved him; he goes to Georgia, as the film unambiguously indicates, solely due to his scientific curiosity—there was no sense of "gratitude" involved. Her statement: "The Metalunans plan to colonize Earth when their planet is eventually destroyed. Cal fights this idea and eventually convinces Exeter to allow him and Ruth to return home alone" (37). The facts: Stating for the third time that the Metalunans were actively planning to invade Earth does not make it true; at no point in the movie does Cal make any real effort to "fight" this idea; Cal never says a word to Exeter designed to "convince" him to allow their return; rather, rescuing Cal and Ruth and returning them to Earth is entirely Exeter's idea. Her statement: "Seeing the Earth he has saved single-handedly from alien invasion, Cal comments, 'thank God it's still here'" (37). The facts: Hendershot has finally descended to an inarguable lie, since Cal has done absolutely nothing to save Earth from alien invasion, single-handedly or otherwise; he has simply stood and watched while the

Zahgons destroyed the Metalunans, making no contributions to the process.

While one can wax indignant about Hendershot's shoddy work, it might be more charitable, and more illuminating, to consider her as a victim of the film, not its victimizer. Whatever their other flaws, critics can usually be trusted to provide honest representations of the texts and films they analyze and to avoid outright mendacity; and I am confident that Hendershot's other publications are not marred by the sorts of lapses that I document here. What, then, would drive an otherwise competent critic to such distortions and dishonesty? The answer is that, in *This Island Earth*, she encountered a film that completely defied all reasonable expectations. This was a science fiction film of the 1950s and as such, one would suppose, it was aimed at young males anxious to watch colorful, melodramatic adventures. There was a strikingly handsome young man featured in every scene of the film; he must be the hero. Heroes in these science fiction films do heroic things: They uncover nasty alien plots, they successfully battle horrible monsters, they rescue fair maidens from distress. Noting that this particular handsome man was an atomic scientist, one would automatically pencil him in as another example of the "the atomic scientist as messianic figure"; and it subsequently becomes difficult, or painful, to notice that this man actually uncovers no plots, battles no monsters, rescues no maidens, in fact does nothing at all. The problem is that *This Island Earth* was a generally faithful adaptation of a story originally crafted in the individualistic and exploratory manner of science fiction literature, and not the more collaborative and controlled manner of science fiction film; hence, it was a film fully capable of breaking all the rules.

Rather more attentive to, and appreciative of, the film's many complexities is critic Raymond Durgnat, whose pioneering analysis of the film in 1967 was apparently, and unfortunately, unknown to Hendershot. While maintaining that *This Island Earth* "has everything against it" because "it's a fantasy, it's science fiction, it's slanted at adolescents, it's a routine product from a studio with no intellectual pretensions, it has no *auteurs*, its artistic 'texture' is largely mediocre," he concludes that "for all that, it has a genuine charge of poetry and of significant social feeling. It's not cliché; with its sense of inner tensions, of moral tragedy, it's myth" (268). Durgnat usefully analyzes the film in terms of several basic "themes": "Brains," "Remote control," "Penetration," "Crescendo of voyages," "Unusual landings," "Crescendo of altruistic suicides," "Tension of malevolence," and a multifaceted "basic opposition" between Metaluna and Zahgon (259). It is also gratifying to observe Durgnat brushing aside as overly simplistic, in the 1960s, the reductionist anti-communist interpretation that Hendershot would cling to so tenaciously in the 1990s: "The film's political moral isn't at all an equation of Russia and Metaluna. . . . in the course of the film Metaluna becomes, successively, the U.N., Russia, Britain and a too-liberal U.S.A." (261-62).

Still, one grows dissatisfied with Durgnat's analysis. His appeals to Freudian imagery are tired and unpersuasive ("Thus Metaluna is both breast and brain" [263]), and his effort to detect an opposition, in this and other American films of the 1950s, between "gentle, reasonable, liberal" Metalunan attitudes and "Zahgonian brutality" or "Zahgonian mindlessness" in the psyche of the American male

(264) is fanciful, since the film provides no glimpse of the Zahgons and no information about them other than that they are hurtling meteors at the home planet of
their enemy—with good reason for all we know. It is especially difficult to find
support in the film for any contrast between Metalunan morality and Zahgon
barbarism since we have previously watched the Metalunans murdering humans
with energy beams, hardly more civilized than throwing rocks at them, and since
Exeter tells Cal that the Zahgon "ability to use meteors as projectiles is a feat we
would be happy to understand ourselves" (80), clearly communicating that the
Metalunans would be more than willing to throw their own rocks at people if only
they could. Like their name, which yields to no plausible etymological analysis, the
Zahgons of the film are an enigma, and Durgnat's descriptions of their culture,
derived entirely from the single detail of their use of meteors as weapons, are
entirely his own invention.

If both thoughtless and thoughtful critics founder in interpreting *This Island
Earth*, it may be because there is embedded in the film a theme that makes all other
concerns, ranging from fears of communist takeovers to unresolved Oedipal
conflicts, seem inconsequential. Jones's novel depicted a capable scientist who,
after coming into contact with extraterrestrial forces, first learns that he is actually
incompetent, then discovers that the extraterrestrial forces are incompetent as well,
and finally reveals the author of his own adventures to be incompetent in portraying extraterrestrial forces. The film adaptation magnifies and emphasizes the
incompetence of the scientist, the aliens, and its own creators, effectively if inad-
vertently conveying the message that humans are, in fact, puny, ineffectual beings
living in a vast universe they cannot control, cannot even affect, perhaps cannot
even understand. It is a message one also finds in another, more impressive science
fiction film, Arthur C. Clarke and Stanley Kubrick's *2001: A Space Odyssey*
(1968), but the very artistry of that film, its rhythms and thematic resonances,
project an aura of human control over the universe that, in a way, contradicts the
atmosphere of awesome mystery and unknown forces that the filmmakers otherwise sought to convey. *This Island Earth*, lacking that artistry, brings the point
home in a less reassuring, more disturbing fashion. Incapable of doing anything to
help or hinder aliens who are incapable of doing anything to avert their own
destruction, Cal and Ruth, representing the human race, can only observe what is
happening around them before they retreat to their home planet.

As an excellent representation of their plight, there is another important
"theme" in the film that should definitely be added to Durgnat's list: "watching
television." Other critics have noted that science fiction films of the 1950s can
display a fascination with the new media of television, often employing various
sorts of television screens to provide a futuristic ambiance. Yet *This Island Earth*
features, and even fetishizes, television to a unique extent. The initiation rite that
brings Cal into contact with alien beings is, essentially, the construction of a big
television set with a triangular screen; the Metalunan interocitors can also emit
destructive energy beams, symbolizing the power of television. When Exeter is
first interviewing Cal and Ruth, the alien says, "Conserving energy is one of our
primary concerns, isn't it, doctor? Suppose then, we tour the plant right from our

chairs" (40), and he has them observe other rooms by means of the interocitor, emphasizing the convenience and appeal of television viewing. Showing Cal where his laboratory will be, Exeter points out that the room provides him with "your *own* interocitor, of course" (41; emphasis in script), as if this were the ultimate mark of privilege and distinction. Talking to the scientists who may represent the salvation of his people, Exeter suddenly rushes them out the door in order to watch television—a message from the Monitor. The interocitors are additionally important because the Metalunans maintain their control over their human scientists by using the interocitor to observe them. Once on board the spaceship, the center of everyone's attention becomes another type of television—the "Stellarscope"—a circular screen that shows Cal and Ruth the receding Earth, the threatening Zahgon meteors, and the planet Metaluna. When Cal and Ruth enter the headquarters of the supreme Monitor, there is no interocitor in sight, but the Monitor addresses "Interocitor Control" (89) and keeps staring upward and offscreen while talking to the humans, as if watching an unseen interocitor screen, suggesting perhaps that television has become so important to this culture that it dominates the Metalunans even when a screen is not visible. This is also suggested by the final scenes of the picture, where the script twice stipulates that the dying Exeter is "glancing off at Stellarscope" (108, 109), watching a television screen until the very end of his life.

The film's increased focus on television is the masterstroke that finally helps to bring Jones's story to a satisfactory, though unsettling conclusion. For, if humans can have no effect on the universe, that does not mean they can only retreat into their gardens; rather, they can still observe and enjoy the wonders of the universe even as they make no attempt to interact with them. The perfect representation of the non-interactive observer is the watcher of television. In depicting an ineffectual alien culture that is obsessed with television and a human scientist who becomes ineffectual when he begins to share in that obsession, the film links this new media with a passive acceptance of one's place in the cosmos. And while one might argue that television is being prematurely indicted as a cause of this passivity, I suggest that it is instead being portrayed as its natural effect. Intimated by a universe that, we learn, we are powerless to control, we enter our suburban houses and watch the universe on television.

In retrospect, one can say—admittedly in a playful manner—that *This Island Earth* poignantly pointed the way to the future world we now inhabit. Human progress into space, including lunar orbits that took astronauts a few hundred miles past the Moon itself, can be precisely defined as only a bit "beyond the Moon." Instead of conquering the universe, humans have stayed within their cocoons and have constructed bigger and better interocitors to provide entertainment that, more often than not, bypasses the cerebral cortex to stimulate the primitive part of the human brain in the back of the head. For those not satisfied with such diversions, space probes and robot explorers have traveled throughout the solar system with their stellarscopes to send us colorful pictures of alien worlds we can admire, without affecting. We are enjoying, then, precisely what one movie poster for *This Island Earth* promised: "A fantastic spectacle of amazing sights never beheld by human eyes" (reprinted in unpaginated appendix to Riley), but nothing more than that.

While some advocates of space exploration regard our growing passivity about exploring the universe as a betrayal of the ideals of science fiction, this stance actually is not, as already suggested, uncommon in a literary genre interested not merely in catering to its readers but in soberly pondering scientific realities. In "Infant Joys: The Pleasures of Disempowerment in Fantasy and Science Fiction," Eric S. Rabkin claims that many science fiction stories are in fact "disempowerment fantasies" and argues that "There is something compelling about the prelinguistic, the child-like, the oceanic, the humble" (9). While he fails to mention *This Island Earth*, he does conclude with discussions of Clarke and Stapledon, the aforementioned science fiction writers most often associated with oceanic and humbling visions of humanity's essential powerlessness in a universe we cannot control or understand. This is the theme that, in his own awkward way, Jones stumbled upon in the novel, and the theme that, in their own even more awkward way, the creators of *This Island Earth* underlined and strengthened. Somewhat uncommon in written science fiction, it is even rarer in science fiction film, which is one reason why *This Island Earth* continues to command attention almost half a century since its release: It is a science fiction film that is uniquely faithful to an important, if often overlooked, motif in science fiction literature.

It occurs to me, belatedly, that an argument such as this might be misused to defend almost any hapless, inane science fiction film—Edward D. Wood's risible *Plan 9 from Outer Space* (1959) considered as a profound statement about human helplessness in the face of cosmic forces. Yet *This Island Earth*, despite its obvious lapses, stands head and shoulders above the other travesties so prevalent in the field. Supported by solid if flawed source material, a respectable budget, and creators who took their work seriously, *This Island Earth* projects an air of sincerity and gravitas that commands respect and invites viewers to regard the film as a commentary on the human condition in a way that *Doctor Who* and Flash Gordon serials cannot duplicate. We humans may be stupid, we may be powerless, the film's characters seem to say, but we are not clowns, and we are not going to allow ourselves to act like clowns or be regarded as clowns.

It is therefore the ultimate irony, in an analysis not devoid of ironies, that *This Island Earth* found itself in the 1990s assaulted by clowns, determined to transform its characters into clowns. Although *Mystery Science Theatre 3000—The Movie* (1996) returned a slightly edited *This Island Earth* to theaters, accompanied by the purportedly humorous commentary of the series regulars, I cannot say anything about this version of the film because I refuse to watch it. Critics, like anyone else, must maintain certain things as holy, and just as someone who respects and admires Catholicism will have no interest in participating in a black mass, I respect and admire *This Island Earth* far too much to have any interest in witnessing the film recycled as fodder for sophomoric insults. So, I must leave it to other critics to explain in what ways, if any, the comments in that film offer additional insights into its singular qualities. (If the religious analogy here seems excessive, there is one website devoted to *This Island Earth* that labels its link for sales of the videocassette of *Mystery Science Theatre 3000—The Movie* as "Blasphemy.") Yet I can observe, however, that the film has successfully resisted this effort to trash and trivialize it: Sales of videos of the original film remain strong, to judge from the number of times it is featured on commercial websites; the film has been shown several times on the American Movie Classics cable channel; and a company named Pulpless.Com announced in 1999 publication of a new edition of Jones's novel, featuring a picture of Exeter on the cover. As we approach the fiftieth anniversary of the film's release, then, *This Island Earth* remains prominent in the media landscape to an extent that few films of its era can match, testifying to its enduring power to fascinate viewers.

It is easy to ridicule, but hard to understand. If I have fallen short of a complete understanding of this novel and its film adaptation, it is not, I think, for want of trying. However, like the enigmatic Zahgons, there may always remain at the heart of Cal Meacham's story some vast mystery that cannot be fully discerned from the limited vantage point of this island Earth.

6

Opposing War, Exploiting War: The Troubled Pacifism of *Star Trek*

In an article published in *Science-Fiction Studies*, "*Star Trek* in the Vietnam Era," scholar H. Bruce Franklin has argued that the original *Star Trek* series (aired from 1966 to 1969) mirrored growing American disillusionment with the Vietnam War, focusing on four episodes which he claims "dramatize a startling and painful transformation in the war's impact on both the series and the nation" (25). In "The City at the Gate of Forever" (broadcast April 6, 1967), a crucial script change argued that antiwar movements only served to improve the chance of an enemy victory. "A Private Little War" (February 2, 1968) showed Kirk re-enacting President Lyndon Johnson's Vietnam War policy on another planet, but gave prominent attention to Doctor McCoy's vehement objections. "The Omega Glory" (March 1, 1968) presented an alternate Earth devastated by war between Americans and Asians, reflecting disillusionment with the war after the Tet offensive. And "Let This Be Your Last Battlefield" (January 10, 1969) concerned a planet that annihilates itself in a racial conflict inspired in part by foreign wars. Thus, Franklin maintains, the producers of the series visibly moved from an endorsement of the Vietnam War to ambivalent concern about the war and finally to outright opposition to the war.

However, there is first of all one fact which significantly undermines Franklin's chronological analysis: The clearly antiwar script for "The Omega Glory" was written by Gene Roddenberry in *June 1965*—as one possible script for the second *Star Trek* pilot—well *before* the two openly or mixed pro-war episodes cited by Franklin. Perhaps he could find political significance in the decisions to not film the episode in 1966, when support for the Vietnam War was still strong, and to finally film the episode in 1968, when support for the war was weakening. However, there is no evidence that either the producers of *Star Trek* or NBC executives ever argued for or against filming a given script for strictly political reasons. A more likely explanation is that "The Omega Glory" was simply regarded as a weak script (which it was), left on the shelf during the first season when better scripts were available, and retrieved near the end of the second season when Roddenberry was visibly desperate for good scripts.

In addition, one could question Franklin's interpretations of "The City on the Gate of Forever" and "A Private Little War." Certainly, Franklin offers valuable supportive testimony from then-co-producer Robert H. Justman that the script intentionally commented on protests against the Vietnam War; but unfortunately unavailable evidence from the late Gene L. Coon and Gene Roddenberry, who actually controlled the series at the time, might suggest otherwise. Also, if it was the producers' intent to criticize antiwar protesters, one would expect that the future leader of the peace movement, Edith Keeler, would herself be criticized in some way—as rather simple-minded and naïve, perhaps, even as manipulative or duplicitous. Instead, Keeler is consistently portrayed as intelligent, shrewd, straightforward, and honest; every word in the script is unalloyed in its praise for her. As for "A Private Little War," this script could easily be read as an open attack on Johnson's Vietnam policy, not simply as an expression of combined support for and uneasiness about the war. At the end of the episode, the troubled expression on Captain Kirk's face when the formerly-peaceful tribal leader eagerly agrees to accept the Federation's weapons conveys a clear impression that his efforts have all been a horrible mistake.

Still, the most compelling data that call Franklin's thesis into question are several Star Trek episodes from all three seasons, not mentioned by Franklin, that explicitly or implicitly criticize the Vietnam War and the philosophy behind American involvement in that conflict. Together, these episodes suggest an alternative characterization of Star Trek as a series which consistently expressed opposition to the Vietnam War and to the concept of war in general from its beginning to its end.

The most interesting of these episodes, and Franklin's most curious omission, is "Errand of Mercy," broadcast near the end of the first season (March 23, 1967). The world of Organia is about to be overrun by the Klingons, so Kirk beams down to the planet to offer Federation assistance in opposing the invaders; however, the Organians refuse any military aid. When the Klingons arrive and occupy the unresisting planet, Kirk engages in acts of sabotage and tries to encourage other Organians to join his efforts; again, they decline. The parallels to the Vietnam War are clear: If the enemy invades a small country, our side must offer them military support and encourage them to resist the invasion; and the passivity of the Organians might be interpreted as a criticism of the Vietnamese government, which was often seen at the time as insufficiently energetic in carrying out their part of the war.

Parallels between Organia and Vietnam do break down at the end, as the Organians finally reveal themselves to be awesomely advanced aliens who possess and exercise the power to immediately stop the growing conflict between the Federation and the Klingons; they then impose on both sides the Organian Peace Treaty, which stipulates that a disputed world will be awarded to the side that demonstrates it can best assist in the planet's development. When Kirk and the Klingon commander angrily insist upon their right to continue their war, their protests seem absurd and childish. The message in this episode clearly applies to the Vietnam War and other superpower conflicts: Arguments about spheres of influence must be settled by peaceful competition and economic assistance, not warfare and military aid. And, while the Organian Peace Treaty was conveniently forgotten in some later episodes, like "A Private Little War," it figured in other episodes like "The Trouble with Tribbles" (December 29, 1967), which shows Kirk protecting a shipment of grain which will enable the Federation to win a peaceful competition over one planet with the Klingons.

Next, several *Star Trek* episodes show Kirk, or Kirk and his crew, essentially coerced or manipulated into armed conflict by some outside force; the situations are resolved when Kirk decides to renounce any further use of force. One striking episode following this pattern is "Arena" (January 19, 1967). As in the Fredric Brown story the episode adapts, Kirk and a reptilian alien captain who are about to engage in war are teleported by an advanced alien race to a barren planet, where they are told to engage in a duel to the death; the winner's race will survive, and the loser's race will be annihilated. In Brown's story, the human soon kills the alien and saves the human race. However, in the *Star Trek* episode, Kirk overcomes the alien but *refuses to kill him*; an alien appears to compliment Kirk for displaying the advanced trait of mercy and presumably goes on to allow both races to survive. Franklin makes much of the fact that one first-season script was deliberately changed to include a pro-war message; but here is another first-season script, actually filmed before "The City at the Gate of Forever," where *source material was deliberately changed to include an antiwar message*—even if it was one of the most general sort.

Another episode, "Shadow of the Gun" (broadcast October 25, 1968, though written in 1967 by Coon under a pseudonym), closely parallels the structure of "Arena": A hostile alien places Kirk and his crew in a surrealistic replica of nine-teenth-century Tombstone, Arizona, where they must play the role of the Dalton gang and be killed by the Earp brothers and Doc Holliday. When they manage to avoid death, Kirk then refuses to kill those foes; the alien, impressed by this gesture of mercy, then agrees to engage in peaceful contact with the Federation. Still, this particular scenario is completely illogical, since Kirk and his crew survive by persuading themselves that the place and the people they see are all illusions. Thus, it is difficult to be impressed by their humanitarian refusal to kill illusions.

A third episode of this sort, "Day of the Dove" (November 1, 1968), involves an alien who feeds off the emotion of anger. He places some Klingons on the *Enterprise*, arms everyone with swords, and grows stronger from the resulting conflicts and hostility. When Kirk realizes that they are being manipulated, he persuades the Klingons to stop fighting, and when they all stand and laugh at the alien intruder, it is deprived of energy and defeated. Since "dove" was at the time a common description of opponents of the Vietnam War (while supporters were called "hawks"), this episode makes explicit reference to that conflict, and its message is unmistakable: Wars do not serve the best interests of either party, but rather are inspired by other, covert parties to serve their own best interests. This is the argument often made by antiwar protesters, who railed against the "Merchants of Death" (arms manufacturers) in the 1930s, and the "military-industrial complex" in the 1960s, as the factions which were actually instigating and supporting various wars.

One first-season episode, "A Taste of Armageddon" (February 23, 1967), brings Kirk to a planet waging war against another planet by means of computer simulation. When the computer announces that an imaginary battle has caused a certain number of casualties, designated citizens dutifully report to be executed. Kirk is outraged by this practice since it makes war too easy, too unproblematic, and thus provides little impetus for peaceful resolution; so he convinces the computer to self-destruct and shuts down the system. Because victories in the Vietnam War could not be determined by conventional means—the amount of territory gained—Pentagon policymakers seized upon "body counts" of dead enemies (usually grotesquely exaggerated) as a gruesome measure of their success. "A Taste of Armageddon" imaginatively presents a war that is literally determined by body counts and in this way argues against any assessment of war by this method, and against wars that must be assessed by this method.

Several other episodes offer general commentaries opposing war and/or the mentality that leads to war. In "The Devil in the Dark" (March 9, 1967), Kirk comes to a mining asteroid to battle an apparently hostile creature fighting against the miners, only to discover that it is really only a mother trying to protect its babies—a reminder that one should always try to understand, rather than demonize, one's enemies. In "The Doomsday Machine" (October 20, 1967), an ancient fighting machine that has outlived its creators endures to threaten innocent worlds and is finally destroyed by an atomic bomb, ironically described as the "doomsday machine" of the twentieth century—an argument against nuclear weapons. In "The Ultimate Computer" (March 8, 1968), a computer placed in the control of the *Enterprise* becomes deranged and starts fighting against other Federation starships—a warning against allowing weapons, not humans, to conduct and control warfare. In "Patterns of Force" (February 16, 1968), a renegade Starfleet captain takes over a planet, makes it a replica of Nazi Germany, and inspires racial hatred against inhabitants of a nearby world as a prelude to an all-out war—an obvious denunciation of Hitler and fascism, to be sure, but also a statement about the evil and the absurdity of wars between different races. In "Balance of Terror" (December 15, 1966), Kirk battles and destroys a Romulan starship, though Kirk develops a strange camaraderie with the Romulan captain that makes his ship's final destruction, along with the deaths of several *Enterprise* crewmen, a tragedy rather than a triumph—a general lament about the destructive effects of superpower wars.

In short, there are any number of episodes from all three seasons of *Star Trek* that offer either explicit arguments against the Vietnam War or general arguments against war. In the context of all of these episodes, it is difficult to argue that the series somehow represents or reflects a gradual shift from support for the Vietnam

War to opposition to the Vietnam War. Rather, it seems, the producers and writers of *Star Trek* were consistently opposed to the Vietnam War throughout the three years the series was on the air.

If this alternative hypothesis is accepted, then there emerges a possible explanation for one puzzling phenomenon. During its three seasons on NBC, *Star Trek* was a consistently unpopular show; the episode that garnered its largest audience was only the 52nd-most watched show during that week in the Nielsen ratings. Yet when the series went into syndication after being canceled in 1969, it quickly became the most successful series in the history of syndication. Why did a show that was so unpopular in 1968 and 1969 abruptly become so enormously popular in 1970 and 1971? The standard explanation involves scheduling: NBC presented the series rather late at night and on nights when it was relatively inaccessible to one of its natural audiences, high school and college students: 8:30 Thursday night (traditionally a major homework night), and 8:30 and 10:00 Friday night (traditionally a night for socializing). In syndication, though, it usually appeared five nights a week at a much earlier time—usually 5:00 or 6:00 PM. Thus, many young people who found it difficult to watch the show during its run on NBC could discover and become addicted to it in syndication.

No doubt there is a great deal of truth in this analysis; however, I suggest there was a second factor involved. Despite the shock of the Tet offensive in February 1968, to which Franklin alludes, I would argue that American public opinion did not really turn decisively against the Vietnam War until May 1970, when President Richard Nixon invaded Cambodia and inspired widespread outrage, massive student protests, and the Kent State killings. Thus, during its network years, *Star Trek* was often presenting an unpalatable antiwar stance to a viewing public that was still largely in favor of the war, which could partially explain its unpopularity at that time. By the time it was in syndication, *Star Trek* was offering antiwar messages to a viewing public largely opposed to the war, which could particularly explain its tremendous increase in popularity. In short, although the pacifist ideology of *Star Trek* was ahead of its time in the 1960s, it perfectly reflected public opinion in the 1970s.

At this point, partisans of *Star Trek* might conclude this analysis by congratulating the creators and producers of the series for their enlightened and humanitarian opposition to war in general and the Vietnam War in particular, and by seeing the eventual popularity of the series as a belated but stirring affirmation of the best aspects of the American character. Unfortunately, despite all of the evidence presented above, there is also ample evidence to support an entirely different characterization of the message embedded in *Star Trek*.

The simple fact is this: Even by the broadcast standards of its time, *Star Trek* was always an extraordinarily violent series. The *Enterprise* frequently battled against enemy starships with phasers and photon torpedoes, with much death and destruction on both sides. Phaser guns and rifles were regularly used against various adversaries on planets and in the corridors of the *Enterprise*. When phasers ran out of power or were not available, Kirk was always ready to engage in a freewheeling fist fight. Various episodes contrived to put almost every conceivable type of weapon in the hands of Kirk and his crew—including swords, knives, pikes, maces, handguns, rifles, and other exotic alien versions of Earth weapons—which they then used enthusiastically and effectively. Viewers learned than when a bit player beamed down to a planet with Kirk, Spock, and McCoy, he or she was sure to die a violent death. Overall, the body count in several *Star Trek* episodes might compare favorably with that in one of Sylvester Stallone's Rambo movies. Episodes might conclude with a ringing affirmation of the dangers or evils of armed conflict, but before that message emerged, viewers were invited to vicariously enjoy the thrill and excitement of armed conflict. All these scenes can be read as encoded endorsements of warfare as an appropriate, and even pleasurable, method for resolving human problems.

Some of the products inspired by the *Star Trek* series build upon this concealed celebration of violence to offer overtly militaristic scenarios. Consider the crude computer game based on *Star Trek* that was widely popular on college campuses in the early 1970s. As a player, your mission was to employ a limited amount of phaser blasts and photon torpedoes to destroy an attacking Klingon ship, aided by informative comments from other crew members. Since I could never accomplish the task, my games always ended with the destruction of the *Enterprise* and the message, "A Captain Kirk you're not!" The game includes no option for peaceful resolution of the conflict; instead, it is an early variant of the Space Invaders game, where you must shoot and kill the aliens before they shoot and kill you. Also, in the 1970s, plastic replicas of phaser guns were marketed as children's toys, and in the 1990s, "action figures" of characters from all three *Star Trek* series became a toy store staple. Obviously, the phasers were not intended for use as decorations during mock peace negotiations, and action figures were not intended for use in simulated conversations between series regulars, crewpersons, and aliens. These are all war toys, pure and simple. Since mass-marketed products can never be completely unrelated to the films or television programs that inspired them, they can be interpreted as commentaries on the original filmed narrative; and we see again that a series overtly against warfare also contained an embedded celebration of warfare. (For further discussion of the merchandise of *Star Trek* as a commentary on the original series, see my "Where No Market Has Gone Before.")

All of the violence in the series that inspired these products, of course, was not what Gene Roddenberry wanted. When NBC executives rejected his original *Star Trek* pilot, now called "The Cage," as "too cerebral," he correctly interpreted that comment to mean "not enough action." Accordingly, when he then sat down to write a possible script for the second pilot, "The Omega Glory," he made it and the other two stories, as stated in Stephen Whitfield and Roddenberry's *The Making of Star Trek*, "strong action-adventure plots" (134) filled with violence. Indeed, another possible reason why Roddenberry waited so long to produce the script was that he was embarrassed by its egregious brutality. Then, while producing the series, he felt obliged to include fights of some kind in most episodes. Leonard Nimoy (Spock) developed the "Vulcan nerve-pinch" only because he did not want to participate in the numerous fistfights and brawls that he could reasonably predict would be recurring features in the coming episodes.

There then emerges a third possible characterization of the political stance of *Star Trek*: that the series did not evolve from a pro-war to an antiwar stance, that it did not consistently maintain an antiwar stance, but rather that it was consistently at war with itself, with creators who by nature preferred pacifism but were driven by circumstance to glorify militarism.

Of course, many commentators, including Roddenberry himself, have noted that he felt forced to fill *Star Trek* with violence to please NBC executives, and it is tempting to point fingers of blame at those executives as narrow-minded conservatives inappropriately imposing a militaristic aura on a series that would otherwise have espoused unadulterated pacifism. However, bearing in mind the very principles that *Star Trek* episodes repeatedly endorsed, one should not rush to demonize the network officials who ultimately controlled the series. Rather, I suggest that the dichotomized character of the series reflects a broader, and more disturbing, problem for all creators who wish to provide both popular entertainment and a serious message.

Many forms of popular narrative, including television programs and science fiction, often adopt the structure and conventions of nineteenth-century American stage melodrama, with stalwart heroes who must rescue virtuous heroines from, and forcefully oppose the machinations of, despicable villains. It is not surprising, then, to see that most episodes of a science fiction television program like *Star Trek* often assume this form, even if the heroine has green skin and the villain looks like a giant lizard. As I have argued in "Man against Man, Brain against Brain," melodrama is a genre that carries an embedded and irremovable ideology. Melodrama asserts that it is possible to divide the world into good people and bad people; that it is proper for good people to react with emotional indignation to the odious acts of evil people; and that it is appropriate for good people to respond to those acts by actively and violently opposing the evil people.

In contrast, a philosophy of pacifism must be founded on completely different principles: that there are no purely good people and no purely evil people, but rather various degrees of good and evil in all people; that people must react calmly and rationally even to apparently outrageous acts of evil; and that people must always avoid violent conflict of any kind and instead strive to achieve some sort of compromise or peaceful resolution. Thus the question arises: How is it possible to convey an argument for pacifism in the context of a genre inherently based on premises opposing pacifism?

There is one possible answer: to tell the Tale of the Repentant Warrior. Here, the melodramatic conflict is set up, the hero goes forth to rescue the heroine and kill the villain, and audiences experience the excitement of violent conflict; but, then, when the fight is over, the hero realizes his aggressive acts were wrong, and he resolves henceforth to beat his swords into plowshares. This, I submit, is the characteristic strategy of many *Star Trek* episodes: Kirk learns, after a great deal of violence and warfare, that violence and warfare are not the proper ways to settle disputes; then, because of the constraints of episodic television, he must forget this lesson and again reach for his phaser at the first sign of trouble in his next adventure, only to eventually learn once again that he was in error.

This is an approach, of course, that is not unique to *Star Trek*. Consider one of the few antiwar science fiction novels of the 1950s, C. M. Kornbluth's *Not This August* (also published as *Christmas Eve*). Here, the Russians have invaded and occupied the United States, so the hero joins an underground resistance movement seeking to locate and launch a "bombardment satellite" that has enough firepower to drive off the Russians. In a story focused on the thrill of covert military activities, however, there is one unusual character, a seemingly deranged preacher who wanders through the countryside calling for peace. The hero shows no sympathy for his message, and one expects the preacher to receive his comeuppance at the end of the novel. However, after the satellite is launched and the Russians are defeated, the hero abruptly realizes that such military action can only lead to an unending cycle of attack and retaliation, so he gets on his knees and joins the preacher in a prayer for peace.

I am suggesting, therefore, that any effort to convey a peaceful philosophy through the medium of popular narrative will most likely result in a curiously compromised story which spends much time celebrating armed conflict before concluding with a denunciation of armed conflict. I further suggest that such stories will emerge even in the absence of outside pressures toward either militarism or pacifism. There is an obvious test case for such an hypothesis: the series *Star Trek: The Next Generation*. In producing this series, Gene Roddenberry enjoyed almost complete freedom to do what he wanted, without any interference from network executives, obliged only to adhere to a few universal standards (such as no nudity and no overt sexual activity). One would expect, therefore, that this series would perfectly reflect Roddenberry's own philosophy and would consistently both preach and practice pacifism. This is usually the case. Captain Picard never wears a phaser or engages in any fights; almost all episodes have little if any violence; and the conflicts are almost always resolved by improved communication, compromise, a court of law, or peaceful negotiation.

However, these generalizations are not *always* true of *Star Trek: The Next Generation*. Consider the episode "A Matter of Honor," where the *Enterprise* and a starship of the Klingons—the former enemy race now officially allied with the Federation—temporarily exchange First Officers. When a metal-eating virus then attacks the Klingons' ship, they assume the *Enterprise* is responsible and approach the ship with threats to destroy it. Luckily, Picard's subordinate Commander Ryker is able to take control of the Klingon ship and demands the surrender of the *Enterprise*, a subterfuge which Picard gladly plays along with to avoid conflict until the true situation can be explained and resolved. This episode starkly mimics many episodes in the first series, with grim militaristic music, scenes of starships maneuvering toward battle, and angry exchanges between the *Enterprise* captain and the Klingon captain. The only difference is that the conflict is recast as an error right before, and not right after, the actual violence.

In addition, the two-part episode "The Best of Both Worlds" features the Borg, described as an implacably evil race of machine intelligences that cannot be swayed by Picard's soothing words or dealt with in peaceful negotiation. The Borg mentally enslave Picard and use him as their commander, so that Ryker must employ unorthodox strategies to destroy the huge Borg spacecraft before it destroys the Earth. Here, even in a series strongly committed to pacifistic thought and action, and even at a time when the superpower confrontation seemed to be ending, one surprisingly sees a story that embodies the basic rationale behind all armed conflict: Some horribly evil foreigners are coming to kill us, so we must kill them first.

While one observes *Star Trek: The Next Generation* only rarely lapsing into the implicit militarism that characterized the original series, this is not true of the third series, *Star Trek: Deep Space Nine*. Creator Rick Berman frequently said he wanted the new series to be "more seedy" than *Star Trek: The Next Generation*; but it became apparent that he also wanted a series that was "more violent." In the episodes of its first year in syndication, space station Deep Space Nine is threatened by hostile spacecraft, occupied by armed rebels seeking to overthrow a nearby planet, and visited by several brutal intruders. Crew members also visit other planets where they engage in violent conflicts with aliens. Again, *Star Trek: Deep Space Nine* is free of intrusive network control and guided by idealistic creators, but the series again drifted into a covert celebration of violence overlaid with an overt message of pacifism. The same can be said of the most recent series, *Star Trek: Voyager*, which places Captain Janeway and her crew in an uncharted region of space filled, it seems, with unrelentingly hostile aliens who consistently resist her conciliatory words and force her—reluctantly—to turn on the phasers and fire away.

Decades ago, film director Cecil B. de Mille declared that "The way to exploit sex is to oppose it." A cynical filmmaker can get away with including presentations of reprehensible activity as long as the film contrives to overtly repudiate such activity. *Star Trek*, I submit, emerged from radically different motives but employed a strategy that paralleled de Mille's. Here, idealistic filmmakers could get away with presentations of a pacifistic message as long as their episodes also contrived to overtly celebrate militarism in the events it depicted. In essence, in order to oppose war, the makers of *Star Trek* had to exploit it.

Overall, their experiences suggests that there may be inherent limitations in the use of popular entertainment to convey some admirable sentiments. And a paradox emerges: Science fiction is regularly celebrated because of the unique imaginative freedom it offers its writers. By setting stories on other worlds or in future times, they can present unsettling messages about present-day society that might not be acceptable in undisguised form. Certainly, it is hard to imagine another television series in the late 1960s that could have gotten away with so many denunciations of armed conflict at a time when America was deeply engaged in a foreign war. Nevertheless, science fiction, because it so frequently has the deep structure of melodrama, also imposes some unique restrictions on writers. Undoubtedly, as implied by the title of a critical anthology devoted to the series, one can argue that *Star Trek* was an unusually productive "enterprise zone" in the often-depressing ghetto of American popular culture. However, certain worthwhile enterprises, such as advocating pacifism, apparently could not be wholly successful within its confines.

7

Even Better than the Real Thing: Advertising, Music Videos, Postmodernism, and (Eventually) Science Fiction

The title of this essay is ambitious, listing four fields of study that could not be covered in one essay or a hundred essays. Even after completing it, I am not entirely sure which of its listed genres are the subjects of this essay and which are merely being employed as a means to understand other genres. Call the following, then, a zero draft, a tentative exploration of ideas, a possible stimulus for further thought and research. Or, bearing my subject in mind, and understanding that I will be offering some extravagant claims within a limited space, call this piece not an expression of ideas, but an advertisement for ideas.

When major art forms of the twentieth century are discussed, advertising is rarely, if ever, mentioned. Nevertheless, observing page after page of glossy advertisements in our magazines, the billboards that grace our highways, the little placards attached to our shopping carts, and the innumerable commercials that clutter our radio and television programs, we must conclude that advertising is the most ubiquitous and characteristic art form of our modern civilization.

As one sign of the power and influence of advertising, there are now several national television networks primarily devoted to commercials. These include, of course, various "home shopping" networks that somehow attract viewers by presenting and promoting an endless series of items such as jewelry, collectible dolls and plates, household decorations, and small appliances. But the most popular of these advertising networks are MTV and its more sedate cousin VH1. For, we must remember, music videos are nothing more than commercials, made and financed by recording companies as a way to persuade viewers to purchase their cassettes and compact discs. Every video shown on MTV and VH1 concludes by displaying the names of the artist, the song, the album that includes the song, and the company that sells that album—all the information a perspective purchaser might require. While these networks are increasingly creating and presenting other types of programming—including news reports, interviews, documentaries, concerts, and cartoons—one of their primary functions remains to select and air short commercial films financed by recording companies. While music videos are not generally recognized as advertisements and have achieved a popularity and respectability beyond those of other advertisements, this does not alter their basic nature.

Seeking to establish a hermeneutics of advertising, a critic would be tempted to begin by noting one obvious characteristic: Unlike other art forms, advertising has *the primary if not exclusive purpose of getting people to buy a certain product.* Yet this cannot serve as a truly distinguishing feature, since many other works have overt or covert messages of some kind. While critics may wish to differentiate between inspiring people to re-examine the nature of justice in modern society and inspiring people to buy a certain toothpaste, this is a difference in degree, not in kind.

What actually makes advertising a unique art form, in my view, is *the assumption of a hostile audience.* It goes without saying that authors write books for a presumed audience of people who want to read books, that directors make films for a presumed audience of people who want to watch films, that songwriters record songs for a presumed audience of people who want to listen to songs, and so on. Yet advertisers begin with the assumption that people do not want to look at advertisements, that they may go out of their way to avoid looking at advertisements. While we properly denigrate the aesthetic value of most of the works that advertisers produce, we should also to an extent sympathize with them, recognizing that as artists they face a singular burden. It is from its assumption of a hostile audience, not its marketing purposes, that the other characteristics of advertising derive.

One resulting characteristic is that advertising can display *hostility toward its audience.* Knowing that their viewers do not like their work, and may severely condemn their work, advertisers might naturally grow to dislike those viewers. Beneath an ingratiating surface, advertisements often convey an attitude of contempt. Many commercials are apparently aimed at an audience of very stupid people, wives who actually believe that changing their brand of coffee might improve their marriage, or men who actually believe that a new aftershave might attract hordes of beautiful women. The familiar devices of repetition and increased volume also communicate a belief that viewers are slow-witted and inattentive. Irritated by such appeals, people come to dislike advertising even more, which in turn inspires advertisers to dislike people even more, creating a cycle of ever-increasing hostility between creators and their audience.

Another key characteristic is *anonymity.* Focused on a frankly mercenary purpose, advertisers have no time and no motive to identify or celebrate themselves. Further, since advertisers assume that viewers dislike their work, and since advertisers in turn dislike their viewers, there is no reason to announce one's name as a way to establish or to build a special relationship between artist and audience. Only within the industry itself, in private discussions and the annual Clio Awards given to outstanding commercials, are the writers and artists who create advertising ever acknowledged or honored.

Other traits of advertising are harder to delineate, and indeed tend to blur together. However, one might tentatively sort them out in this fashion.

One of these characteristics, undoubtedly, is *physical attractiveness*. If you are showing people something that they really do not want to see, and you wish those images to be persuasive in some way, you should at least try to make those images as appealing as possible. Print advertisements and commercials invariably present the most beautiful women, the most handsome men, and the most adorable children. Homes are spacious, impeccably decorated, and virtually spotless. Cars drive through magnificent and spacious natural settings without another car or human artifact in sight.

In keeping with this drive for the attractive, advertising often projects a general *aura of artificiality*. People and places, quite overtly, are presented as artificially attractive. Advertisements may attempt to mimic other forms of more palatable entertainment. Print advertisements in news magazines try to look like articles, while extended television commercials (the infamous "infomercials") try to look like talk shows. Yet these attempts rarely succeed: The advertisements remain recognizable as fake news articles or fake talk shows. And a dramatic break with mimetic realism may help to attract attention. A famous perfume commercial showed a beautiful woman in a swimming suit, lying next to a pool; a handsome man on the other side of the pool dives in, swims towards her, rises from the pool, approaches her, and vanishes. As the commercial itself acknowledges, the whole scene is a "fantasy." And in general, one might argue, many advertisements and commercials present a fantasy world, an obviously artificial environment and story.

A further characteristic might be termed *compression*. If your audience is hostile, you must make your presentation as brief as possible, so that they can get the message before they have the chance or inclination to turn away. This was a lesson the makers of print advertisements and commercials learned gradually. In old magazines, we can see many advertisements with several paragraphs of small print, explaining the virtues of the product in extraordinary detail, with a small picture of the product and its endorser somewhere in a corner. Commercials from the 1950s were one minute long and often featured nothing more than a man dressed as a doctor facing the camera and lecturing about the effectiveness of a certain pain reliever. Today, print advertisements may present only one large glossy picture, whose message can be discerned in an instant, with perhaps a single sentence of explanatory text. Today, the typical length of commercial is 15 or 30 seconds, and one characteristic format is a brief narrative of contemporary life, noticeably involving the product in question, radically condensed to fit that time frame.

Another characteristic of advertising is *relentless borrowing*. Ordinarily, we would have little interest in or regard for a unkempt bum with ragged clothes and scraggly beard, and ordinarily we would see nothing significant in a man reaching for a salt shaker. But with several establishing scenes, a film director can make that bum a sympathetic character and can make that reach for the salt shaker an evocative emotional moment. Advertisers do not have the time to be original in these ways, and hence they must rely on images and tableaux from other art forms with pre-established import and resonance. The use of celebrity spokespersons is one obvious result: When Yoplait undertook to sell French yogurt to American consumers, they needed a representative who projected down-home, working-class American values. Instead of troubling to create such a character, they simply hired actor Jack Klugman, who had portrayed many such roles in film and television, to extol their product in print and in commercials. Other scenes in advertisements and commercials duplicate iconic moments in life and in literature—the graduation ceremony, the baseball players rushing to surround the pitcher after a victory, and so on—so as to instantly convey the desired emotional impact.

Finally, all advertisements must project *an atmosphere of dissatisfaction or incompleteness*. Even commercials with a crude and apparently complete narrative about a housewife who re-establishes domestic harmony by switching to the proper detergent convey to women viewers the unsettling reminder that their own domestic harmony is less than ideal and the suggestion that their own relationships might be improved by using the detergent. Other advertisements effectively arouse interest by deliberate incompleteness. One extensively discussed print advertisement, for Benson & Hedges cigarettes, featured a group of normally dressed people facing a man wearing nothing but a pair of pajama bottoms. In newspapers and in magazines, people debated the questions: Who exactly is this man, and what is his relationship to the other people in the room? Why is he wearing only pajamas when everyone else is fully dressed? Some modern commercials even adopt a serialized format, with a commercial ending with on a note of suspense and the message "To Be Continued."

We can observe all of these characteristics in the form of advertising that I regard as the major precursor of the music video: the film preview. Of course, previews are designed to induce people to go see the film. Since people go to theaters to see movies, not previews, the audience may be naturally hostile to the previews, regarding them as something that delays presentation of the desired featured film. Sometimes, in their efforts to oversell a rather routine film as a modern masterpiece, previews convey a belief that audiences are rather gullible. This is most conspicuous, perhaps, in the previews of previous decades with their effusive accolades splashed on the screen in large print. The people who assemble previews are typically professionals with no other connection to the films in question, and they remain unknown outside the film industry. Previews can be artificial in that they may deliberately misrepresent the film, emphasizing, for example, the comic scenes in a generally serious film. (The preview for *The Paper Chase* [1973] showed the law student hero insulting the professor in class, followed by a scene of the students applauding—suggesting that the students were applauding the student's insult—but the clips actually came from two widely separated scenes in the film.) Previews are necessarily and visibly condensations of longer works, they always include footage from the most attractive and expensive scenes, and they emphasize those scenes that are most derivative and evocative outside of their original context. Finally, they are always incomplete, deliberately withholding vital information about the film in order to persuade curious people to see the entire film. A superior film preview can be both an interesting work of art and a powerful marketing tool; for example, while *An Officer and a Gentleman* (1983) was little more than a compendium of clichés, routinely filmed and, with the exception of Louis Gossett, Jr., indifferently acted, its preview was magnificent, reducing the trite and predictable story to its appropriate length of five minutes and effectively employing moments from its best scenes to briefly stir the emotions. Certainly, that preview was one major reason for the film's otherwise inexplicable success.

Generally, music videos also display the characteristics of advertising. One need not belabor the points that, as noted, videos are designed to sell products, and that videos emphasize appealing images of glossy attractiveness. Videos are not entirely anonymous: Performing artists are always identified, MTV and VH1 have adopted the habit of identifying directors as part of the opening and closing credits, and programs that "annotate" videos like *Pop-Up Video* and *Artist's Cut* may offer behind-the-scenes information. Still, the vast majority of people involved in creating videos—actors, dancers, choreographers, cinematographers, editors, writers, and makeup artists—always remain unknown. What merit some discussion are the features of artificiality, borrowing, compression, incompleteness, and the mutual hostility of creator and audience.

With their obvious and unconcealed use of computer graphics and special effects, videos acknowledge and advertise their own artificiality. Performers who move their lips while the song plays do not really pretend that they are actually singing. In fact, they are often lip-synching in postures or situations—flying through the air (Paul McCartney's "Off the Ground"), swimming underwater (Hanson's "Weird"), riding on a motorcycle (k. d. lang's "Freedom"), or lying half-buried in the ground (Peter Gabriel's "Digging in the Dirt")—where they could not possibly vocalize or be heard. In one video, Annie Lennox's "Why," the singer, most of the time, does not even bother to lip-synch, does not even go through the motions of pretending to sing. Viewers are repeatedly reminded that they are watching an ersatz performance, not a real performance.

Seeking maximal impact in a minimum of time, music videos are obliged to borrow familiar images and themes from other sources. Like commercials, videos often employ well-known actors in small parts to immediately convey a certain mood or attitude. Celebrities who have appeared in videos include Christie Brinkley, Macaulay Culkin, Chevy Chase, John Goodman, Arsenio Hall, Magic Johnson, John Malkovich, and Eddie Murphy. When actual celebrities are unavailable, impersonators may be featured, as in the Go West video "King of Wishful Thinking," which apparently features, among other people in the background, Elvis Presley and Pope John Paul II. Videos often mimic familiar films, like Madonna's "Material Girl," virtually a restaging of a scene from *Gentlemen Prefer Blondes*, or Meatloaf's "I Would Do Anything for Love (But I Won't Do That)," a homage to innumerable monster movies. There are also numerous videos which refer to or parody other videos, one noteworthy example being Genesis's "I Can't Dance."

Next, while virtually all films and television programs are edited down from a large amount of footage, they attempt to project a sense of completeness, as if the entire film presents only the scenes that were actually filmed. In contrast, music videos flaunt their status as the edited-down remnants of larger works. When preparing a video, the director might first film the performer singing the entire song in a conventional setting, a concert stage or a nightclub, perhaps filming in black and white. Next, the director films the performer singing the song in some spectacular outdoor setting, perhaps standing on top of a mountain in a vast expanse of desert. The director then shoots some scenes conveying some standard narrative reflecting the lyrics of the song, such as an on-and-off romance involving the performer and an attractive model; if the performer is getting to be a bit elderly, a younger actor may be employed in these sequences as a more plausible surrogate lover. Finally, the director assembles the videos using bits and pieces of these sequences, showing the performer singing two lines while on stage, then two lines while standing on the mountain, then a few seconds of the narrative footage while the singing continues. In these ways, viewers are clearly aware that they are observing only a small part of the entire work, as in a film preview.

As one indicator of the affinity of videos and previews, it should be noted that in the case of a song from a film soundtrack, the video may simultaneously serve as a video and a preview, with footage of the singer(s) interspersed with scenes from the film, possibly along with some new footage showing the singer and the film stars interacting. For example, Billy Ocean's video of the song "When the Going Gets Tough," from the film *The Jewel of the Nile*, shows Ocean performing the song with the film's stars Michael Douglas, Kathleen Turner, and Danny deVito serving as backup singers, and occasional scenes from the movie also appear. The Wallflowers's video "Heroes," from the film *Godzilla* (1998), features footage from the movie and, at one point, the giant tail of Godzilla threatening the rehearsing band members.

Finally, with so much footage visibly withheld, and with cutting so rapid that it becomes almost impossible to notice what is happening in one shot, music videos are conspicuously incomplete, and project a feeling of dissatisfaction, to inspire viewers to complete their lives by purchasing the album in question or, at least, to inspire them to watch the video again.

Despite all these overt features of advertising in music videos, there is one possible difference: Do creators assume a hostile audience, and express hostility towards the audience? Obviously, many people want to watch videos and appear to appreciate their creators, and recording artists seem to enjoy making videos for that appreciative audience. Because many people choose to watch MTV and VH1, those networks can sell time to other advertisers who present conventional commercials between the videos. Videos can become marketable items in themselves. When MTV refused to air Madonna's racy video "Justify My Love," she successfully sold copies of the video in stores, and artists such as the Rolling Stones and Bruce Springsteen have marketed videocassettes featuring a compilation of their videos.

Despite all these signs of a receptive and appreciated audience, however, there is evidence in several videos of a relationship founded on hostility. Consider one of the most fascinating and powerful videos ever filmed—Dire Straits's "Money for Nothing." As the story goes, Dire Straits singer Mark Knopfler overheard someone in a bar criticizing recording stars—they get "Money for nothing and their chicks for free." Building on that hostility toward musical artists, the band then created a song and video that expressed hostility towards their audience.

"Money for Nothing" includes footage of the band performing the song on a concert stage, though some scenes are visually augmented by bright neon colors over the film images. Primarily, however, the video is a cartoon, featuring two crudely drawn men who work hard every day at menial jobs, delivering refrigerators, televisions, and microwave ovens, while they are simultaneously fascinated by, envious of, and angry at the performers they watch on MTV videos. The video also includes brief clips from imaginary videos, complete with identifying information in the lower left hand corner. Finally, the video is manifestly a commercial for both the song and MTV itself: The logo of MTV is seen in the video, MTV is mentioned several times in the lyrics, and at the end, guest vocalist Sting repeatedly sings in the background about wanting his MTV, citing the well-known advertisements that first promoted the network.

The message here could not be clearer: We are members of the wealthy, pampered, exploitative elite who create videos, and you are the poor, oppressed, exploited people who watch them. We are, in the standard manner of advertisers, tantalizing you with images of the good life to persuade you to buy our valueless products—we are trying to get your "Money for Nothing." And you *know* that there is this huge gap between us, you *know* that we are simply trying to take advantage of you, and you poor slobs *still* want to watch our videos, you *still* want your MTV.

Another video which projects a similar viewpoint is U2's "Even Better than the Real Thing." Again, there are brief bits of footage showing U2 performing the song in some kind of murky nightclub. We see singer Bono mouthing the lyrics and smoking a cigarette as he endlessly falls head over heels down the side of a skyscraper. Other group members are seen playing their instruments while tumbling in the same way. There are clips—so brief as to be almost subliminal—of people impersonating various rock icons, including the Beatles dressed as Sergeant Pepper's Lonely Hearts Club Band, Jimi Hendrix, and Elvis Presley. With other apparently random images, we see clips from various television programs—commercials, news reports, talk shows, a woman screaming in an old horror movie.

While this video lacks the viewpoint characters who drive home the point in the Dire Straits video, U2 here presents the same announcement of self-conscious exploitation and contempt for its audience: MTV and its cousins are offering you nothing but random, worthless, ersatz images, designed to distract you, take advantage of you, and ultimately numb your mind. And you ignorant fools *know* it, and you *still like it*. You like it better than the "real thing"—the real thing being, apparently, more satisfying real-life and aesthetic experiences.

What is remarkable about these videos is not only their message but their popularity in spite of their seemingly unpalatable message. "Money for Nothing" was one of the most widely viewed videos of its era, and even today it still shows up occasionally on VH1. "Even Better than the Real Thing" won an MTV Award as the Best Rock Video of the Year. It is hard to argue that these videos are aberrations; rather, their widespread acceptance suggests that they are actually representative. (One should also note that one of the most popular programs ever aired on MTV, the cartoon *Beavis and Butthead*, satirically portrayed MTV viewers as lazy, ignorant teenagers who waste large amounts of time sitting on the couch and making idiotic remarks about various music videos when they are not getting into mess after mess due to their abject stupidity. The cartoon all but announces to its audience that "We think you are brain-dead morons," yet its large audience did not seem to mind.)

We can conclude, then, that at least to some extent and on some level, viewers are in fact hostile to the people who make music videos, and the makers of videos are hostile toward the people who watch them. People recognize that videos are simply commercials aimed at exploiting them; they recognize that their creators dislike and belittle them. Yet despite all of this evident hostility, people still like music videos. In effect, the MTV audience has accepted commercials as its characteristic and chosen form of entertainment, even though they are crass, artificial, incomplete, and hostile.

Perhaps this strange fondness for advertising is not unique to MTV and its cousins. In general, one could maintain, people today have embraced advertising to an unprecedented extent. In the 1950s, there was a great deal of concern and outrage about advertising. Books like Vance Packard's *The Hidden Persuaders* exposed the tricks of advertisers, novels like Sloan Wilson's *The Man in the Gray Flannel Suit* questioned the ethics of advertising, and speculative works like Frederik Pohl and C. M. Kornbluth's *The Space Merchants* grimly foresaw a future world controlled by insidious advertisers. *Mad* magazine relentlessly parodied various print advertisements, and television variety shows regularly included parodies of especially obnoxious commercials. Today, however, one simply does not observe any visible worries about the effects of advertising or any efforts to make fun of or criticize advertising. If the genre has not exactly been celebrated, it has at least been accepted as part of the media landscape. (To be sure, there are criticisms of particular advertising campaigns, like the purportedly racist Taco Bell chihuahua or the Budweiser commercials with talking frogs and lizards apparently designed to appeal to children; but there are few if any general denunciations of advertising itself.) The success of MTV, then, may be only one sign of a growing, if unstated, recognition of the value of advertising, even as people continue to feel some hostility toward it.

Everything I have said about advertising will, of course, sound extremely familiar to many scholars, for they will recognize in this description the widely discussed characteristics of the modern literary and artistic movement known as "postmodernism" (to finally use one of the two terms I have been avoiding). The existence of this movement has been powerfully promoted by critics like Fredric Jameson in works like his *Postmodernism*, and by Larry McCaffery in his anthology of stories and essays, *Storming the Reality Studio*. In these and other analyses, virtually all of the characteristics I have found in advertising have been ascribed to numerous other modern works of literature and art.

To be specific, postmodernism recognizes that a work may combine, without any sense of contradiction, a true commitment to aesthetic value and a crassly exploitative intent. Postmodernism delineates a fundamentally confrontational relationship between artist and audience. Postmodernism "decenters" the author as someone who has a special relationship to or propriety interest in the work. Postmodernism emphasizes attractive surface features instead of layers of deeper meanings, and postmodernism breaks down previously-accepted dichotomies between the real and the artificial. Postmodernism tries to condense what were once larger works into small moments in large works. Postmodernism sanctions extensive borrowings from other genres and works. And postmodernism projects the sense of an inchoate collage, a visibly incomplete and ragged combination of elements. Of course, most works celebrated as postmodern are considerably more profound than most advertisements; but in listing these surface features at least, one notes undeniable parallels. The novelty in my analysis is that other critics see postmodernism as a fusion of various other works and traditions. Instead, I would venture to offer the theory that advertising is the true wellspring of this movement and has throughout its history contained all its features in combination. Postmodern fiction is the child of advertising, and its appearance is yet another covert sign of the widespread acceptance and aesthetic triumph of advertising.

The triumph of the defining art form of capitalism can be properly seen as the triumph of capitalism, and critics may properly view the emergence of postmodern literature and art with both fascination and outrage. Here, I cannot completely discuss the reasons why this form of expression has become widespread or fully consider the effects of its many manifestations. My one comment here would be that the contemporary ascendance of advertising might be seen as only logical, that advertising is the appropriate art form for people who have become (to state it positively) realistic and mature, or for people who have become (to state it negatively) cynical and disillusioned.

Realistic (or cynical) people recognize that all forms of entertainment are to an extent exploitative efforts to persuade them to spend money, that artists are not their spokespersons or representatives but rather belong to a separate elite class, that there is natural hostility between creators and themselves, and that there is no reason to esteem, or even learn the names of, the people who create entertainment. And yet, realizing all of these things, they are still willing to be entertained. Busy, unhappy people whose days are devoted to installing microwave ovens and moving refrigerators are willing to settle for works of entertainment that offer only an attractive surface, works that are visibly artificial, works that radically condense narratives and experiences, works that borrow from other works and traditions for quick emotional impact. Finally, people who have lost any hope of ever improving their unhappy conditions will accept works that are similarly incomplete and unsatisfying, in contrast to works that offer illusory images of completeness and satisfaction.

If advertising is in fact the form of art which inspired and defined postmodernism, there is one more question to explore: Why have other critics failed to identify the key role of advertising in this development? Of course, advertising has not been totally ignored: McCaffery's "Introduction: The Desert of the Real" in *Storming the Reality Studio* notes that "advertising" is one of the three key developments in the era of postcapitalism and, while discussing the breakdown of earlier distinctions, mentions "art and advertising" as one of those blurred barriers (4, 14). Veronica Hollinger's "Cybernetic Deconstructions: Cyberpunk and Postmodernism" notes William Gibson's "nearly compulsive use of brand names" in the quintessential postmodern novel *Neuromancer*, suggesting a link between cyberpunk and advertising (212). Arthur Kroker and David Cook's "Television and the Triumph of Culture" includes some discussion of television commercials. And Brooks Landon's "Bet on It: Cyber/video/punk/performance" and George Slusser's "Literary MTV" observe at length connections between cyberpunk and those advertisements known as music videos. These are, however, mostly tangential references in critical analyses focused on a number of other variegated sources which, critics argue, combined to produce postmodernism. The emphasis on borrowing and jagged collage is said to stem primarily from novelists like William Burroughs and Thomas Pynchon. The hostility of artist and audience is said to stem primarily from punk rock. The breakdown of previous distinctions is said to stem primarily from performance artists. And the fascination with the artificial and the technological is said to stem primarily from (to finally use the other word I have been carefully avoiding) science fiction.

Indeed, it is science fiction, rather than advertising, that is characteristically cast as the main source of, and inspiration for, postmodernism. Granted, critics are highly selective in their use of science fiction, focusing on the cyberpunk writers of the 1980s and a few obvious precursors like Alfred Bester, Philip K. Dick, and Samuel R. Delany. Still, even this limited examination implicitly celebrates the larger tradition of science fiction from which those writers emerged.

My counterhypothesis—that advertising primarily inspired postmodernism—is arguably a better (at least a simpler) theory, since advertising already combines all of the features of postmodernism, while other theories of its development demand, somewhat implausibly, a sudden merging of a number of disparate sources. A possible objection would be that advertising, the most overt of all expressions of capitalism, could not have inspired forms of art that can seem violently opposed to capitalism. However, science fiction itself, the preferred candidate as the precursor to the postmodern, was often, as H. Bruce Franklin has noted, "technocratic," unashamed in its advocacy of modern technology and its accompanying superstate (*Future Perfect* 394). If critics can posit that such a literature could engender a movement with values opposed to capitalism, it seems equally logical that advertising itself might engender a movement with values opposed to capitalism.

However, these two theories of the development of postmodernism might be reconciled, at least to an extent. If I can plausibly argue that advertising primarily inspired postmodernism, and if several noted critics can plausibly argue that science fiction primarily inspired postmodernism, one might posit there is some intimate connection between advertising and science fiction. In fact, the case can be made that science fiction, earlier and more so than other forms of popular fiction, embraced the standards and concerns of advertising.

First, Hugo Gernsback, who created science fiction as a marketing concept (if not as a genre), was undoubtedly a profit-minded individual, and his efforts to promote science fiction, such as the proclamation of "Science Fiction Week" and the founding of the Science Fiction League, were clearly and largely inspired by greed (in *The Way the Future Was: A Memoir*, Frederik Pohl described the League as Gernsback's "buck-hustle" [18]). Thus, one could argue, modern science fiction was, from its earliest moments as a recognized genre, tainted by mercenary concerns. In addition, the modern genre has typically been focused on selling a product, which could be briefly described as "the future" and more extensively described as the promotion of scientific research and technological innovation. In these ways, science fiction functioned as a sort of advertising.

In the tradition launched by pulp magazines, pseudonyms have often been employed in science fiction for various reasons: to allow an editor to conceal publishing his own stories (F. Orlon Tremaine, presenting his own stories in *Astounding Stories* as by Warner van Lorne), to help writers start a new career (John W. Campbell, Jr., escaping from his space-opera past by writing as Don A. Stuart), to avoid having two stories by the same author in the same magazine issue (one reason why Robert A. Heinlein was frequently assigned a pseudonym), or simply to be playful (Henry Kuttner with his innumerable pseudonyms). Some magazines and publishing houses imposed house names on several authors, and today, many well-known authors lend their names to works they did not write. Massive references have been compiled solely to identify which authors wrote which stories under which pseudonyms, and some works have still not been attributed. So, an aura of anonymous writing often permeates the field.

Second, science fiction has always been associated with colorful and attractive pictures of monumental, pristine future cities and exotic alien landscapes, best exemplified by the cover paintings of Gernsback artist Frank R. Paul. To this day, such images remain a key element in the appeal of science fiction. It is not without significance that the first Guest of Honor at a World Science Fiction Convention was not a writer or editor, but illustrator Paul—demonstrating the importance of surface glamour and attractiveness in the promulgation of science fiction. Today, innumerable print advertisements and cover illustrations continue to emphasize that importance.

Artificiality? By nature, a science fiction world is an artificial world. While accompanying commentaries may try to stress that science fiction deals with very possible futures, there has always been a countervailing feeling of make-believe, of a story involving an attractive imaginary world that never existed and could never exist.

Compression? When the only real market for science fiction was the magazines, writers were virtually obliged to condense their narratives into short stories, or to present them as a series of short stories. In some cases, stories were later expanded into novels, or series of stories were "fixed-up" as ersatz novels—so that condensation remains a factor, although now only the necessary first step in the creative process. Even today, when markets for longer works are plentiful, science fiction stories often reach readers in the same two-step process, first appearing as condensed versions in magazine serials or series of stories, later appearing as complete works.

Relentless borrowing? The use of disparate generic models, or the mixture of different generic models in one work, has always characterized modern science fiction. Examples include Gernsback's own juxtapositions of dime-novel adventures with scientific lectures; various attempts to create science fiction utopias, satires, and Gothic novels; the imitations of modernist writers like James Joyce and John Dos Passos during the New Wave of the 1960s; and the homages to *film noir* and Raymond Chandler often found in the cyberpunk fiction of the 1980s.

A sense of incompleteness or dissatisfaction? The task that Campbell assigned his writers—to create a fully developed future world as a background to their stories—is impossible to achieve, so such stories often end with readers feeling that they are still not really familiar with all the fascinating aspects of that world. The modern tendency to generate sequels may in part reflect an urge to correct such necessary incompleteness. As sequels in turn generate an endless series of works set in that world, a sense of incompleteness becomes a deliberate narrative strategy, to always leave readers wanting more.

There is one missing element in all of this, however: the assumption of a hostile relationship between creator and audience. Granted, the general public has always been thought, not without justification, to despise science fiction, and a certain defensiveness about the quality of the genre has often been detectable. In response, science fiction fans have disliked those outside their community, calling them "mundanes." However, one cannot deny that science fiction writers have continually enjoyed a warm and intimate relationship with readers in that community. When John Clute's "Fabulation" argues that science fiction is essentially modernist, not postmodernist, he might have based his argument on this key difference between genre science fiction and more recent literary movements.

Despite the absence of the hostility associated with advertising, however, a hypothesis can still be sustained based on other similarities. Science fiction was the first modern genre to powerfully assimilate the motives and features of advertising, and, for that reason, it is a natural case of mistaken identity for modern critics to perceive science fiction, not advertising, as the true source of postmodernism. If accepted, this hypothesis suggests three interesting conclusions.

First, many critics note with proper dismay that modern science fiction seems inextricably linked to various forms of marketing. Publishers employ the names of famous authors and "shared worlds" to generate an unending series of almost identical works: Literature reduced to Product. Every big-budget science fiction film inevitably inspires a novelization, comic book, video game, "action figures," and innumerable other products and toys; the film serves to sell these products, and these products in turn serve to sell the film. While other forms of modern writing also display this pressure towards commercialization, science fiction has arguably suffered the most. Perhaps that is because the modern genre has always, at some level, reflected the concerns and traits of advertising, so that it remains naturally more amenable than other genres to such exploitation.

Second, if both music videos and science fiction are seen as closely related to advertising, one would expect to find some affinity between the two art forms. Such a connection is manifest. MTV has always identified and celebrated itself as a product of modern scientific technology, as aptly indicated by the most famous of all its promotional symbols: a scene of astronauts Neil Armstrong and Buzz Aldrin on the Moon, raising not the flag of the United States but the flag of MTV. High-tech special effects are a key element in all MTV programming, and many videos imitate images and themes from science fiction, most evidently in the works of Michael Jackson. His famous video "Thriller" is a homage to old monster movies; *Captain Eo*, the extended video once exhibited daily at Disneyland and Walt Disney World, is a pastiche of *Star Wars*; the direct-to-video film *Moonwalker* climaxes with Jackson's metamorphosis into a Transformer-like fighting machine; and his video with sister Janet Jackson, "Scream," depicts the pair in a massive spaceship, escaping from a hostile world. Other videos that employ science fiction imagery range from the quaint evocation of Georges Méliès in the Smashing Pumpkins's "Tonight" to the high-speed, computer-generated animation in Peter Gabriel's "Sledgehammer" and the glitzy evocation of *Star Wars* in the Backstreet Boys's "Larger than Life." Since science fiction naturally combines with all forms of advertising, the argument would go, science fiction naturally combines with music videos.

Finally, it may be a deliberate decision, not simply an error, when postmodernist critics ignore advertising and celebrate science fiction as one key foundation of their movement. When the existence of a new genre or literary movement is announced, one of the first things that proponents do is to identify certain past works and past creators as their precursors, whether there is a true relationship between them and the new movement or not. These declarations have short-term and long-term benefits. In the short run, the assimilation of older works adds some respectability to the new development, and in the long run, those older works provide stimulating and exemplary models to inspire contemporary creators to improve their work. For example, when Gernsback first marketed science fiction, the stories he was offering may have been little more than juvenile adventures, but he did not identify this negligible tradition as the ancestor of science fiction; rather, he claimed, science fiction was the literature of Edgar Allan Poe, Jules Verne, and H. G. Wells. He reprinted their stories in his magazines, and he urged writers to emulate these masters in their own works. In the short run, the association with these great writers made science fiction more respectable, and in the long run, the example of these great writers served as one inspiration for improvements in the content and style of modern science fiction. Today, many writers of science fiction in fact display the strong influence of writers like Poe and Wells. Thus, what was a blatantly false picture of the roots of science fiction in 1926 has now arguably become "the true history of science fiction."

Now, proponents of postmodernism may be emphasizing its roots in science fiction, not advertising, for the same reason. In the short run, selected writers of science fiction offer some sense of tradition and respectability to the nascent movement of postmodernism, and in the long run, those writers may inspire contemporary postmodern writers to move in worthwhile directions. Thus, all these critical pictures of the roots of postmodernism in science fiction, punk rock, or performance art may be false today, but may also become true in the future.

Of course, there is an irony here. For decades, science fiction was widely regarded as the most reprehensible literature of them all, one that deserved no respect, and one whose influence could only be pernicious. However, even science fiction is more respectable than advertising, and even science fiction is more stimulating than advertising. Thus, in contrast to advertising, science fiction emerges as respectable literature, so that science fiction, instead of advertising, is employed as a device to make postmodernism respectable and to improve its works. As a worthwhile precursor to postmodernism, therefore, science fiction is even better than the real thing.

8

Legends of the Fall:
Going Not Particularly Far
Behind the Music

In the early 1980s, the cable network MTV attracted attention because of its novel format of showing nothing but music videos. By the late 1990s, MTV was attracting attention because of its novel new policy of actually showing music videos in prime time. Clearly, in the two decades of its existence, significant changes have occurred in the concept of "music television."

The problem facing MTV and its sister network, VH1, has always been simple enough: Nonstop presentations of music videos attracted relatively low ratings, as likely viewers were regularly drawn away from videos to watch more appealing programs on other stations. The music networks, then, needed "event" programs that would attract viewers to watch at particular times. While videos themselves might be transformed into event programs—an hour devoted to the top ten videos of the week, or a compilation of videos by one major artist—other types of programming also had to be created to boost ratings.

The responses of MTV and VH1 to this challenge have been highly variegated. Filmed concerts—*MTV Unplugged*, VH1's *Duets* and *Storytellers* series—were obvious options. MTV developed unique "reality" shows that brought together some carefully selected "typical" teenagers, placed them in interesting environments, and filmed their actions, reactions, and interactions: the stationary *The Real World* and the peripatetic *Road Rules*. VH1, during one period, strangely emphasized comedy programs. Variations of almost every type of television program, with a music angle, have been tried with mixed success, including game shows (VH1's *My Generation* and *Rock'n'Roll Jeopardy*), talk shows (ranging from the serious sex talk of MTV's *Lovelines* to the celebrity fluff of VH1's *The RuPaul Show*), awards shows (*MTV Video Awards*, *MTV Movie Awards*, *VH1 Fashion Awards*), news programs (*MTV News*), theatrical movies (VH1's *Rock'n'Roll Picture Show*), and animated programs (MTV's *Liquid Television, Beavis and Butthead*, and *Daria*).

Throughout the 1980s and early 1990s, the older and more established MTV, designed for teenagers and young adults, invariably seemed far ahead of the newer VH1, less certainly aimed at older adult viewers. MTV innovated, and VH1 lamely followed in its path. More recently, however, VH1 has apparently taken the lead, largely thanks to two of its programs that have garnered unprecedented attention—and unprecedented ratings.

The first of these was *Pop-Up Video*, which showed music videos accompanied by small captions offering inside information and humorous commentary. While annotated presentations of previous viewed films had been seen before, most prominently in the abysmal jokes of the *Mystery Science Theater 3000* crew, the use of written (as opposed to spoken) annotations was especially effective as an accompaniment to a music video. Viewers could still enjoy the song even as they read the comments, and what *Pop-Up Video* had to say about its videos was often genuinely interesting and genuinely amusing. Nevertheless, as is the case with *Mystery Science Theater 3000*, the program was also displaying genuine contempt for music videos, products to be recycled for someone's additional amusement and not works of art. For example, watching the Pop-Up version of the Verve Pipe video "Freshmen," which employs a stark, minimalist setting to appropriately mirror the grim irony of the song, one might well object to the all the silly captions with nonsense rhymes designed to convey the sophomoric boredom of the annotators, who apparently prefer bright colors and jazzy special effects in their videos. The overall effect is not unlike watching the *Mystery Science Theater 3000* version of *Schindler's List*. It is worth noting that the attempts of MTV to imitate *Pop-Up Video*—programs offering complete song lyrics, artists' comments on videos, or captions displaying the costs of various effects—have tended to be more respectful, and uncoincidentally have been less successful. As videos, like advertisements, convey contempt for their audience, it seems most fitting that music networks should display contempt for their videos.

Of even greater interest, however, is the other major success of VH1, its *Behind the Music* documentary series, which presents one-hour biographies of various performers or groups (although a few episodes have had broader topics, like the music of the year 1998, the Lilith Fair, Studio 54, Woodstock, rock photographers, and the film *The Rocky Horror Picture Show*). A companion series, *Legends*, offering biographies of especially noteworthy musicians, has also been well received. While MTV has presented its own biographies—a series of "Rockumentaries" years ago, and the more recent *Biorhythms* series, uniquely lacking a narrator—these never achieved the popularity and visibility of *Behind the Music*, which increasingly dominates VH1 programming, with a new episode almost every week, one or more episodes rebroadcast every weeknight, and "marathons" of several old episodes back to back on weekends. In late 1998, after the first broadcast of the *Behind the Music* episode about country and pop singer Shania Twain, VH1 proudly announced that the program had drawn the largest ratings in the cable network's history. As another sign of their growing popularity, episodes now sometimes conclude by offering a video of the program, with some added unaired minutes, for mail-order sale.

These documentaries have examined a wide variety of musical artists, though a definitive list is hard to come by. Some programs are heavily promoted before their appearances; others slip in and out of the schedule virtually unheralded. After programs are first aired (sometimes before their official debut times as "sneak previews"), some are rerun again and again and again; others are never rerun at all, presumably because of low ratings. Bibliographical information appears nonexistent, and my polite e-mail request for information from VH1 was not answered. To the best of my knowledge, in addition to the six exceptional cases listed above, these are the individuals and groups that have been profiled by *Behind the Music* as of November 1999: Bad Company, the Bay City Rollers, Black Crowes, Blondie, Sonny Bono, Eric Burdon and the Animals, Glen Campbell, the Carpenters, David Cassidy, Harry Chapin, Cher, Joe Cocker, Natalie Cole, Alice Cooper, Jim Croce, David Crosby, Culture Club (episode later reedited and retitled "Boy George"), Def Leppard, John Denver, Depeche Mode, Dr. Dre, Duran Duran, Gloria Estefan, Melissa Etheridge, Marianne Faithfull, Fleetwood Mac, Leif Garrett, Gloria Gaynor, Andy Gibb, the Goo Goo Dolls, Grand Funk Railroad, Heart, Iggy Pop, Rick James, Jan and Dean, Jefferson Airplane, Billy Joel, K.C. and the Sunshine Band, Gladys Knight, Lenny Kravitz, Julian Lennon, Jerry Lee Lewis, Lynyrd Skynyrd, Madonna, the Mamas and the Papas, MC Hammer, Meatloaf, John Mellencamp, Metallica, Bette Midler, Milli Vanilli, Keith Moon, Alanis Morissette, Mötley Crüe, Willie Nelson, Stevie Nicks, Ted Nugent, Tony Orlando, Ozzy Osbourne, Donny and Marie (Osmond), Tom Petty and the Heartbreakers, Poison, Quiet Riot, Bonnie Raitt, R.E.M., Lionel Ritchie, Robbie Robertson, Selena, Rick Springfield, Steppenwolf, Sting, Donna Summer, Thin Lizzy, TLC, Peter Tosh, Shania Twain, Vanilla Ice, Barry White, Weird Al (Yankovic), and Buddy Holly, Richie Valens, and the Big Bopper, the last three collectively profiled in an episode entitled "The Day the Music Died." For purposes of later comparisons, these are the artists and groups profiled as *Legends*: the Bee Gees, David Bowie, Johnny Cash, Eric Clapton, the Doors, John Fogerty, Aretha Franklin, Marvin Gaye, the Grateful Dead, Jimi Hendrix, Elton John, Janis Joplin, B. B. King, Led Zeppelin, John Lennon, Curtis Mayfield, the Pretenders, Queen, Bruce Springsteen, Tina Turner, U2, Stevie Ray Vaughn, and the Who.

To someone unfamiliar with the programs, the title *Behind the Music* might suggest a behind-the-scenes look at the business of creating, recording, and performing music, examining how artists compose their songs, how they polish arrangements in the studio, and how they choose and rehearse songs for concert performances. As it happens, VH1 did briefly present a few documentaries along these lines, under the umbrella title of *Classic Albums*, which offered in-depth examinations of the crafting of famous albums like the Grateful Dead's *American Beauty* and Fleetwood Mac's *Rumours*. However, this clearly was not the sort of behind-the-scenes look that viewers were clamoring to see, and that series has vanished from sight. Instead, the focus of *Behind the Music* is almost entirely biographical, and the music figures in the story only in terms of how it affected the artist's life: A popular album brings personal satisfaction, wealth, and/or fame, while an album that fails to become popular leads to disheartenment, financial troubles, and/or obscurity. The words that flash almost subliminally across the screen at the beginning of each episode—fame, fortune, passion, glory, success, heartbreak—further emphasize that this is a program emphasizing the *effects* of music on its performers, not the music itself. As Randy Newman put it, "It's not 'Behind the Music,' it's 'Not About the Music'" (cited in Milward, "How to Clean Up").

Still, this emphasis on biographical reality could be viewed as salutary, as an enlightening and beneficial contrast to the playful and glamorous unreality so often featured in music videos. Episodes of *Behind the Music* can get very bleak indeed: Musicians die, due to drug overdoses, drunken excesses, or reckless driving; musicians attempt suicide in response to one reversal or another; musicians go to jail or experience public humiliation for their sins; musicians go bankrupt or face major struggles with the Internal Revenue Service and larcenous ex-associates. In short, one could argue, these documentaries demonstrate that the smiling faces of music videos regularly conceal the more troubled, even nightmarish, daily existence of many artists, and that they offer sobering lessons to young people who might otherwise seek to follow in the footsteps of their celluloid heroes.

Unfortunately, there are three aspects of the *Behind the Music* programs that undermine any endeavor to view them in an entirely positive light.

In the first place, episodes of *Behind the Music* go into production only with the full cooperation of their subjects, as evidenced by extensive clips from interviews with the artist or artists, along with numerous family members and friends. According to John Milward, "The first step" in preparing a *Behind the Music* episode "is always to secure the cooperation of the artist" ("How to Clean Up"). This not only explains why certain prominent artists have never been profiled—they did not wish to be profiled by VH1—but it also accounts for some surprising omissions, and an obvious absence of forthrightness, in certain aspects of some stories. To get artists to cooperate, producers may feel, or be, obliged to accentuate the positive. Evidence introduced in the Vanilla Ice episode seems to show clearly that the artist intentionally lied about his background and experiences on several occasions, but the producers blandly present his vague denials, do not press for explanations, and move on without further comment. While the John Denver episode notes his arrests for drunk driving in the 1990s, it inexplicably fails to report what was common knowledge in the 1970s: that Denver regularly smoked hashish and made no effort to conceal it. Julian Lennon's well-publicized problems with cocaine and other drugs are also unmentioned. The career of K.C. (of K.C. and the Sunshine Band) is incongruously described without a single reference to any romantic relationship, suggesting to any reasonable viewer that the singer is a gay man determined to remain in the closet. The John Mellencamp episode makes no reference to his widely praised drummer, Kenny Aronoff, and provides no explanation as to why he eventually abandoned Mellencamp to work with John Fogerty and others. Clearly, one cannot watch these episodes fully confident of receiving the truth, the whole truth, and nothing but the truth. Albeit without definite evidence, these visible omissions in some episodes engender additional suspicions that other episodes are being less than forthright in depicting, for example, the newly warm relations between reunited band members or the enthusiasm of peers for their latest music.

In addition, the artists who agree to be profiled by *Behind the Music* may have their own specific hidden agendas, further distorting the presentations of their life stories. To be sure, some artists who have seen better days, like Jerry Lee Lewis or Tony Orlando, may simply appreciate the opportunity to get some attention from the media again; but other, less admirable motives may be involved in the decision to serve as the subject of a documentary. A few artists visibly have scores to settle, or axes to grind: For example, John Kay, lead singer of the group Steppenwolf, eagerly defends a morally questionable deal that deprived his former bandmates of all income from their classic records; Jim Farber notes that Billy Joel's lengthy discussions of his bad business deals, and his reasons for ending up in them, seem "suspiciously self-serving" ("VH1 Blends Music with History"); Madonna seizes the opportunity to defend herself at length against various criticisms; and Ted Nugent is more than happy to have another forum (besides his radio program) for expressing his right-wing opinions.

However, the most common ulterior motive behind these documentaries is, unsurprisingly, commercial. The artist or group in question is often coming back after a long absence, or is not selling as many records as before. Clips near the end of the program show the artist(s) recording in a present-day studio or rehearsing for an upcoming tour; the cover of the latest or upcoming release of the artist(s) is prominently displayed; and the new music is described by interviewees in glowing terms. Although the Blondie episode was most overtly designed to promote a reunion album, any number of other episodes—such as those featuring David Crosby, Grand Funk Railroad, Lynyrd Skynyrd, Julian Lennon, Poison, Bonnie Raitt, and Vanilla Ice—include big plugs for new releases or insistent reminders that the artist(s) are still touring. The program's creator, Jeff Gaspin, notes that the series "has proven to sell records" and admits that "We are a marketing arm for the artist, there's no question about it" (cited in Milward, "How to Clean Up"). Like music videos themselves, then, these episodes of *Behind the Music* function primarily as advertisements, blatantly intended to interest viewers in their subjects and to persuade them to buy their new records and/or attend their forthcoming concerts. It is reasonable to assume that in many cases, artists have aggressively campaigned for an appearance on *Behind the Music* to garner themselves some publicity, and in at least one case the fans are even getting into the act. Surfing the Internet for data on the series, I stumbled upon a plaintive plea from a devotee of Cyndi Lauper urging fellow fans to write letters to VH1 demanding an episode of *Behind the Music* devoted to her, which the fan clearly envisions as a way to promote her long-moribund career.

While one can blame artists or their kin for slanting stories to present everything in the most favorable light or for bringing some hidden agenda to their documentaries, the producers of the series—or perhaps human nature itself—must be held responsible for the third and most disquieting aspect of *Behind the Music*, the distorting influence of its chosen genre.

To explain this problem, one must first consider the oddity of launching two different series—*Behind the Music* and *Legends*—devoted to biographies of rock artists. Why didn't VH1 place all its documentaries, of both contemporary music's all-time greats and its fascinating lesser lights, under the title of *Behind the Music*? Further, told that two series with those titles existed, one would expect *Legends* to focus exclusively on the unquestionable giants of the field, while *Behind the Music* examined less important figures. In many cases, to be sure, exactly that criterion was applied: John Lennon obviously belongs in the company of *Legends*, while the notorious non-singing singing duo, Milli Vanilli, obviously does not, demanding an episode of *Behind the Music* to tell their story. Still, some of the artists profiled by *Behind the Music*—such as Cher, Fleetwood Mac, Billy Joel, Madonna, John Mellencamp, and Sting—actually seem to be more important figures in rock music history than some of the artists profiled by *Legends*—such as Johnny Cash, John Fogerty, Curtis Mayfield, the Pretenders, Tina Turner, and Stevie Ray Vaughn— suggesting that some criterion other than sheer musical greatness must sometimes come into play in determining which series will examine which artists. The program's creator Jeff Gaspin has suggested that the artists themselves make the choice: "Early on, we'd approach an artist and they'd say, 'I'd rather be on "Legends."'" But now that *Behind the Music* has proven to sell records and get the top ratings, people don't want to be a 'Legend,' but a 'Behind the Music'" (cited in Milward, "How to Clean Up"). But if this is always the case, that raises a further question: Why have the *Behind the Music* documentaries become more popular than the *Legends* documentaries, so much so that artists now often shun what would seem the more prestigious venue?

My hypotheses are that the two series are devoted to telling two different types of stories; that in some cases artists may find themselves in one series or the other because their experiences seem easier to shape into one type of story; that once biographies are scheduled for one series, the stories are further distorted in the preferred fashion even if it is not totally appropriate; and that the characteristic story of *Behind the Music* is more dramatic, and more involving, than the characteristic story of *Legends*.

Science fiction writer Robert A. Heinlein once opined that there were only three basic types of stories: Boy Meets Girl, The Little Tailor (the person who triumphs against overwhelming odds), and the Man Who Learns Better. While strong romantic elements figure in many of VH1's documentaries, the two documentary series each seem devoted to one of Heinlein's other two models: *Legends* describes Little Tailors, while *Behind the Music* describes Men (and Women) Who Learn Better.

For the most part, the *Legends* documentaries are exercises in hagiography. To add an aura of special gravitas, episodes of *Legends* are sometimes narrated not by an anonymous professional announcer (like all episodes of *Behind the Music*) but by musical artists of some renown themselves, like Sheryl Crow, Levon Helm of the Band, Kris Kristofferson, and Steven Tyler of Aerosmith. The artists are portrayed as entering the music business already blessed with such tremendous talents that they are sure to succeed. Popular acclaim and prosperity come quickly and easily, and they move on to one triumph after another. There may be problems along the way, ups and downs in their careers, but nothing that is really serious enough to threaten the stature of the artists. Though some may tragically die at a young age, the others seem destined, at the end of the program, to continue making wonderful music and to enjoy further success indefinitely.

Consider, for example, the *Legends* version of Bruce Springsteen's life. This classic Little Tailor figure—a poor New Jersey teenager—quickly displays his amazing musical gifts as a singer and songwriter. Gathering a band together, he immediately attracts attention and gets a recording contract in the early 1970s. While the poor sales of his first two albums briefly threaten his ascent to rock godhood, the spectacular quality of his third album puts him simultaneously on the covers of *Time* and *Newsweek* and makes him internationally famous. A dispute with a former manager stalls his career for a few years, but he roars back with two successful albums and a hit single. The 1980s bring even greater triumphs with his landmark album *Born in the U.S.A.* and a string of popular singles. His troubled first marriage and a split with his E Street Band bring another career lull in the late 1980s, but he carries on in the 1990s with more noteworthy albums and an Oscar-winning song. Overall, then, despite a few stumbling blocks in the way, the career of Bruce Springsteen is presented as a long, triumphal march through rock'n'roll history.

In contrast to this spirit of continuity in the typical episodes of *Legends*, the stories of *Behind the Music* typically take on a stark, three-part structure. In the beginning is phase one, the Rise. As with the stars of *Legends*, the artists' rise to fame and fortune is characteristically rapid and spectacular, but in the world of *Behind the Music* this success does not always seem entirely deserved. There may be indications that some combination of friends in high places, hype, and sheer luck have elevated the artists more highly and more quickly than their talents alone would warrant.

This inexorably brings on phase two, the Fall. The reasons for the artists' decline can vary. Excessive use of drugs and alcohol is often a factor, leading to breakdowns on stage, car accidents, near-fatal overdoses, or arrests. Other health problems unrelated to drug use may threaten the artists' lives and careers. Bad business deals with greedy agents or duplicitous recording companies can lead to grave financial difficulties. Feuds with band members or partners may bring a premature end to uniquely fruitful musical collaborations. Deaths of loved ones, or broken romantic relationships, can plunge the artists into deep depression. Ruinous revelations about the artists' past lives can bring tons of negative publicity. Or musical tastes may simply change, resulting in low record sales and general disregard for the artists in the musical community and among the general public. More than a mere bump in the road, a genuine, career-threatening crisis confronts the typical artist of *Behind the Music*, which sometimes culminates with one moment when the artist identifiably hits rock bottom—by attempting suicide or nearly dying in some other fashion.

Not every artist survives the Fall, and *Behind the Music* does include the cautionary tales of Karen Carpenter, Andy Gibb, Philip Lynott of Thin Lizzy, and Keith Moon of the Who to illustrate that it is entirely possible to hit rock bottom, die, and never come back. The far more common outcome, however, is phase three, or the Return. With the help of family and friends, the artists pull themselves together, check into a rehabilitation center, and emerge clean and sober. Lawsuits are settled, new financial managers are brought in, and the artists get their business affairs in order. Abandoning their wild lives of constant hell-raising and one-night stands, the artists get married, settle down, and have children; they recover from depression, reunite with old collaborators, and go back to the studio to record some new music. And they tell the camera that they have never been happier in their entire lives.

Of course, the Return is rarely a complete return to their former heights. The artists still must live with certain irretrievable losses. Their music is much less popular with contemporary listeners and record-buyers, and they will probably never reach the top of the charts again or achieve their former prominence in the music world, though they claim that such aspirations no longer concern them. Older and wiser, they are willing to embrace their now-diminished stature, or even complete obscurity, while they tend their gardens.

As an example of a typical *Behind the Music* episode, consider the Vanilla Ice story. Robert van Winkle, a young Dallas teenager with a fondness for rap music, begins performing in local clubs as the white rapper Vanilla Ice. He is quickly offered a record deal, and that leads to a heavily promoted single, a version of "Play That Funky Music, White Boy" which goes absolutely nowhere. Then one disk jockey begins playing the single's B-side, "Ice Ice Baby," and that immediately becomes an astonishingly huge hit, the first rap song to hit Number One on the charts. Soon, Vanilla Ice is enjoying widespread media attention, sold-out concerts, and even a lucrative merchandising deal for a Vanilla Ice doll. Then, everything falls apart: An investigative reporter determines that Vanilla Ice has been telling outrageous lies about his background, bringing harsh criticism and a loss of credibility; there are legal problems because "Ice Ice Baby" conspicuously "sampled" from David Bowie and Queen's hit "Under Pressure" without providing credit or royalties; he is publicly ridiculed in other rap videos and on television comedy shows; and sales of his second album are hugely disappointing. In response, Vanilla Ice first retreats from the music business altogether, racing cars for two years, then releases another album that is entirely ignored. Now using drugs heavily and deeply depressed, Vanilla Ice attempts suicide. However, after hitting this low point, the rapper kicks his drug habit, settles down with a good woman, produces another, better album, and announces a newfound contentment with his life.

Now, to argue that this documentary about Vanilla Ice follows a different "generic model" than the documentary about Bruce Springsteen might engender some exasperation. For heaven's sake, a response might go, one necessarily presents the story of a genius like Springsteen as an unbroken string of triumphs, while one necessarily presents the story of a one-hit wonder like Vanilla Ice as a spectacular rise and spectacular fall. To be sure, documentaries cannot entirely ignore the facts, and life stories cannot be infinitely distorted to fit preconceived patterns. Still, the disparate rhythms of the two series do have a definite influence on the stories they choose to tell and on the way they choose to tell them.

Consider Madonna and Billy Joel. Both have had careers similar to Springsteen's in longevity, and if they have not always enjoyed as much critical respect, they have undoubtedly been more successful than Springsteen by other measures, such as overall record sales, numbers of hit singles, and numbers of awards and honors. Since they have rarely been away from the charts for long, their careers could easily have been presented as continuous success stories in the manner of *Legends*. However, producers either detected a three-part structure in their stories and scheduled them for *Behind the Music*, or, having decided for other reasons to feature them on *Behind the Music*, bent over backwards to discover and impose such a structure on their stories. Madonna? After a decade of hit after hit, she experienced a major crisis in the early 1990s, when her film career was floundering and her new, more sexually explicit music attracted criticism and did not sell tremendously well. However, she recovered to triumph in the film version of *Evita* and to release one of her most popular and acclaimed albums, *Ray of Light*, in 1998. Billy Joel? After a decade of great success, he hit bottom in the mid-1980s, when he discovered that dishonest management had essentially left him dead broke and his record sales were slumping. However, he stormed back with a major hit in 1989, "We Didn't Start the Fire," and soon earned a second fortune to replace the one he had lost. Still, some public disapproval and disappointing sales figures do not necessarily represent a significant crisis for prominent artists like Madonna and Billy Joel, and, for that matter, during the same general period, Bruce Springsteen was experiencing similar setbacks. He was widely criticized for firing the E Street Band, and sales of his simultaneously released albums *Human Touch* and *Lucky Town* fell far short of expectations. Yet *Behind the Music* portrayed every artist as experiencing and overcoming a catastrophe, while *Legends* portrayed the similar situation of each of its artists more as a bump in the road. *Behind the Music*, in sum, relentlessly strives to portray its subjects as falling into the abyss, then climbing out of the abyss, whether they actually did so (like Joe Cocker, Rick James, and Meatloaf) or whether they only experienced milder disappointments and problems (like John Mellencamp, Bette Midler, and Ted Nugent).

Indeed, seeking to picture its artists as burdened with troubles during their cataclysmic second phases, *Behind the Music* sometimes must visibly stretch. For Shania Twain, a brief, and relatively mild, public challenge to her claimed Native American heritage (on the grounds that her Native American father was her adoptive, not her biological, father) is trotted out to function as her career-threatening crisis; and for Gladys Knight, it is what seems like a rather restrained addiction to gambling. In other cases, undoubtedly saddening but hardly unusual events, like divorce or the death of a parent or close friend, may be overdramatized to the breaking point. In the case of John Mellencamp, even the death of a beloved *grandparent* is depicted as a crushing blow to the struggling, angst-ridden artist. Exactly why audiences are supposed to feel so sorry for these artists is open to question: Aren't these things that everybody has to deal with in life? Is having the ability to write songs or play the guitar somehow supposed to make a person immune to the normal vicissitudes of life? Why are these people being celebrated for facing problems that ordinary people deal with all the time? Again, one must attribute these excesses to the influence of the series' chosen generic model: In the middle of their careers, artists in the conceptual universe of *Behind the Music* must suffer, and if they display no obvious symptoms of suffering (such as a near-fatal accident or jail sentence), it becomes necessary to seize upon every conceivable source of pain in their lives and exaggerate it to the greatest extent possible.

In sum, these VH1 documentaries invite suspicions for three reasons: cooperating artists or their family members and associates will inevitably seek to accentuate the positive and ameliorate the negative in their lives; some of them may bring specific hidden agendas to the proceedings; and the producers of the documentaries will endeavor to shape the story to fit either the pattern of continuous triumph (*Legends*) or spectacular rise followed by spectacular fall and eventual recovery (*Behind the Music*). Warped and distorted by all of these factors, the biographies presented become artifice more than journalism, attractive fictions created out of a mosaic of facts, in which every detail may be true while the overall picture is false.

As a footnote, there has now emerged another VH1 series, *Where Are They Now?*, with hour-long segments consisting of, in effect, miniature *Behind the Music* documentaries: A famous music star or group of the past is briefly profiled—the Rise—the narrator asks "Where Are They Now?" and the artists appear on camera, describing how they fell out of public view—the Fall—and how they have put their lives back together—the Return. While some featured artists have also been profiled by *Behind the Music*, like David Crosby and drummer Rick Allen of Def Leppard, the series seems primarily to serve as a vehicle for telling the stories of rock stars whose careers were not quite prominent enough, or whose stories were not quite involving enough, to qualify for a full-length *Behind the Music* documentary.

It is also interesting to note that VH1 has, at times, parodied its own documentaries. In a promotional clip for the short-lived satirical program *Random Play*, people were depicted playing the "Behind the Music" board game, in which players advance when they pick a card announcing a hit record, but go backward when they pick a card announcing a drug addiction. In addition, one promotional clip for the episode on Weird Al Yankovic showed the artist apologizing because he was too busy to get addicted to crack cocaine; another showed him first breaking down in tears because his record's sales were disappointing, then looking up somberly and asking the camera, "Will that work for you?" The humor in all these advertisements explicitly derives from the expectation that *Behind the Music* documentaries must, as a matter of form, invariably chronicle both spectacular rises and spectacular falls.

Discerning the narrative patterns imposed upon the VH1 documentaries, we can understand why the music documentaries aired on MTV have proven considerably less popular, even though they also focus on popular artists and appear to be just as factual and candid as their VH1 counterparts. Since the "Rockumentaries" were usually only 30 minutes long, and since *Biorhythms* programs have no narration, these programs have considerably less power to *shape* their stories, and they are not as enjoyable as a result. One might argue, given the recent increases in various types of "reality" programs on television, that people are coming to prefer fact to fiction. Yet the vast differences in the popularity of the two music networks' documentaries suggest, less hearteningly, that people are coming to prefer *fact in the form of fiction*. And VH1 is delivering the goods, while MTV isn't.

To many, these charges will seem harsh, especially since published commentaries on the *Behind the Music* documentaries typically praise them enthusiastically as honest and hard-hitting. Jim Farber says that

VH1 doesn't like to be known for nostalgia.
But over the past few years, the cable channel has mined the past for a higher purpose: to become pop's own history channel. . . . It produces original shows that cast their gaze on history with the freshness of "20/20" hindsight—like its excellent "Legends" series or even better "Behind the Music" programs. . . . And like any good history lesson, the specials offer as much current perspective as possible, the better to get their subjects (or their survivors) to cough up the stories they hid when it was all happening. ("VH1 Blends Music with History")

And according to Jim DeRogatis,

Behind the music—theoretically that's where all music journalism is supposed to take us, but . . . the rock press doesn't bring us there nearly enough these days.
Who'd a thunk that VH1 would?
In 1999 the major music magazines accept that there's no room for probing journalism or real criticism. . . . All of which makes it surprising refreshing to pause while channel surfing on VH1's *Behind the Music*. . . . The things people say in these stories are actually revealing, as opposed to the carefully crafted sound bites delivered on the newsstands. . . . The producers know their stuff. A number of veteran New York music journalists write for VH1, some of them alumni of the late *Musician* magazine. They don't shy away from asking the tough questions, and they are rewarded with candor. ("[A] Bum's Note[s]")

Still, as DeRogatis's comments suggest, it may be that these programs's "freshness" and "candor" emerge only in contrast to the sheer fluff elsewhere available on the subject of popular music. Yet the fact remains that, to people who are actually well informed about the careers of, say, Sonny Bono, David Crosby, John Denver, and Julian Lennon, their *Behind the Music* biographies will seem horribly incomplete, superficial, and misleading.

As Heinlein's categories indicate, the mythic patterns promulgated by these programs are hardly new in human history, and one of them—the *Legends* model—seems relatively innocuous. It is the myth of the superhero, the being blessed by the gods with powers and abilities far beyond those of mortal men, the superman destined to overcome every challenge he faces. This story is implicit in the innumerable music videos displaying musicians in concert, triumphantly standing in the spotlight while hordes of admirers scream and gyrate to show their adoration. This heroic pattern may come to the forefront in extended videos like Michael Jackson's *Moonwalker*, where the singer finally emerges as a Transformer-like superhero, rescuing children from powerful villains. Such stories lack genuine drama, since no force can plausibly threaten such mighty heroes, and that is why mature audiences often find them uninteresting. Still, such portrayals of *Legends* are essentially harmless, because even young people can recognize that these sagas are unrealistic, or applicable only to a few rare individuals.

More pernicious, even if more involving, are the characteristic stories of *Behind the Music*. These suggest that even persons without remarkable talents may, by means of good fortune or special circumstances, achieve astonishing success; and even if those people proceed to make every mistake in the book—even if they do everything they can to destroy themselves with alcohol, drugs, reckless driving, ruinous relationships, or bad business deals—they can still survive, climb back from the abyss, and attain a blissful and satisfying, if not quite as elevated, existence. In short, episodes of *Legends* validate perfection as the road to success, but since few people imagine they have achieved, or ever will achieve, the level of perfection to travel on that road, there is little chance that these stories will influence anyone. In contrast, episodes of *Behind the Music* validate relying on good fortune and happy-go-lucky blundering as the road to success, and since any people can readily imagine themselves traveling on that road, it is entirely possible that young viewers might become more inclined to leave it all behind and set out to conquer the music world in the manner they have observed.

At this point, one might protest that, as noted, the *Behind the Music* documentaries are filled with statements about the evils of drinking and drug-taking, and musicians invariably assert that becoming clean and sober has infinitely improved their music and their lives as well. Yet the episodes typically depict drinking and drug-taking young artists reaching the top of the charts, while reformed older artists are sitting in their backyards and enduring small record sales and relative obscurity. Effectively, then, these documentaries are conveying another, less wholesome message to their viewers: Live wild and party hard while you're young, because that is the path to success, and wait until you're older to sober up and settle down and raise a family. The dangerous myth that wretched excess and self-destructive impulses are essential to musical creativity is being reinforced by the design of the narrative even as it is contradicted by the artists' testimony.

The trouble is that life does not always conform to the patterns projected by *Behind the Music*. People who reach rock bottom don't always climb back up, and don't always achieve inner peace; so it is foolish for troubled people to trust in time to invariably heal all their wounds and solve all their problems. And this is, as it happens, perfectly illustrated by the subjects of the very first *Behind the Music* program.

To introduce their chosen narrative template, the producers of *Behind the Music* could have made no better choice than the duo of Rob Pilatus and Fab Moran, who performed as Milli Vanilli, because no act in rock history has ever risen so high and so rapidly only to fall so low and so dramatically. Their first album was an instantaneous success, their videos became MTV staples, they headlined sold-out arena concerts, and they earned a Grammy Award as the year's Best New Artist. Then there came a stunning revelation: During their rise to rock stardom, Rob Pilatus and Fab Moran had never sung a note on their records. The singing on their debut album was entirely the work of anonymous session men, and in concert, they were always lip-synching to the pre-recorded singing of those other singers. Viewed from the proper perspective, it was hard to blame Pilatus and Moran for the situation. They were young and ambitious, they signed a contract, and the man who controlled their careers insisted upon using other singers. Still, huge waves of anger and outrage immediately and effectively ended their careers, even though they briefly attempted to carry on as genuine singers by performing as Rob and Fab.

As unsurprisingly documented by *Behind the Music*, the abrupt crash landing of Milli Vanilli soon led the young men to financial problems, heavy drug use, and deep depression. But Fab pulled himself out of it, picked up his guitar, and started writing and performing his own songs as Fabrice Moran. He achieved only modest success, and found himself playing only in very small clubs, but he told *Behind the Music* that he felt happy and satisfied with his status, since he was now finally able to express himself with his own music. In the conceptual universe of *Behind the Music*, this is the way it is supposed to be.

Unfortunately, Rob didn't seem to be following the script. By all appearances, he had not managed to forget about the awful past, he had not recovered from his depression, he had not gotten himself clean and sober, and he was not moving on with a new career. In an effort to impose some positive imagery on a situation that could inspire no genuine optimism, the producers got him to take off his shirt and filmed him walking along a beautifully scenic beach, as if to iconically suggest that he was somehow communing with nature or belatedly finding some peace of mind. But that suggestion was false, as events quickly demonstrated.

Several months after the Milli Vanilli episode of *Behind the Music* first aired, Rob Pilatus committed suicide. The producers were obliged to reedit the episode and add a new, incongruous ending to their carefully crafted documentary.

It will always be impossible to determine exactly what drove Pilatus to finally kill himself, but any search for the answer must consider the one major event in his life between the fall of Milli Vanilli and his death: the airing of the *Behind the Music* episode chronicling his career. Before its appearance, Pilatus could ponder his continually pathetic situation in the context of one consoling thought: "Hey, nobody else has ever gone through what I've gone through, so nobody can blame me if I can't get myself out of the hole I've fallen into." But VH1's documentary destroyed all such rationalizations. "Look at Fab!" his friends might say, or Pilatus himself might privately say. "*He* went through *exactly* what you went through. But *he* came back; *he* pulled himself together. So why can't *you*?"

It is no sin to be unable to recover from a horrible experience that somebody else can recover from; all people are different, whatever visible similarities in their situations there may be, and the private hell that Pilatus endured may have been far more excruciating than the private hell that Moran endured. Thus, the pattern of that *Behind the Music* documentary, Moran's ability to conform to that pattern, and Pilatus's seeming inability to conform to that pattern may have served as a final, crushing blow to Pilatus's ego and his self-esteem.

Just possibly, Rob Pilatus represents the first person in history killed by a documentary.

If anything good can be said to have come out of his death, it is that the new, updated Milli Vanilli story now stands as the most honest *Behind the Music* episode ever aired. It is one of those rare occasions when changing realities force-fully intervene to contradict advertised illusions, reminiscent of the time when a former Marlboro Man returned to television, as an older man dying of lung cancer, in a public service announcement warning young people about the dangers of smoking cigarettes. The unsettling new coda to an episode that previously strug-gled to be so reassuring persuasively communicates that, no matter what young viewers may wish to believe, and no matter what television producers may wish to tell their young viewers, recovering from setbacks and achieving a sense of con-tentment with life is not always easy, and sometimes it is not even possible.

Whatever else that advertising can offer in the way of entertainment and en-lightenment, people should never turn to advertising in order to discover the truth. The impulse to sell at all costs will invariably distort the presentation of facts, no matter how honest or truthful the commercial may seem. This is not necessarily damaging because the vast majority of consumers in a capitalist society will understand the nature of advertising and will accordingly respond to its messages in an appropriately skeptical manner. As suggested previously, MTV and VH1 may be best regarded as advertising channels, dedicated to selling CDs and cassettes by means of attractive music videos, and the documentaries increasingly emphasized by VH1 might logically be characterized as other means to achieve that goal, glorifying artists, and the rock lifestyle itself, in an effort to sell more products to consumers. These motives are not evil or insidious, but the methods being em-ployed here—in essence, advertisements disguised as journalism—invite criticism, because in this situation, the fantasies of advertising may deceive even the most cynical viewers, leading them to accept a false, and possibly dangerous, belief in the inevitably redemptive rhythms of careers in the world of rock music. However, to approach such realizations is to venture much further *Behind the Music* than VH1 wishes its viewers to go.

9

Hollywood Strikes a Pose:
Seven Tales of Triumph, Treachery,
and Travail in Old Tinseltown

When asked by David Pringle to contribute to a proposed volume entitled *Hollywood: The Best 100 Novels*—a project now indefinitely delayed—I was initially hesitant about venturing beyond my usual areas of expertise. However, when I began reading some Hollywood novels, everything seemed comfortingly familiar. The patterns and conventions of the genre seemed immediately clear, and I could recognize the ways that individual authors were following, or interestingly departing from, those patterns and conventions. The story of entering, conquering, and being conquered by the world of Hollywood may in fact be the central myth of twentieth-century America, if not the western world, permeating all media and making any alert observer an expert on its permutations.

What follows, then, are examinations of seven major examples of the Hollywood novel, not quite a comprehensive survey but one which, I believe, will provide enough data to convey a rough holographic image of the entire genre. To provide the aura of an *ad hoc* history of Hollywood in the twentieth century, I have arranged the novels chronologically according to the periods they focus on, beginning with Charles E. Van Loan's and Gore Vidal's stately portraits of the silent era and moving on to Stuart Kaminsky's intimate snapshot of Hollywood in 1940, Thomas Tryon's and Darcy O'Brien's expansive overviews principally of the 1940s and 1950s, and Jacqueline Susann's and Richard Sale's salacious sagas of the 1960s. If things seem bright and cheerful at first, only to grow progressively darker and more depressing, that may only be appropriate.

Today, we do not normally envision movie-making as a sporting event, but in the early days of the industry—with bulky hand-cranked cameras, extensive location shooting, and plots that relied heavily on slapstick, violence, and authentic stunts—everyone involved in the process worked up a sweat. So it is only fitting that Charles E. Van Loan's *Buck Parvin and the Movies: Stories of the Motion*

Picture Game (1915)—nine pioneering stories about Hollywood during the silent era—came from a writer previously noted for sports fiction, and that he described making movies as a "game." The generic echoes are obvious: Producer/director/ actor Jimmy Montague (modeled on Hobert Bosworth) is the coach, gruff and demanding but ultimately likeable; the actors and extras are his players, trying to carry out their assignments and desperately improvising when things go wrong, while the coach shouts advice from the sidelines; Buck Parvin is the veteran player who, though not admired for his acting talents, earns a place on Montague's team as a hard-working stunt man; and getting the scene properly filmed, with the action properly executed and the camera focused on the stars, is equivalent to scoring the winning touchdown.

Two other aspects of these stories may also surprise contemporary readers. First, we are accustomed to novels that focus on the sordid personal lives of Hollywood insiders; but to Van Loan, the most interesting thing about movie-makers is the fact that they make movies. Almost every scene takes place during filming, and he provides a wealth of interesting information about the early indus-try: how silent movies were planned, how convincing outdoor actions were staged, how directors employed editing to minimize filming difficulties, and so on. Sec-ond, we are accustomed to novels that present Hollywood producers and stars as powerful people, but these workers in a fledgling industry often find themselves in thrall to powerful outsiders: the company executive in "Snow Stuff" who insists he knows how to make movies better and more cheaply than the director; the domineering novelist of "Author! Author!" who does not understand that his novel must be changed to make it into a successful film; the high-priced stage actor of "Man-Afraid-of-His-Wardrobe" who is not prepared to ride horses or engage in rough-and-tumble action; and the wealthy housewife of "This Is the Life!" who does not realize that acting involves more hard work than glamour. These people cannot be directly challenged; but like playful college students dealing with a stuffy old dean (another generic echo), the movie-makers overcome their opponents with elaborate pranks: The executive is captured on film stealing a kiss from the leading lady, discrediting him in the eyes of his colleagues; the novelist is scared off the set when Buck tells him that the film's Indian actor is an uncontrollable savage (when he is really an articulate Harvard graduate); the stage actor quits when he is forced to ride a horse through dangerously deep water; and the would-be actress returns to a life of domestic ease after the director makes her perform one onerous task after another.

Though this atmosphere of collegiate hijinks seems outdated, Van Loan does confront—naïvely—what will become one major theme in Hollywood fiction: how movie-making blurs the distinction between reality and illusion. Because film is still a relatively new phenomenon, the people who observe films and the process of creating them may mistake staged events for actual events. In "The International Cup," an Englishwoman sees her beau-turned-actor kiss an actress in a movie, imagines that the woman is a true rival for his affections, and so breaks her coquet-tish silence and contacts him. In "The Extra Man and the Milkfed Lion," a smitten extra sees an actress register fear in a lion's cage and, believing she is really in danger, attacks the lion. And in "Desert Stuff," an addled prospector mistakes the trained camel Buck is riding for a wild animal attacking him and shoots the camel down. More interestingly, actors may start behaving as if their scenarios are real. In "Buck's Lady Friend," Buck in one scene is supposed to be angry with the leading man, but as the cameras roll, he suddenly suspects that the man is flirting with his girlfriend, his feigned anger becomes real anger, and what was supposed to be a restrained slap becomes a haymaker. And in "Water Stuff," an actress must jump off a ship into the water and swim to a raft, but because she lied to the director about her swimming ability, her jump leaves her floundering and about to drown. Recognizing that her phony danger has become real, Buck dives in and effects an unscripted rescue; and since the alert cameraman filmed the action, the director decides to use the exciting footage in his movie, adding new establishing scenes involving Buck and the actress. Here, a feigned peril becomes a real peril, then is re-transformed into a feigned peril.

While one can extract from these stories a message about the pitfalls of confusing acting and real life, there is another lesson for prospective Hollywood novelists: The process of movie-making, once the tricks of the trade are revealed, can remain interesting only if staged dramas are turned into actual dramas. Since it is hard to believe that the day-to-day business of movie-making routinely leads to genuine perils and passions, a writer can regularly accomplish this only through implausible contrivance. Van Loan's contrivances have a certain charm, but this is not a viable long-term strategy for an emerging literary tradition; so it is not surprising that later novelists shifted their focus away from the set—where the dramas are always real.

As a collection of stories, not a true novel, one cannot logically fault this book for lacking unity or a sense of closure. But its format is strangely fitting: *Buck Parvin and the Movies* is a youthful, inchoate book about a youthful, inchoate industry. Today, the literature of Hollywood offers readers more than enough maturity and cynicism; Van Loan usefully reminds us that once upon a time, and sometimes even now, movie-making might be properly seen as an exciting game for overgrown children.

To readers who are not familiar with Gore Vidal's work, *Hollywood: A Novel of America in the 1920s* (1990) will seem misleadingly titled. Part of a series of Vidal novels chronicling American political history, it largely takes place in Washington D.C., from 1917 to 1923 and devotes most of its attention to the careers of Presidents Woodrow Wilson, Warren G. Harding, and various real and fictional colleagues. Yet Vidal does include the adventures of several Washington figures who move from the world of politics to the world of filmmaking: George Creel is sent by Wilson to encourage filmmakers to produce anti-German films and build support for American involvement in World War I; William Randolph Hearst abandons his New York political ambitions and settles in California to promote the film career of his mistress, Marion Davies; Will Hays leaves Harding's cabinet to become the public guardian of Hollywood morality after the Fatty Arbuckle scandal; the novel's protagonist, Washington newspaper publisher Caroline Sanford, improbably launches a new career as a middle-aged movie star after an amateur film produced by Hearst reveals that she is unusually photogenic; and she later plans to become a film producer, in partnership with her lover, director Tim Farrell, so that they can make movies to covertly promote American values. All these migrations suggest that an important power shift was occurring in America at this time: Before 1920, the American public was primarily influenced by Washington; after 1920, Hollywood would be an equally important influence. While the argument in itself is not startling, the way that Vidal describes the development of Hollywood offers a fundamental challenge to traditional attitudes toward the movie industry.

Hollywood novels typically present the rags-to-riches stories of lowly upstarts who manage to rise to the top because of their talents; depending on the author's idealism or cynicism, the talents involved may be acting, deal-making, or back-stabbing, but everyone seems to agree that Hollywood was a business created and dominated by energetic newcomers, and continually reinvigorated by the appearance and success of talented new outsiders. However, Vidal insists, that wasn't the way it happened at all. Rather, he tells a riches-to-riches story: As soon as the wealthy and powerful scions of the political establishment realized that movies could be a valuable tool, they moved in to take control of the industry. Some, like Creel and Hays, openly functioned as dictators, ensuring that filmmakers offered only approved political opinions and promoted wholesome moral values; others, like Hearst and Caroline, insinuated themselves into the industry through their wealth or connections. Not really a new force in American society, the movie industry was only another instrument of familiar old forces. Hollywood thus serves to provide additional support for Vidal's general thesis about America: While history books record the apparent rises and falls of various elite groups, the country has actually been governed at all times by the same elite group, an incestuous network of families and friends who openly or secretly dominate every powerful institution.

Of course, absorbing Hollywood into this system was not unproblematic, as suggested by Caroline's experiences. When she assumes the persona of Emma Traxler, mysterious actress from Europe, it is a sign of her genuine unease in this new environment that she often feels like two separate people, Caroline and Emma, with two separate identities. Gradually, though, she adjusts: She masters the conventions of film acting and the rhythms of Hollywood socializing; she discovers new passion in her affair with Tim; while she previously thought in terms of newspaper headlines, she learns to think and speak like title cards; and she has a secret face-lift because in Hollywood, on and off the screen, power is often linked to physical attractiveness.

But her major problem is figuring out how to use this new medium: "What to do with so novel a means of—what? George Creel would say propaganda. But that was too simple and eventually the audience would learn all the tricks" (143). With the arrival of the puritanical Hays as overseer, she finally resolves to influence people's dreams, not their thoughts and opinions, by making films about an "ordinary American town" that would "appeal to as many people as possible, yet with a certain intrinsic design that, if successful, would subtly alter the way everyone observed the world" (387, 385). At this moment, significantly, she starts to feel like one person again: She has learned to be both Caroline—a powerful influence on America—and Emma—a Hollywood icon. In this way Vidal explains the history of American film from the silent era to the 1930s—with its gradual shift to celebrations of idealized small-town values, to Shirley Temple and Andy Hardy—as the result of a deliberate plot by America's political elite.

As someone who emerged from that powerful group, Vidal expresses no outrage about this situation, although particular people are singled out for criticism; *Hollywood* is an exposé without indignation. Apparently he shares Caroline's opinion: "She was entirely on the side of the rulers, ridiculous and unpleasant as so many of them were. She felt a certain generalized pity for the people at large, but there was nothing she could do for them except report murders in the press, and commit suicide on the screen" (266). Indeed, except for cameo appearances by servants and passers-by, Vidal deals exclusively with the rich and famous. Everyone else is part of an undifferentiated herd, whose opinions are easily swayed in any desirable direction by political leaders or popular movies. From this perspective, Hollywood does not give the public what it wants, but rather makes the public want what it is given—or as Caroline and Tim put it, in an exchange that conveys both condescension and a sense of moral rightness, Hollywood will "invent the people" because "They're waiting to be invented, to be told who and what they are" (360).

It is Vidal's peculiar mission, then, to maintain on the one hand that all cherished beliefs about America—government by the people, movies created by popular demand—are nothing but glorious illusions, and to imply on the other hand that this is, after all, the best of all possible worlds.

Stuart Kaminsky's *Murder on the Yellow Brick Road* (1977) seems designed to please Raymond Chandler fans: Here is another hard-boiled detective, Toby Peters, in the mold of Philip Marlowe, working the same mean streets of Los Angeles in the 1940s, narrating his adventures in the same laconic style. Fans of Hollywood fiction should be pleased as well, because Peters is investigating the murder of a midget on a leftover set from *The Wizard of Oz*, and, exercising a freedom Chandler did not enjoy, Kaminsky features as characters many celebrities associated with MGM Studios and Hollywood during that era, including Judy Garland, Victor Fleming, Clark Gable, Mickey Rooney, and Louis B. Mayer. Even Chandler himself makes a brief appearance, tagging along after Peters in search of story material. Yet these readers may be strangely disappointed by this novel, for one reason: Unlike Chandler and other Hollywood novelists, Kaminsky seems to be giving them the real thing.

In the guise of a hack writer churning out stories for the mystery pulps, Chandler was a frustrated poet who imbued his narratives with evocative detail and stunning metaphoric language. And in the guise of a cynical opportunist, Marlowe was a knight in shining armor, always ready to give up a desperately needed paycheck to restore justice or rescue a fair maiden. In contrast, Kaminsky deliberately limits his language to what an actual detective of the time might have to say. There are some colorful observations and apt descriptions, but nothing beyond the predictable repertoire of an average Joe. And Peters seems genuinely interested first and foremost in supplementing his meager income: While he prolongs his investigation ostensibly to help a wrongly accused midget, Peters then seems to forget all about him. However, the detailed, itemized bill that he submits to MGM at the end of the novel speaks volumes about his true motivation. Peters is apparently a man for whom trouble really is only a business.

As a former bodyguard for Warner Brothers and as a product of Hollywood, Peters reflects what Kaminsky asserts is the true attitude of people in the movie industry: that their work is simply a business. True, the story behind the murder suggests a searing exposé: A studio employee conspires with midgets to produce pornographic films combining stolen outtakes from *The Wizard of Oz* with new footage of a Garland double being raped by naked Munchkins, featuring sets and costumes from the movie. An excitable critic might perceive an allegory—beneath the wholesome facade of Hollywood's Oz lurks a seedy netherworld of lust and depravity—but nothing else in this novel supports this interpretation. This sordid undertaking is clearly presented as an anomaly, not standard procedure. The film executives Peters meets are not saints, but neither are they sinners: They want to find the murderer, like good citizens, but they also want to keep the story out of the papers, since it might harm the image of their studio and movies. Garland is understandably nervous about the murder, but she is not—not yet, at least—a bitter, out-of-control alcoholic; Gable is presented not as a wonderful guy, or worthless heel, but simply as a calm, rather ordinary person. What movie people seem most determined to avoid is passion, mirroring the dogged lack of emotion that Peters maintains. Even the murders are a matter of cold calculation: One midget has threatened to reveal the scheme, so he logically must be eliminated, and when Peters tracks down another midget who might provide damaging information, it makes sense for the murderer to try to kill him too.

The only exception to this pattern is Cassie James, MGM costume designer, Garland's companion, and the woman eventually exposed as the brains behind the clandestine filmmaking and the murderer as well. She is a cauldron of suppressed emotions: First a frustrated actress, she then watched in further frustration as her sister's promising career in the movies led instead to degradation and death. Since Garland won two roles her sister had competed for, Cassie sees the actress as the agent of her sister's ruin—and that secret anger destroys her. Had she simply stabbed the midget and left the body for some random person to discover, she might have gotten away with murder; but she wanted to hurt Garland, so she arranged by an accomplice's phone call to have Garland discover the body, and Garland is the one who calls Peters and gets him involved in the case. Then, simply to upset Garland, she puts poison in her pitcher of water. Because of these unnecessary actions, that only Cassie could have arranged, Peters can finally identify her as the killer; yet he almost fails to figure it out because he has become romantically involved with her. Thus, Kaminsky indicates, you get into trouble when you let your emotions interfere with your business.

Perhaps to impress his professorial colleagues, Kaminsky tosses out some raw meat for scholarly interpretation, including ongoing reports on the 1940 presidential election—suggesting a political subtext—and vivid descriptions of Peter's surrealistic nightmares featuring Oz characters—suggesting hidden parallels between the film and his story. What is truly striking about this novel, however, is that despite his colorful settings and characters, Kaminsky surprisingly makes the world of Hollywood seem rather dull—just as the actual life of a small-time detective in 1940s Los Angeles was probably rather dull. The predominant color of this story is grey: As he examines the corpse, Peters notes that "the yellow brick road. . . . didn't lead to Oz, but to a blank grey wall" (2); Mayer "wore a grey suit" (23); even the famed Brown Derby restaurant is really "a greyish dome" (60).

Of course, it is the business of the Hollywood novel to destroy illusions. But while the murder on the Yellow Brick Road shatters the image of a happy young girl frolicking in a wonderland, it does not substitute a picture of wicked witches carrying out depraved schemes; rather, one sees grey men in business suits engaged in damage control—making this, perhaps, the most disillusioning Hollywood novel of them all.

Arguably, Thomas Tryon had the perfect background to write the Great Hollywood Novel: a previous career as a motion picture actor, and experience writing horror novels.

While lacking overt supernatural effects, the four portraits of fading movie stars that comprise Tryon's *Crowned Heads* (1976) mimic the structure and tone of horror stories, as an initial atmosphere of calm realism gradually builds to a surreal, or even feverish, climax. Their unifying element is a familiar horrific theme, the loss of personal identity: Hollywood has imposed false personae on these people, ones they cannot accept and cannot escape. Renowned for her late return to film stardom displaying an amazingly preserved youthful beauty, the mysterious, Garbo-like actress Fedora actually recruited her daughter to impersonate her, aided by her natural resemblance and plastic surgery, while she assumed the identity of an old friend; and of course, neither mother nor daughter are happy playing these roles. Minor actress Lorna Doone, widely regarded as a mentally unbalanced nymphomaniac, is driven to play that part while vacationing at a resort, sleeping with every man she meets (except the one she really desires), shoplifting, starting some fires, wounding the man who scorned her, and finally dying in an apparently willful embrace with a poisonous snake that repeatedly bites her. (Her nickname was "Cookie," and she correspondingly crumbles.) Former child star Bobby Ransome, barely surviving in New York while beguiling his acquaintances with attractive lies, does attempt a comeback performance as his real self; but the actress who once played his stern governess marches on stage and forces him back into his celluloid Bobbitt character, performing his old songs to thunderous applause. And beloved Willie Marsh, "the Grand Old Man of Hollywood," was repressed all his life by his domineering and ever-present mother Bee; soon after her death, he allows his house to be ransacked by "guests" (actually thieves), does not object when they burn the only manuscript of his autobiography, *Salad Days*, and finally lets them literally crucify him in a private chapel rather than revealing the location of a priceless mirror that is really a worthless duplicate. The bizarre conclusion to Willie's life makes Tryon's title bitterly ironic—a crowned head may also wear a crown of thorns—and suggests that all popular stars become martyrs, suffering or even dying so that others may be entertained. A further irony is that unlike true monarchs, these people cannot really control their worlds, or even their own lives. (A later sequel to *Crowned Heads*, *All That Glitters* [1986], brought some of these characters back in minor roles while focusing on new Hollywood horror stories, including a man who prolongs the career of an actress modeled on Mae West by impersonating her, thus abandoning his own identity.)

In describing how miserable these people become, Tryon often appears to indict motherhood: Fedora dooms her own daughter to a sad life of deception; Lorna's evident lack of self-esteem might be attributed to her mother, who once "told her she was just a dumb bunny and to keep her mouth shut or people would find out how stupid she really was" (107); Willie's oppressive mother (known as the Queen Bee) makes all his decisions for him and never allows him to marry or do anything he wants to; and while his own mother stayed in England, Bobby's mother figure in the movies is the one who finally does not let him grow out of the role of lovable little Bobbitt. In the strange scene where Willie reveals himself as a closet trans-vestite, parading before the intruders in makeup and women's clothing, Tryon may be paying tribute to the most famous horror story about the evil influence of mothers: Robert Bloch's novel and Alfred Hitchcock's film *Psycho* (1959, 1960). Like Norman Bates, these over-mothered or under-mothered characters can be destructive toward others—Lorna's casual arson and violence, Bobby's lies that ultimately hurt his friends; but also like Bates, their primary aim seems to be self-destruction—seen most graphically in Lorna's and Willie's suicidal willingness to die.

More broadly, Tryon indicates that Hollywood acts like a mother to its per-formers: Like a good mother, Hollywood offers them unconditional love and protection from the harsh world; but like a bad mother, Hollywood keeps treating them like children and refuses to allow them to mature and become their own persons. The connection is clearest in the Willie episode: Immediately after he realizes that "I hate you, Bee. . . . I have hated you all my life," he abruptly an-nounces to his tormentors that the life of a movie star is "Bullshit. . . . a crock" (375). Finding out that he hated his mother, and finding out that he hated Holly-wood, were his simultaneous—and parallel—revelations.

As if sensing that this picture of Hollywood life is too negative, Tryon adds a coda to his novel, also called "Salad Days," which goes back to the 1950s when the lives of his characters intertwined, then drifts even further back to the 1930s, when Fedora and Willie enjoyed an idyllic picnic at the beach and watched a young Lorna twirling the baton with her high school band. By ending his novel this way, Tryon implies that Hollywood stardom is indeed pleasant at the beginning—just as one's early childhood is often pleasant—but gradually becomes horrifying—just as continued existence in a child's role becomes horrifying. To put it another way, the true joys of movie life, after initial success, are found only in nostalgia, looking at scrapbooks and souvenirs and reminiscing about the Salad Days. Yet this is surely an artificial and unsatisfying kind of joy, as phony as the cheap replicas of valuable curios that fill Willie's house.

Thus, while there is nothing autobiographical in Tryon's portraits—no characters resemble him—the novel does serve to explain and justify his unusual decision to abandon a successful Hollywood career for the less glamorous life of a novelist. Yet, as he looks back with both revulsion and genuine sympathy at the sad kinds of people he once knew, Tryon does not seem surprised that they could not or would not follow his example and walk away from the world of Hollywood, even as it was visibly destroying them. After all, no matter how terrible she becomes, it is always difficult to leave your mother.

Drawing on his experience as the son of western star George O'Brien and actress Marguerite Churchill, Darcy O'Brien wrote his first novel, *A Way of Life, Like Any Other* (1977), about the son of a fading movie actor and former actress. The narrator's early years are idyllic, as he frolics at his father's ranch being pampered by servants and celebrities like Charles Laughton. But the family fortunes decline and his parents divorce, forcing him to live with his mother in relative poverty while she anesthetizes her sorrows with alcohol, travel, and a disastrous second marriage. When she moves to Europe, he stays with the family of director Sam Caliban, then moves in with his father, though they achieve only moments of rapport. Finally, he leaves for college on the East Coast and, perhaps, escapes from Hollywood forever.

On one level, O'Brien is relating the familiar story of how Hollywood destroys people, first by giving them too much too soon—driving them to dangerous self-indulgence—then by taking it all away—leaving them to wallow in despair. But the effects of Hollywood are more subtle: Existing in a world of play-acting, people learn to put on an act all the time and never communicate their true feelings or personalities. His mother never talks about her bitterness, but blithely insists all her problems can be solved by another man, another drink, or another environment. His father never admits his career is over, but keeps reporting his imminent comeback in some unlikely forthcoming film. The sense of Hollywood as a constant false front is best conveyed by the narrator's encounter with the Calibans. He first believes he has found an Ozzie-and-Harriet world: hard-working father, loving mother, well-adjusted son. But the wholesome facade collapses: Caliban turns out to be a compulsive gambler whose Las Vegas adventures lead to death threats and impending financial collapse; his wife turns out to be mentally unstable and, unable

116   *Science Fiction, Children's Literature, and Popular Culture*

to deal with reduced circumstances, eventually must be committed to an asylum; and the son turns out to be sharing a mistress with his father, dissipating illusions of a virtuous family life.

However, O'Brien does not indict his characters as frauds, but rather suggests that they pretend to be other people because, having done so for so long, they no longer know who they really are. As its most insidious effect, Hollywood not only takes away people's prosperity and sincerity, but their self-knowledge as well. Desperately seeking an ersatz sense of identity, his mother immerses herself in supposedly superior European culture, and his father retreats into Catholicism. Caliban keeps up an optimistic front because he does not know what actual person exists behind that front. As one irony underpinning the novel, characters regularly remove their clothes: We first see the narrator as a boy sunbathing in the nude, and he ends an awkward recitation for Laughton by contriving to have his pants fall down; later, he has long conversations with his mother while she takes a bath, and joins his father at a health club where they shower and sauna together; and his mother's husband idiotically tries to end an argument by exposing his penis. But while they frequently reveal their bodies, they never bare their souls.

From everything said so far, this novel might recall other critiques of Hollywood life; but O'Brien fails to follow the usual pattern. First, he refuses to play the moralist: While characters receive little praise, they are not vilified, and despite their excesses they remain contributing members of society. Portraying the father as a born-again Catholic seems particularly designed to counter the notion that all actors inevitably sink into decadence. Further, while other works introduce outside observers—like the journalists in *Crowned Heads* or the film *Sunset Boulevard*—to watch and comment on these deluded people like anthropologists studying exotic natives, O'Brien's narrator is also a product, and victim, of Hollywood. Never given a name, he also does not communicate his true feelings, because he also does not appear to know what those feelings really are. Like those he describes, he acts out a series of roles: cute little boy to his father's friends, dutiful son to his parents, regular guy to his best friend, and—finally and most distastefully—snotty young rebel to everyone. One finishes this book not understanding what he truly thinks about himself or those around him, and not knowing what he will do with the rest of his life. Crafting his narrative this way was O'Brien's courageous but, in one respect, risky choice, as this becomes a novel with a viewpoint character readers cannot sympathize with or get to know at all.

If a lack of communication and self-knowledge is the terrible fate awaiting those who work in Hollywood, one must ask whether the movie industry itself is to blame. One scene in the novel offers a clue: in the Caliban home, the narrator sees "a magnificent mural" where "Sam Caliban was depicted sitting in his director's chair, watching a parade of characters from his pictures. . . . Martians, monsters of all kinds, ape women riding giant lizards, toads wearing space suits, the abominable hermaphrodite, Pilar the Pygmy Love Goddess." Caliban then explains his film-making philosophy: "I know what's gonna entertain your average person who goes to see a movie. Why? Because I'm an average guy myself. . . . I make 'em happy. So what's wrong with that?" (60-61). Well, if you dedicate yourself to making people happy, you may neglect to tell them anything about yourself; and if you spend your life in the company of colorful imaginary beings, you may start acting like an imaginary being yourself, and thus learn nothing about yourself.

However, undermining the notion that these characters' problems are the fault of Hollywood is the title *A Way of Life, Like Any Other*. Is that a sincere assertion that Hollywood is only a reflective microcosm of American society, or another of O'Brien's ironies? Like other questions raised by this deliberately dissatisfying novel, the issue remains unresolved.

If you descend into Jacqueline Susann's *Valley of the Dolls* (1966), you are not expecting literary quality; indeed, there is little to say about Jacqueline Susann's masterful prose, complex characters, or symbolic depth. Yet slick promotion and a popular movie adaptation cannot fully explain the phenomenal success of this book, once cited as the bestselling American novel of all time (with 29 million copies sold). In fact, if not excellent, *Valley of the Dolls* is certainly extraordinary; and the chord it struck in the American consciousness still merits attention.

Before Susann, almost all Hollywood novels were written by men about men; here is a novel written by a woman about women. Despite its reputation as mind-less fluff, it is an amazingly angry book. Its message is that all the worlds of show business—Hollywood, Broadway, television—ruthlessly exploit and degrade women. Anne, first almost forced into marriage by an assertive millionaire, achieves success as a television model but not happiness, as she passionately loves a man who cannot and will not remain faithful to her. Jennifer, with a beautiful body but little talent, goes to France and becomes a sensation making movies with nude scenes, then commits suicide when a mastectomy threatens to remove the one thing about her that her senator fiancé really loves—her breasts. Neely wins acclaim as a singing movie star, but the pressures of constant filming make her an alcoholic, drug addict, and "monster" who is finally committed to an insane asylum. Meanwhile, the men in these worlds enjoy placid lives, with wealth and influence largely derived from capitalizing on these women's tormented labors.

Overall, Susann paints a relentlessly unpleasant picture of women in show business. Women can gain success and power, but these are fleeting things, based solely on physical attractiveness. When they age and start to lose their beauty, they face three unpalatable options: kill themselves, like Jennifer; retreat into passive acceptance of their reduced and marginal status, like Anne; or become raging bitches, clinging desperately to what they have gained with temper tantrums, shrill demands, and assaults on potential rivals, like Neely and Broadway star Helen Lawson. In this milieu, even women who look like villains turn out to be victims. When Jennifer has an affair with singer Tony Polar, she sees his sister Miriam as a dominating meddler, completely controlling his life and keeping him from marrying her; but she later learns that Tony actually has a congenital mental problem that gives him the permanent mind of a ten-year-old, and that Miriam has sacrificed her own life to constantly take care of him and keep his career going.

With a title featuring Susann's made-up slang word for tranquilizers, "dolls," and pictures of little capsules at the beginning of each chapter, this novel might also be viewed as a polemic against drug abuse; but the real addiction that destroys these women is their desire for success and fulfillment in the destructive worlds of show business. Anne, who stumbles into a career she did not seek, takes the longest to succumb to drugs; Neely, who eagerly throws herself into the high-pressure business of movie-making, succumbs most quickly and disastrously. The word "dolls" encapsulates for Susann everything that is wrong with show business: A derogatory term for attractive but unintelligent women is "dolls"; to attract men and get ahead, women must put on makeup, or "doll" themselves up; and men treat women like "dolls," controlling them, pampering them for a while, then discarding them when they get old and worn out.

While her largely unsuccessful experiences as an actress undoubtedly made Susann thoroughly aware of this situation, she can offer no solutions to her characters' dilemmas. Women cannot band together to fight for justice, for show business forces them to be rivals: Older actresses must use their power to resist the encroachment of young actresses, and younger actresses must use their beauty to gain an advantage over older actresses. Helen insists on firing a young actress in her new musical who she fears might upstage her; Neely responds to Helen's insults by pulling off her wig and flushing it down the toilet. (Neely's—and Susann's—message is clear: in show business, once you've lost your youth and beauty, you're all washed up.) Women are thus driven into catfights, not camaraderie; and the men are either exploitative—like Anne's philandering husband—or pleasant but ineffectual—like Anne's former boss, a theatrical attorney.

In a manner that makes her own ineptitude as a writer a strange advantage, Susann cannot impose structure on her novel, as her characters simply confront one problem after another, and she cannot bring her book to either a conventionally satisfying happy ending or a conventionally instructive tragic ending. Instead, she limply concludes by envisioning future cycles: Anne will endure with patience and pills a series of her husband's affairs followed by reconciliations; Neely will fight her way back to the top, destroy her career again with irresponsible behavior and drug abuse, then start again from the bottom. Like her unhappy characters, Susann cannot control her own world, so that the novel she creates both describes and exemplifies the problems of women in show business.

Valley of the Dolls is more than an indictment of Hollywood, though the movie industry where Neely crashes does emerge as stressful and damaging; Anne hopes that "This phantom that Hollywood had created would eventually disappear and the real Neely would return" (307). It is more than an indictment of show business, though there are specific criticisms of its people and practices. It is finally an indictment of men, and of a society that allows men to mistreat and abuse women. Thus, the millions of women who thought they were reading a diverting entertainment about glamorous actresses may have absorbed and responded to an unexpected message. In future histories of feminism, women like Betty Friedan and

Gloria Steinem will be credited as the brains behind the modern movement; but scholars searching for evidence of the heart, the rage and passion, behind the drive for female equality might profitably look at Jacqueline Susann.

In some of its self-descriptions—studio publicity, ghostwritten autobiographies, and puff pieces in movie magazines—Hollywood presents itself as a warm, close-knit community of talented people dedicated to producing superior entertainment while devoting their spare time to their families, charities, and other worthwhile causes. To many, though, these portrayals are unconvincing and unsatisfying; they would prefer to believe that Hollywood is a sordid cesspool of sin and corruption. Therefore, in other self-descriptions—"hard-hitting" novels, "kiss-and-tell" memoirs, and the tabloid press—Hollywood cheerfully admits that it's all true. After all, Hollywood always gives the public what it wants.

With astonishing exuberance, Richard Sale's *The Oscar* (1963) sets out to fulfill this second assignment. Here, Hollywood life apparently involves little more than endless drinking, fornicating, and back-stabbing. Antihero Frank Fane is the least worthy Oscar candidate only because he is slightly more reprehensible than the other nominees: Alcorn, a hopeless alcoholic; Chichester, a closet homosexual; Prescott, a right-wing Neanderthal; and Bundee, a respected family man with a secret mistress. To emphasize this novel's accuracy, Sale employs an unusual device: factual footnotes providing tidbits of Hollywood lore and anecdotes about Sale's experiences as a screenwriter. *The Oscar* is thus an annotated exposé. Yet Sale breaks down the division of fiction and fact in a note describing a fictional conversation with the real Rock Hudson about the fictional Fane, wherein Hudson complains that telling Fane's story would misrepresent a community that also includes many fine, upstanding people. This disclaimer seems to undermine everything that Sale is asserting about Hollywood—yet that note was an insider's wicked joke, since Sale surely knew that Hudson, then publicly presented as a paragon of virtue, was actually a promiscuous homosexual who frequented Hollywood's sleaziest gay bars. For those in the know, mentioning Hudson spectacularly confirmed Sale's thesis.

The centerpiece of the indictment is Fane, first encountered after he has seduced Bundee's mistress for sheer vindictiveness, though he avoids a beating at Bundee's hands when the radio announces that both actors had just been nominated for the Oscar. He hypocritically publishes an advertisement announcing his apparent withdrawal from the race, then sponsors a luncheon where he tricks other nominees into declaring their intentions to vote for him. He tries to arrange for a young homosexual holding a check from Bundee to be arrested while sleeping with Chichester, in order to ruin the reputations of two nominees with one blow. And we are only halfway through *The Oscar*. Readers may feel like washing their hands after reading this novel.

Perversely, readers will also be rooting for Fane, hoping his Byzantine conspiracies and loathsome double-crosses will work, perhaps even accepting his argument that, as an outsider trying to claw his way into Hollywood's elite, he has the right to use every dirty trick in the book. Like Richard III, Fane is fascinating and alluring in his pure evil, and the novel is strongest when Sale straightforwardly depicts Fane as a demonic schemer. Consider his masterstroke: When detective Barney Fluger tries to blackmail Fane by threatening to reveal the pornographic playing cards Fane once posed for in the nude, Fane sweet-talks his secretary into giving him the cards, then anonymously sends them to several Hollywood figures so he can portray Barney as the paid tool of Bundee's wife. Thus, Fane contrives to ruin his own reputation in a manner that gives him an advantage in the Oscar race. Here is another man who might take Machiavelli to school.

However, to make Fane a symptom of a general malaise, not merely a cancer in the community, *The Oscar* seems driven in less successful directions—to psychoanalyze him, to rationalize and explain his behavior. Certainly, one can say Fane grew up in a loveless world and so was forced to love only himself; his narcissism, suggested by his compulsive habit of looking in the mirror, is underlined by one setpiece. Distraught because his plot to sully Chichester and Bundee seems about to backfire, Fane drinks himself into a stupor watching his old movies: "He put on another feature, and opened another bottle of bourbon, and staggered back to the lounging chair, waiting to be fascinated by his own image" (200). Despite numerous affairs with beautiful women, there are hints—his brief career as a gay model, his exhibitionist habit of walking around naked, the friendship he strikes up with Chichester, and the singular guilt he feels about betraying that actor—that repressed homoerotic desires may be warping his behavior. His senseless attempt to seduce a lady friend of his new wife, a good woman he seems attached to, and the resulting end of their marriage may be other signs of that, but they also suggest a self-loathing, self-destructive personality that drives Fane to dangerous and convoluted schemes that finally ensure he will lose the Oscar he so desperately covets. However, if you start to feel guilty about hating Fane, or start to feel sorry for Fane, you are falling into his trap, giving him an edge he will ruthlessly exploit. One of the fascinating things about *The Oscar* is that Fane seems to manipulate not only those around him, but his author as well; he is finally not as evil as we want him to be or, one suspects, as evil as Sale originally intended him to be.

There is much to criticize about the inept film version of *The Oscar* (1966), but screenwriter Harlan Ellison saw Fane for what he was, removed the unflattering portraits of his colleagues, and focused on one story: the rise and fall of Frank Fane, the ultimate Hollywood heel. Ellison thus sees Sale's efforts to offer broader criticisms of Hollywood as nothing more than Fane's self-serving smokescreen, the lame argument that inexcusable behavior may be excused if other people are doing it. However, while Sale presents Fane as an example, and Ellison presents him as an exception, both novel and film deny Fane his Oscar and suggest that, in the end, people like Fane will be recognized and punished. For whether its protagonists are saints or sinners, the drama of Hollywood is always a morality play.

10

In Defense of Stone Tablets:
Isaac Asimov Explains Why
Science Fiction Is Skeptical about
"New Information Technologies"

When I was asked to attend a conference on "New Information Technologies" and speak about science fiction, I knew immediately what any ambitious, upwardly-mobile, science fiction critic should plan to say: Wearing my mirrorshades, black leather jacket, and Nine Inch Nails t-shirt, I should have sauntered up to the podium and announced, "Hey, there, something's happening and you don't know what it is, do you, Mr. Lit-Crit Jones? Well, it's time for you to leave your stale old mainstream fiction behind and get connected to the with-it world of postmodern science fiction, where all the hip-to-high-tech writers can clue you in about what's happening now and what's going to happen tomorrow." Unfortunately, as these retro references have already suggested, I can't do the Larry McCaffery hipster routine very persuasively, and in any event, since my scruples are stronger than my ambitions, I could not bring myself to offer opinions that I believe to be false. So, I told the people attending the conference that I didn't think they had a lot to gain from looking at science fiction, though it may have been far from expedient to say that so bluntly.

First, regarding the development and use of new information technologies, I believe that science fiction is, generally and unsurprisingly, a conservative genre, one which will most likely be one of the very last fields to embrace and fully explore the potentials of any radically different new media. Second, regarding what science fiction texts have tended to predict about new information technologies, I believe that science fiction, based on its record in other areas, is most likely wrong in most of its predictions, and that science fiction therefore offers insight into the probable impacts of these new technologies only by means of comparisons between its faulty predictions and the actual outcomes in those other areas.

As other commentators have noted, science fiction has tended to avoid new and innovative approaches, which, in light of its historical interest in and fondness for scientific progress, might be seen as paradoxical. My friend Brooks Landon—Larry McCaffery in a business suit—has waxed eloquent about what he regards as this deplorable situation in his *Science Fiction after 1900*: the cyberpunk writers, he says,

have proved oddly wedded to older models of writing. In failing to imagine that the computers that so radically reshaped the cyberpunk semblance could also radically reformulate narrative structure itself, cyberpunk may eventually prove to be no more than a last gasp of print fiction as it slips under the steamroller of electronic culture. . . . cyberpunk writers have proved all too willing to continue to employ the tired furniture of linear narrative, leaving the exploration of hypertext narrative to writers who remember that writing is itself a technology and who take seriously the implications of computers for narrative itself. (165-66)

But this really isn't paradoxical or "odd" at all, if one recalls C. S. Lewis's famous dictum that "To tell how odd things struck odd people is to have an oddity too much," so that "Gulliver is a commonplace little man and Alice a commonplace little girl" ("On Science Fiction" 65). Similarly—and I am far from the first to argue this—since the characteristic subjects of science fiction include aliens, other worlds, future societies, new inventions, and many other strange things, it is necessary for these strange stories to be presented in a commonplace manner to avoid having a strangeness too much. The history of science fiction in the twentieth century suggests that there has always been a dogged conservatism in its style of presentation, an inclination to resist new techniques until they have long been accepted elsewhere. Thus, we find that science fiction readers of the 1960s were shocked and sometimes appalled when writers dared to try writing like James Joyce and John Dos Passos in the 1920s, and one reason that *Neuromancer* so stunned those readers in the 1980s was that William Gibson boldly and innovatively imported into science fiction the attitudes and style of the Raymond Chandler detective stories of the 1940s. These two examples seem to suggest that there is typically a forty-year gap between the introduction of a new approach to literature and its appearance in the form of science fiction; and, come to think of it, full-length feature films were around for about forty years before science fiction films became a common and recognized genre, and comic-strip narratives were around for about thirty-five years before Buck Rogers and Flash Gordon brought science fiction firmly into that milieu. So here is an answer to Brooks Landon's puzzlement: Today, why are there are no science fiction hypercard narratives or fractal fictions? Because they are not scheduled to appear until the year 2030.

Now, in arguing that the literature of science fiction tends to be conservative in its manner of presentation, I do not wish to imply that the *readers* of science fiction are necessarily conservative about "new information technologies." In fact, science fiction fans were among the first to take full advantage of the Internet, and one of the most penetrating critics of cyberspace, Clifford Stoll, is a long-time science fiction fan. Further, while it was not science fiction, one major writer in the genre, Geoff Ryman, did produce the innovative "novel for the Internet," *253* (published in print form in 1998), while other members of the science fiction community have enthusiastically taken to various sorts of science fiction role-playing games and computer games, which are arguably new, interactive forms of narrative.

Still, one must acknowledge that the prose narratives of science fiction undeniably remain, by and large, conventional in their approach; and there may be something else at work here that reflects more than a mere desire for some necessary continuity in one's otherwise innovative life. Based on the research of William Labov and others, I believe that the human psyche has within it an inborn pattern of story-telling that is just as instinctive as the inborn pattern of language itself: the introductory abstract, the background information, the rising action, the pondering of possible alternative developments, the resolution, and the final, reflective coda. In order to communicate one's story and ideas more clearly and effectively, a writer will tend to fall back on this ancient approach. What most distinguishes science fiction from other forms of contemporary literature, as I have suggested elsewhere ("The Words That Could Happen"), might be its overpowering urge to *communicate*. Even the most simplistic space opera of the *Star Trek* or *Star Wars* school may contain an embedded message about limitless human potentialities and our destiny to inhabit and conquer the universe—a message which, even if erroneous, remains appealing and strongly felt. More thoughtful writers wish to explore and convey their ideas about possible new scientific developments, their broader implications, and their possible impact on future human societies.

If one's strongest impulse is to communicate data, the natural choice is an old and familiar format—in the case of science fiction, what Brooks Landon would condescendingly call "the tired furniture of linear narrative." If writers try to be innovative, they may lose potential readers who wish to avoid innovations; and even the more adventurous readers willing to examine the innovative text may be at times confused or unable to follow all of its myriad threads, again hindering the author's ability to communicate. It's a simple principle: One does not invent a new language in order to yell "fire" when a building is burning down. Many science fiction writers believe, however fallaciously, that their messages are just as important, and just as urgent, and so they stick to tried-and-true approaches. To continue the argument, then, it is the other writers of the "postmodern" school, not believing quite so fervently in the importance of what they are saying, who are willing to play around a bit, experiment with new forms, even if they lose a few readers or fail to get some ideas across. This would further explain why science fiction writers tend to adopt new techniques only forty years after their development. They characteristically wait for a time when the once-novel approach has become familiar and unthreatening, and hence has become an effective and widely acceptable means of communication.

If science fiction, then, is unlikely to offer timely examples of new forms of narrative, perhaps its stories about the future can provide some guidance as to what new forms might appear, and how they will impact on society. But I doubt this as well. A while back, I pondered why it was that the predictions made in science fiction were so often wrong, and I created a list of typical "Fallacies" underlying those predictions. One of them I called "the Fallacy of Replacement": the assumption that, once a new and seemingly better way to do something is invented, everybody will abandon the old way and universally embrace the new way. Thus, in Hugo Gernsback's *Ralph 124C 41+*, after Ralph invents a way to record one's thoughts directly on paper, it "entirely superseded the pen and pencil" (48), and once his society invents "Tele-Theatres" to broadcast plays and operas into the home, people understandably stop bothering to go to theaters. But my favorite example of the fallacy is David H. Keller's story "The Revolt of the Pedestrians" (1928), describing a future world where motorized transportation is so ubiquitous that the legs of most people have atrophied, leaving only a downtrodden minority of "Pedestrians" still capable of walking who rail against their increasingly paved-over world.

In reality, of course, new devices and systems rarely *replace* the old ones. Instead, the new ways do become popular, but the old ways remain in use, as they are still best in certain situations. Consider land transportation. Virtually every way of getting from one point to another ever devised by human beings is still in use today. People still walk—even though, by purchasing a wheelchair, they could achieve Keller's utopian ideal of life on wheels. People still ride horses—indeed, police officers have discovered they are ideal for swift and flexible travel in urban environments. People still enjoy carriage rides and bicycles; people still use skateboards and roller skates—oops, excuse me for un-hipness; of course, I meant "roller blades." Consider forms of entertainment. Films did not replace plays and operas, television did not replace films, and other, seemingly archaic sorts of performances like puppet shows, ballets, concerts, and mime shows are still found today. Or, more relevant here, consider various ways to communicate. People still talk, either in person or by telephone, people still use pens and pencils to write letters and memos, people still use typewriters, and all of the new ways of communicating by means of computers, whether it is disks with word-processed texts or Internet chat groups, have not eliminated these earlier methods. Do people still communicate by chiseling on stone tablets? Sure they do—in graveyards and on public monuments; and it's hard to see why anyone would ever want to replace them with talking microchips.

There are some exceptions to this pattern of endurance, to be sure. Technologies have become entirely extinct, like silent movies (unless one wants to argue for music videos as a transformation thereof) or slide rules, for example. But there are, on reflection, amazingly few successful devices or systems once employed by humans that have entirely vanished.

Thus, when I examine science fiction predictions about new information technologies, I feel that they typically view them as becoming excessively dominant. For example, James Gunn's *The Joy Makers* (1961) concludes with a grim vision of every citizen permanently hooked up to devices perpetually stimulating the pleasure centers of their brains. Well. Despite the absence of advanced technologies, a few alcoholic drinks or a few puffs of marijuana can do a pretty good job of stimulating human pleasure centers, but vast numbers of people prefer to eschew those pleasures, and vast numbers of people would undoubtedly prefer to eschew those pleasures even if they did become available by means of electrodes in their brains. Will three-dimensional, interactive "virtual reality" narratives completely replace old-fashioned novels and movies? I don't think so. I have mild acrophobia, and when I started playing Super Mario 64 with its advanced, three-dimensional graphics, I surprisingly found myself a bit *disturbed* when my little cartoon Mario was walking across a thin board balanced precariously above a vast chasm. I found that I much preferred the older, less advanced games where the dangerous heights were not so realistically portrayed. And you tell me that, in the future, I will prefer to enter a virtual reality environment where I will be able to see, hear, and feel myself walking across that thin board, buffeted by heavy winds, looking down at the tiny trees far below me? No way! And there will be many others, I believe, who will find boring old novels and flat, two-dimensional movies just fine for them, thank you.

What a few perceptive science fiction stories suggest, perversely, is that new forms of technology may bring, as one of their effects, a new appreciation for, and heightened use of, old technologies. For enlightenment in this area, we must turn to the late Isaac Asimov, a brilliant and imaginative science fiction writer famed for his disinclination to fly and for a monotonous lifestyle centered on his home typewriter. It is not surprising, then, to see this writer frequently depicting the enduring appeal of yesterday's techniques in the worlds of tomorrow. In one satirical story modeled on James D. Watson's *The Double Helix*, "The Holmes-Ginsbook Device," two future scientists lamenting the limitations of microfilm struggle to invent a remarkably effective new way to store and retrieve information—a book. In "The Fun They Had," some future children wax nostalgic about the good old days when children went to school and learned from human teachers instead of teaching machines.

However, Asimov's subtlest story along these lines is surely "Someday," where two boys living in a future world of widespread computers excitedly discuss an amazing discovery: There actually exists an ancient way to communicate and do mathematics *using pencil and paper*, ideal for "*secret message stuff*" (186). In a splendid move, Asimov makes the central figure—almost the central *character*—in "Someday" a *story-telling machine*, whose endless variations on fairy tales are considered dull and old-fashioned by the boys, who ignore the machine while they focus on trying to master the mysteries of *handwriting*. Similarly, then, as we enter a future filled with virtual reality booths, hypercard novels, and other exotic new forms of narratives, we may unexpectedly find ourselves more and more fond of the ancient forms of communication that have endured for millennia.

Actually, this is already happening. My wife teaches a class at California State University, Fullerton entitled "Oral Interpretation of Children's Literature." It is basically a class about how to read to children, and how to tell stories to children. Now, if you are talking about "information technologies," you can hardly get more primitive than that. And yet, the class has been a popular class, and it seems to be growing more popular every year; there are always several sections offered each semester, and my wife always begins each semester with a packed house and a list of students hoping to fill the few precious openings that may arise. There has recently been, in fact, a general resurgence of interest in the simple art of oral storytelling, evidenced by scores of conferences, instructional books, videotapes, and television programs.

The new popularity of simple storytelling has another implication as well: In excited discussions about new technologies and their impact on narratives, the usual focus is the notion of "interactive texts" where readers participate in deciding what sort of story they will hear. Lush descriptions, or stripped-down prose? A story that is G-rated, or X-rated? Scenes of graphic violence highlighted or expunged? A happy ending or a sad ending? You, the audience, can decide. Yet I think it is false to believe that most readers and viewers really desire this sort of power. Simple games, of course, depend on interactiveness, but the joy of experiencing a genuine narrative lies in surrendering control to a masterful storyteller, whether the person is talking to you, writing to you, or constructing a film for you. Storytelling is a challenging and difficult art, and most people are lousy storytellers. Place the average person completely in charge of the story, and she is likely to put together a lousy story, one that she will regard not as perfectly tailor-made to her preferences, but as predictable and boring. (I mean, consider your own, private, sexual fantasies; they serve a purpose, no doubt, but would you really want versions of them as your daily leisure reading activity?) Thus, enhancements in the quality of communication will no doubt be welcome, but I suspect that the simple, linear, one-size-fits-all narrative will remain the norm, no matter how its telling is improved or enhanced.

Overall, then, while the future will undoubtedly bring hosts of new ways to tell and absorb stories, the new ways will take their place beside, and will not replace, the old ways. Though it is important to anticipate and embrace the new, we should never fall into the fallacy of believing that the old invariably goes away. All in all, the information technologies of the future, despite some cosmetic differences, may turn out to bear some striking resemblances to the information technologies of the past.

When I examined my original text one more time before printing it out, I suddenly felt surprised and dismayed by its message: Here I was, a science fiction critic who should be dedicated to and excited about the future, literally writing "In Defense of Stone Tablets"! Have I, and the genre I examine, really degenerated into a kind of reactionary old-fogeyism, so that other critics representing other genres must now champion the new?

Perhaps it is true; nevertheless, it is also possible that it is the world around science fiction, and not science fiction itself, that has changed—leading to this apparent lurch into irrational conservatism.

John W. Campbell, Jr., once argued that science fiction needed to "function as a frontier literature," exploring prospective developments not yet addressed or examined in other contemporary forums ("We *Must* Study Psi" 217). But I might recast that and argue that science fiction really needs to function as a *heterodox* literature, always focusing attention on the important facts and concerns that others would prefer to ignore. Now, in the 1940s and 1950s, when Campbell was reforming, solidifying, and promulgating the underlying ideology of science fiction, there were widespread efforts, in prose fiction and elsewhere, to promote belief in perpetual continuity in human affairs. As Campbell put it, "The essence of 'main stream literature' is that There Are Eternal Truths And Nothing Really Changes" ("Non-Escape Literature" 228). In contrast, science fiction argues that "change is the natural order of things, that there are goals ahead larger than those we know" ("Introduction," *The Astounding Science Fiction Anthology* xiii). And during the era of President Eisenhower, sock hops, and *The Adventures of Ozzie and Harriet*, this was a novel and important message.

But things are, after all, a little bit different now. Everyone has read Alvin Toffler, and everyone knows that constant and ever-accelerating change is the natural condition of modern technological society. Today, all citizens are constantly bombarded with news about the latest scientific and social innovations. Whereas people in the 1950s read *The Saturday Evening Post* with Norman Rockwell paintings proclaiming the homespun constancies of small-town American life, people in the 1980s read *Time* magazine announcing that "The Computer" was its Man of the Year. Let's face it: when a bunch of academic scholars have organized a conference about "New Information Technologies," it's painfully obvious that the word has gotten around—the times they are a'changin', and they're changin' fast.

Therefore, if science fiction is to remain the literature of heterodoxy, its message must shift. In a world that freely accepts and even embraces the idea of change, science fiction writers must remind people that everything is not going to change, that some of the things people do today are pretty much exactly what people did a century ago, and that many things that people do in the next century will be pretty much exactly what we are doing now. When school districts are literally letting all their textbooks fall to pieces while they scramble for funds to put computers in every classroom, the role of science fiction may be to remind people that books are still valuable and worthwhile objects, not quite replaceable by a television screen hooked up to silicon chips. By this logic, Isaac Asimov, far from being a hidebound conservative, represented the bold vanguard of a new, and necessary, argument in favor of maintaining some essential continuities in a world that is getting a little over-excited about change.

So, perhaps it was not really incongruous or disheartening for a science fiction critic to come to a conference on "New Information Technologies" and speak in favor of stone tablets—because, I might now argue, challenging orthodoxy is what science fiction is all about.

11

Partial Derivatives:
Popular Misinterpretations of
H. G. Wells's *The Time Machine*

The Time Machine is the story of a journey, both temporal and intellectual; and, since few of its readers have shared H. G. Wells's intelligence and vision, most of them unsurprisingly have never completed the journey. To be sure, they finished reading the novel, but mentally they stopped at an early stage, accepting an interpretation of the story that is later contradicted in the text; and the stopping points chosen by various readers, as evidenced in contemporary commentaries and adaptations, can be related to the circumstances of their distinctive eras. Further, while prediction is always uncertain, I can guess where the next generation of interpreters are most likely to stop reading the novel.

Since I am sometimes discomfited by the glib generalizations of social historians, I will begin by placing all of mine on the table. For purpose of argument, let us divide the history of North America and Western Europe since publication of *The Time Machine* into three, roughly equal periods. The time from 1895 to 1930 might be called the Era of Scientific Optimism: All sorts of new technological marvels—electrical devices, radio, automobiles, aircraft—had suddenly appeared, large numbers of amateur inventors following the example of Thomas Alva Edison were exploring the possibilities created by these innovations, and prospects for future improvements in all areas of life seemed unlimited. Then, the Great Depression of 1929, and collapse of the world economy, apparently eliminated all chances for quick and easy solutions, scientific or otherwise, to fundamental problems, so that people were forced to return to the attributes of their ancestors: hard work, violence directed at enemies, and constant vigilance against possible threats. Call the period from 1930 to 1965 the Era of Struggle; and having inculcated these qualities, people of that time endured the hardships of the Depression, overcame the armies of Germany and Japan, and maintained a nervous attentiveness towards the perceived Communist threat of the 1950s. Finally, in the mid-1960s, a genera-ion came of age who had never had to work hard or struggle, and who saw no reason to work hard or struggle; instead, they wished to devote themselves to peace, to the pursuit of various forms of happiness—sex, drugs, music, games— and to the rediscovery of nature. Call this period from 1965 to the present the Era of Complacency—though I will later argue that we may be witnessing the emergence of a fourth distinct era. Of course, such rough characterizations will not be universally accurate—some visionaries at any time will anticipate the attitude of a latter era, while some older people will retain the attitude of an earlier era—but charitable readers will probably grant the general soundness of this potted history.

Now, as it happens, if people stop reading *The Time Machine* at certain points, they can find an interpretation of the text that perfectly accords with the expectations of those three eras; and that is generally what occurred with the readers of those eras.

Consider, first, the consequences of reading only Chapter I of *The Time Machine*, "Introduction." There, the Time Traveller explains to his friends the general principle of time as the fourth dimension; discusses a series of photographs of a man and a graph of weather conditions as traces of movement through time; posits that, just as aircraft gave humans a new freedom to move up and down, another device might provide a similar ability to move backward and forward in time; and demonstrates the practicality of time travel by making his model machine vanish into another time period. At this point, the novel might seem to be primarily a discourse on the theory and practice of time travel, and one might interpret the novel as an exploration of the possibilities and problems raised by the creation of a working time machine.

This is how Hugo Gernsback (1884-1967), amateur inventor and enthusiastic advocate of the Era of Scientific Optimism, described *The Time Machine* when he reprinted the novel in the May, 1927 issue of his *Amazing Stories*. Here is the complete introductory blurb, which was written either by Gernsback or by his associate T. O'Conor Sloane:

How will this earth of ours appear 100 years from now, 1,000 years from now, 100,000 years from now? No one, of course, knows. Suppose it were possible to build a machine that could project us into the future, a machine which, with the present-day knowledge of Einstein's science, is not as impossible as it might have appeared even a generation ago. Time, as the term is understood today, is but a dimension. It should, therefore, be possible to either go backwards or forwards into this dimension, the same as can be accomplished in any other dimension. H. G. Wells has attempted such a machine in his present story, and while fantastic in the extreme it may not be as fantastic a hundred years from now as it appears at present. The Time Machine is one of the classics of scientifiction, and is certainly one of Wells' most famous works. (Blurb to *The Time Machine* 148)

Having previously defined science fiction as a narrative offering scientific education and stimulating scientific ideas—"a charming romance interwoven with scientific fact and prophetic vision" ("A New Sort of Magazine" 3)—Gernsback must struggle to fit *The Time Machine* into this Procrustean bed. First, the blurb

implies, Wells wrote this story as an entertaining diversion, a way to satisfy people's curiosity about the future: "How will this earth of ours appear 100 years from
now, 1,000 years from now, 100,000 years from now?" Second, Wells wanted to
provide scientific information about the nature of time: "Time, as the term is
understood today, is but a dimension. It should, therefore, be possible to either go
backwards or forwards into this dimension, the same as can be accomplished in any
other dimension." Finally, Wells sought to suggest or inspire the construction of a
machine that might travel through time: "Suppose it were possible to build a
machine that could project us into the future. . . . H. G. Wells has attempted such
a machine in his present story, and while fantastic in the extreme it may not be as
fantastic a hundred years from now as it appears at present." In this reading of the
novel, there is no hint that Wells is engaged in any social commentary on class
divisions in modern society, or building to a grand cosmic vision; only the comment that the novel is "one of the classics of scientifiction" suggests that it has
other literary values.

It might seem that this threadbare, reductive interpretation of the novel could
have little impact on Gernsback's readers, but there is evidence to the contrary. I
examined all letters published in *Amazing Stories* in the six months after the
appearance of *The Time Machine*, and while there were some general words of
praise or criticism directed at Wells, and a few brief compliments for *The Time
Machine*, the only three letters with substantive commentary on the novel—all in
the "Discussions" section of the July 1927 issue—focused on purely technical
issues. The briefest of these complained that "Wells has the objectionable method
of giving us the opinion that he could make it a better story if he wished to," calling
The Time Machine "as simple a story from a theme that is promising as possible."
The reader then described how he felt the story might have been improved: "Sup-
posing he had made the story in the time that the ruins were new? He doesn't even
describe the machine or how it functions" (414). In offering the first suggestion,
the reader apparently wished to have the more detailed scientific information that
would be necessary in depicting an advanced civilization at its peak, and the second
suggestion requires no comment: He wanted to know more about the time machine
itself. A second letter announced "a terrible flaw in the story": noting the scene
where the Time Traveller took "a headlong fall from his suddenly stopped machine," the reader logically concluded that "He could have taken a fall, but if he
did, he would be thrown far out in time and would have to wait for his machine to
catch up with him" (410). A third letter presented, in a rambling and ill-tempered
manner, several objections to the notion of time travel: that the occupant of the
time machine is not affected by the rapid changes all around him, that a person
could not go back and meet himself, that a backward traveler should logically grow
younger, that a time traveler could not go back to before his birth since that would
be "an effect going before a cause" (410), and that such a traveler might generate
a paradoxical situation by shooting his younger self. In all cases, no attention is
paid to the larger issues raised by the novel; instead, the only topics of interest are
the time machine and the logic of certain developments in Wells's story or, gener-

ally, in any scenario involving time travel.

Interestingly, these are precisely the concerns emphasized in the first sequel to the novel, *The Return of the Time Machine*, written during the 1930s by the German Egon Friedell (1878-1938), a man of Gernsback's generation. Readers of Wells who come to Friedell are invariably disappointed, since his novel says so little about humanity's future, offering only brief and uninvolving pictures of life in two eras of the near future. However, it is a novel with a radically different agenda. Whereas Wells's novel was really about the future, with the time machine introduced only as a mechanism to get the viewpoint character into the future, Friedell's novel is actually about the time machine, the theory of its operation, and the issues and problems it might generate.

After some tedious framing devices, Friedell has the Time Traveller (now identified as James Morton) attempt a journey into the past, only to find that nothing happens. He identifies the problem as "The resistance of Earth Time" (64) and comments to the effect that all objects on Earth have a residual momentum directed toward future movement, and that in order to reach the past, one must first travel into the future to build up necessary energy for a return trip (Friedell even introduces an equation to explain the phenomenon). So Morton jumps to the near future, where he observes a London of floating platforms and talks to a projected image; but while going back, he encounters some sort of resistance and decides to return into the future. There he meets two Egyptians, representing an ancient tradition, who introduce some new issues. First, they are disturbed by the very idea of a time machine, since it seems to contradict the idea of history; the disturbance, they suggest, may have been one of the Selenites, beings that not only are four-dimensional but also possess the natural ability to travel through time; and they claim that Morton must have misinterpreted the bleak future he visited, since the Eloi and Morlocks may have been part of an alternative future, not Morton's, or they may have represented only one stage in a process leading to a new and more glorious humanity. Finally traveling toward the past, Morton now has an adventure that oddly reflects two concerns of Gernsback's letter-writers: the machine stops abruptly, since it cannot exist in a time before it was built, and the quick stop catapults Morton further back in time, where he is apparently stranded until his natural aging process reunites him with the stalled time machine. In providing these detailed explanations and throwing out new ideas about time travel, *The Return of the Time Machine*, more than *The Time Machine* itself, seems close to the spirit of Gernsback's blurb and, indeed, seems exactly the kind of novel that Gernsback's letter-writing readers evidently craved.

As a footnote, it is interesting to find science fiction writer J. B. Priestley (1894-1984), only ten years younger than Gernsback, expressing in part this approach to *The Time Machine* in a 1964 introduction: First, as "a rather personal note about Wells and the Time problem," he says, "I am deeply, almost bitterly, sorry he lost interest in this subject soon after writing *The Time Machine*. . . . He had early, as the introductory chapter to *The Time Machine* plainly shows, a flair for this kind of thinking" (vi). He later notes a technical problem in the story:

"Strictly speaking, [Wells] should not have allowed his Traveller to venture outside the machine. It was only the machine that could move freely along the fourth dimension" (viii). While Priestley elsewhere acknowledges the larger issues in the novel, he still wishes to engage the text in the same manner as Gernsback and his readers.

After some preliminaries, Wells's Time Traveller advances to 802,701 A.D., and in Chapter V, significantly entitled "In the Golden Age," he is initially puzzled by the docility and stupidity of the Eloi and attempts to develop an explanation. Shortly thereafter, in Chapter VI, "The Sunset of Mankind," he announces his first major "interpretation upon the things I had seen . . . as it shaped itself to me that evening" (287):

Strength is the outcome of need: security sets a premium on feebleness. The work of ameliorating the conditions of life—the true civilizing process that makes life more and more serene—had gone steadily on to a climax. . . . I saw mankind housed in splendid shelters, gloriously clothed, and as yet I had found them engaged in no toil. There were no signs of struggle, neither social nor economical struggle. The shop, the advertisement, traffic, all that commerce which constitutes the body of our world, was gone. It was natural on that golden evening that I should jump at the idea of a social paradise. . . . No doubt the exquisite beauty of the buildings I saw was the outcome of the last surgings of the now purposeless energy of mankind before it settled down into perfect harmony with the conditions under which it lived—the flourish of that triumph which began the last great peace. This has ever been the fate of energy in security; it takes to art and to eroticism, and then come languor and decay. (287-289)

Of course, even while describing this vision of a "social paradise" complacently enjoying "perfect harmony," the Time Traveller calls it a "half truth" and a "wrong" theory (287, 289); but a person who stopped reading at this point might see the Eloi as representing the ultimate and desirable goal of humanity: to achieve a perfectly relaxed and contented existence, albeit an unchallenging or even decadent one.

This is the misinterpretation of *The Time Machine* announced on the cover and first page of the 1968 Bantam Books edition of the novel, which appeared at the height of the era of the "hippies," or, in my schema, the first prominent manifestation of the Era of Complacency. Implausibly, the edition casts *The Time Machine* as Wells's prediction of hippies and "Flower Power." The front cover calls the novel "the science-fiction masterpiece that heralded the coming of the flower children!" The back cover began by promising "Primitive Adventure in the Lush Land of the Flower People" and proceeded to describe the Time Traveller's discovery of the future: "Earth was ruled by a gentle race of slender creatures who dwelt communally in perfect happiness. Their tranquil days were spent at play or at love, and the greatest gift they could bestow was a garland of flowers." The first page claimed that Wells "describes a civilization of beautiful pacifists who spend their time in pursuit of pleasure and whose symbol of love and respect is the flower." The unsettling presence of the Morlocks is not entirely ignored—the back cover devotes one sentence to the "grotesque mutants . . . who worshipped only cruel strength and the taste of human flesh," and the psychedelic cover painting shows both the flower-strewing Eloi and the monstrous red Morlocks—but the overall thrust of this edition is clear: Wells was predicting the then-current era of the hippies, the age of peace, love, and happiness, and he was doing so in a manner that indicated his approval of the phenomenon. In 1976, with the hippie era a thing of the past, Bantam reissued the book with a different cover and blurb, but something of the spirit of the 1968 blurb remained in its language: "A primitive adventure in a lush land. . . . He found himself in another age of creatures who dwelt together in perfect happiness."

A similarly benign and celebratory view of the Eloi is conveyed by the dust jacket description of *The Time Machine* for a 1996 omnibus, *The H. G. Wells Reader*:

The Time Traveller discovers a harmonious world inhabited with gentle creatures. He explores their palatial buildings, tastes their delectable fruits, and experiences firsthand a utopian society where there is no social or economic stress. All goes smoothly, until he returns to find that his Time Machine is missing. Is he stranded on this strange planet forever?

Here, the Morlocks are not even mentioned, and the language is almost a paraphrase of the Time Traveller's first impression of the Eloi: "palatial buildings" for "splendid shelters," "utopian society" for "social paradise," and "no social or economic stress" for "no signs of struggle, neither social nor economical struggle."

That such endorsements of the Eloi lifestyle represent a characteristic interpretation of our present age is also suggested by one of the strangest versions of *The Time Machine* now available: the Great Illustrated Classics edition "adapted by Shirley Bogart," first published by Baronet Books in 1992. The very existence of this sort of book provides evidence that we now live in an Era of Complacency: Today's young readers are thought to be incapable of reading Wells's not especially challenging prose, and so must be provided with a simplified and homogenized version of the text to enjoy the story. Furthermore, the people who prepared this edition were obviously not energetic in their research, since the introductory "About the Author" passage refers to the author as "Henry George Wells" (4). For its first twelve chapters, Bogart's text follows Wells's story with reasonable fidelity, although in a painfully crude and simplistic manner. Here, for example, is Bogart's version of the Time Traveller's first theory excerpted above:

While I was in this curious mood, one question led to another. "How did the people on my planet get so soft and empty-headed?"

I could only guess at the answer. "I'll bet that not having to work has ruined humanity. Man needs to struggle, to face hardships in order to be strong, energetic, and intelligent."

Then how did I explain these little people? "With no wars, animals, or diseases to fight, the weak people survived better than the strong, because they weren't as restless, and they lived a life of contented idleness." (90, 92)

The description of the Eloi seems a bit harsh, but this is explained by the ineptitude of adapter Bogart, who cannot maintain the careful separation between stages of understanding in Wells's text and thus prematurely drifts into the more critical attitude later shown by the Time Traveller.

However, in addition to Bogart's butchering of Wells's prose, something extraordinary happens in Chapter 13, "The Golden Age of Science." Returning from his chilling vision of a dying Earth, the Time Traveler (as it is spelled here) thinks about "how sadly lacking in accomplishments my trip had been. What wondrous healing salve, what formula for peace, what marvelous new hope for my race was I bringing back to share?" (203). He decides, then, "to make one more stop. . . . Three hundred years from home, I figured, I would reach the Golden Age of Science. Like Prometheus, the Greek god who brought men fire, I'd return with some dramatic new way to help my fellow man" (203-204). There follows an entirely new adventure not found in Wells's text. Stopping at that time, the Time Traveler finds himself in a laboratory where he is overcome by "Apathy-Gas" (206) and taken prisoner. The Time Traveler is then told that because of increasingly awful conditions in the twenty-first century, "four scientists" who formed "the *World Science Governing Board*" were granted control of the entire world, and their intelligent guidance soon brought "A glorious interval. . . . War outlawed. Disease cured. Life extended. Harmony and good fellowship everywhere" (218, 220). But this "Golden Age of Science" lasted only "One generation," because "the children of the founding four wanted to take control, instead of holding a universal election" (220). The result was two warring factions, one based at the North Pole and one at the South Pole (a curious echo of *The Return of the Time Machine*, where at roughly the same time the war that destroyed London "started with a discussion about the two Poles" [91]), and at this point the explanation is appropriately interrupted by an enemy attack. "In the confusion," one man attempts to seize the time machine, announcing "I'm going back in time. With all my knowledge, I'll dazzle the old world. They'll *worship* me!" (224). However, the Time Traveler manages to overcome him and return to his own time—and to Wells's story.

It is hard to explain why this inane adventure, unrelated to any other events in the novel, was so crudely tacked on to Wells's narrative. I would guess that the editors of the series insisted upon a certain uniform length for all texts, and when Bogart's version came out a bit short, she decided, or was told, to add another chapter. But everything in this episode constitutes a criticism of human ambition. First, the disastrous encounter results from the Time Traveler's own ambition to be like Prometheus—not exactly a positive role model—and to gain glory by bestowing some blessing on his own time. Significantly, he comes to regret his decision to stop: "I should have gone straight home in Time" (212). Second, the idyllic future world briefly achieved is destroyed by the personal ambition of the scientists' children. Finally, the time machine is almost taken away by a man with the ambition to become a godlike figure in a past world.

In all cases here, then, everything would have been better if the persons involved had been more complacent, more content with their lot in life; and this message is perfectly conveyed in this edition's emasculated version of the novel's last paragraph. In Wells's text, of course, the narrator first announces the necessity for continuing human activity despite knowledge of a grim future: He "saw in the growing pile of civilization only a foolish heaping that must invariably fall back upon and destroy its makers in the end. If that is so, it remains for us to live as though it were not so." Then there is a final moment of sentimentality: the flowers "witness that even when mind and strength had gone, gratitude and a mutual tenderness still lived on in the heart of man" (335). In Bogart's final paragraph, only the sentimentality survives: "And now, whenever Filby worries about what the future holds for mankind, he finds some comfort in two strange, white flowers that he has kept all these years, although they're brown and flat and brittle by now. For they remind him that even in wretched times, concern, gratitude, love and devotion to others can still live on in the heart of man!" (238). There is no mention of any need for ongoing struggle, only the "comfort" of knowing that whatever else happens, "love"—a popular term in the 1960s not offered by Wells—can still survive. This is an interpretation of *The Time Machine* that only a hippie would provide.

Uncoincidentally, a similar trivialization of Wells's final message occurs in Marvel Comics's 1976 adaptation of *The Time Machine*, where the Time Traveller says, "I'll go into the future again. I'll find Weena who proved that even though mankind was becoming extinct there was room for love in the heart of man" (cited in Haining 36). Again, the only important quality suggested by Weena's example is the un-Wellsian "love."

As we return—happily—to Wells's text, the Time Traveller's initial explanation of the Eloi is soon shattered by his growing knowledge of the second, underground race, the Morlocks. In Chapter VIII, "Explanation," he develops the notion that the growing separation of the elite aristocratic class and the lower working class eventually led to their evolution into two species, the Eloi and the Morlocks, and he begins to see the visible decline of the Eloi in less positive terms: "The too-perfect security of the Overworlders had led them to a slow movement of degeneration, to a general dwindling in size, strength, and intelligence" (302). Soon, he further realizes that the Morlocks actually dominate and feed upon the Eloi, revealing their plight to be even worse:

I pitied this last feeble rill from the great flood of humanity. . . . These Eloi were merely fatted cattle, which the ant-like Morlocks preserved and preyed upon—probably saw to the breeding of. . . . Then I tried to preserve myself from the horror that was coming upon me, by regarding it as a rigorous punishment of human selfishness. Man had been content to live in ease and delight upon the labours of his fellow-man, had taken Necessity as his watchword and excuse, and in the fulness of time Necessity had come home to him. I even tried a Carlyle-like scorn of this wretched aristocracy-in-decay. But this attitude of mind was impossible. However great their intellectual degradation, the Eloi had kept too much of the human form not to claim my sympathy, and to make me perforce a sharer in their degradation and their Fear. (311)

Now, to a reader who is not fully attentive to Wells's criticisms of the aristocracy, the story might seem a cautionary tale, no longer celebrating complacency but rather warning against it: The Eloi or their ancestors had relaxed, felt secure, grown lazy and decadent, so a formerly subordinate group of people had been able to rise up and become their masters and oppressors.

This sort of message was often heard in America during the Era of Struggle, though it was most manifest in the 1950s, when American and European citizens who had triumphed over the Depression and the Axis powers were repeatedly urged to remain on guard against the new and subtler menace of Communist infiltrators. Thus, there is a distinct element of fear and paranoia in the blurb to *The Time Machine* in the August, 1950 issue of *Famous Fantastic Mysteries*: "Defenseless, alone, he blazed his nightmare trail into tomorrow, the grim Traveler who dared to gamble the world—to live again a million years too late" (10). In the Era of Struggle, the Time Traveller is "grim," "Defenseless," and "alone" in the face of tomorrow's "nightmare"—providing a striking contrast to the more comforting blurbs of 1968 and 1996 in the Era of Complacency.

Since science fiction films of the 1950s were often overt allegories about the need to detect and resist hidden menaces like communism, the most famous misinterpretation of *The Time Machine*, the 1960 film produced and directed by George Pal, unsurprisingly takes this approach to Wells's story, depicting the Eloi as people who grew too soft and passive and thus allowed themselves to become the slaves of evil masters who literally came from the underground. A poster for the film, presented in Ronald V. Borst's *Graven Images* (220), perfectly evokes the paranoia of the 1950s by depicting Rod Taylor (the Time Traveller) and Yvette Mimieux (Weena) running on the surface while monstrous Morlocks watch from below the surface. The grafting of an anti-communist subtext onto the story is also suggested by the *New York Times* review describing the Eloi as "beautiful but thoroughly brainwashed boobs" (19), brainwashing being of course the Communist tactic most feared at the time.

Looking at David Duncan's original script for *The Time Machine*, dated April 16, 1959, one sees how Wells's story has been homogenized and distorted to present a simple message about the need for activity and ambition. First, he removes the issue of class division: According to the records Taylor discovers, the Eloi and Morlocks emerged only because some survivors of "the war between the East and West" decided "to take refuge in the great caverns and find a new way of life far down below the earth's surface," while others chose to "take [their] chances in the sunlight, small as those chances may be" (78); only "by some quirk of fate" did the Morlocks "become the masters and the Eloi their servants." Since, then, there is no particular reason why the Eloi developed into submissive victims, the only problem for Taylor is to re-educate and re-motivate these people.

When he first observes the Eloi's passivity, he sees this as irresponsibility:

"What have you done? Thousands of years of building and rebuilding creating and re-creating so that you can let it crumble to dust. A million yesterdays of sensitive men dying for their dreams. *For what?* So you can swim and dance and play" (65). He regards the Eloi as "The human race reduced to living vegetables!" (71) and announces he must return to his own time "so that I can die among *men!*" (65). Then, when he realizes that the Eloi are being preyed upon by the Morlocks, he likens them to "fatted cattle" and "sheep" (85, 86). Finally, after some of the Eloi follow his example and actively resist the Morlocks, Taylor concludes, "From now on they would have to work to survive. And looking at their faces, I somehow knew that they could start all over again" (105). Darko Suvin, in *Metamorphoses of Science Fiction*, sees Wells's *The Time Machine* as an elaborate fable of devolution (222-42); Duncan instead makes it a fable of *re-evolution*, as the Eloi advance, under Taylor's tutelage, from being "vegetables" to "cattle" to real "men" (as proven by their new propensity to violence).

Since the Eloi's rise to manhood is symbolized by their fighting, *The Time Machine* becomes a movie at war with itself, since it also includes an extended prelude, clearly borrowed from Wells's 1936 film *Things to Come*, depicting the evil of war, as the Time Traveller successively witnesses the horrors of World War I, World War II, and a nuclear war in 1970. Yet, after expressing his disgust with the stupidity of these repeated conflicts, Taylor enters the world of the Eloi and promptly teaches them how to wage war. The celebratory scene showing how the Eloi have learned to battle against the Morlocks is therefore both alien to Wells's philosophy and deeply incongruous in the context of the film.

The same divided message emerged even more clearly in Pal's planned sequel to the movie, *The Time Machine II*, which was never filmed because Pal could not obtain the necessary financial backing but eventually surfaced in the form of a novel, published in 1981 as by Pal and Joe Morhaim. Despite its development in the 1970s, creator Pal, born in 1908, failed like many of his generation to adapt to contemporary moods and continued to project the attitude of the 1950s. Again, there is an antiwar introduction: The Time Traveller and a pregnant Weena, returning to the past so their child can be born there, are interrupted by the London Blitz of 1941 and killed while their son is born. Thirty years later, the son, named Chris Jones, discovers his heritage, duplicates his father's work, and travels in his own time machine to meet his parents, though they refuse to believe that he is their son. He then travels further into the future and encounters, like Wells's Time Traveller, a desolate landscape with something like a giant butterfly and a giant crab. But Pal adds hordes of other giant insects—notably giant bees and giant ants—as well as a small band of humans barely surviving the attacks of those insects. "They are masters now" (110), the discouraged leader tells him; but Chris encourages them to fight back and fortuitously locates an ancient arsenal of functioning superweapons—heat guns, freezing guns, and paralyzing guns, perhaps the products of his father's rebuilding efforts—and trains the humans to use them against the giant insects. Again, after an opening scene illustrating the devastation of war, the unfolding story proclaims the dangers of apathy and the corresponding need for violent resistance.

Now, if these misinterpretations of *The Time Machine* seem derived from a partial reading of the novel, one rejoinder might be to follow Wells's story through to its powerful conclusion, the extraordinary final paragraph somehow combining nihilism, renewed commitment to action, and respect for simple human emotions. Perhaps, however, most contemporary readers are not quite ready for that complete journey, and they may prefer to stop at another point well before the end of the novel: the Time Traveller's own final conclusions, suggesting another misinterpretation that might be increasingly attractive to readers of the 1990s.

After achieving the interpretation above, the Time Traveller journeys to the Palace of Green Porcelain, where the items in the museum may have served to place matters in perspective, and in Chapter XII, "In the Darkness," he experiences a horrible night of fighting with the Morlocks and escaping a forest fire. There, for the first time, he seems to recognize the underlying humanity of the Morlocks; observing them trapped by the fires, "I was assured of their absolute helplessness and misery in the glare, and I struck no more of them" (320-21). Further, he has already deduced that the Morlocks, unlike the Eloi, have retained some intelligence and knowledge of machinery; in most respects, then, they, and not the Eloi, are the Time Traveller's true descendants. All of this leads to the more balanced interpretation of affairs he offers in Chapter XIII:

So, as I see it, the upper-world man had drifted towards his feeble prettiness, and the under-world to mere mechanical industry. But that perfect state had lacked one thing even for mechanical perfection—absolute permanency. Apparently as time went on, the feeding of the under-world, however it was effected, had become disjointed. Mother Necessity, who had been staved off for a few thousand years, came back again, and she began below. The under-world being in contact with machinery, which, however perfect, still needs some little thought outside habit, had probably retained perforce rather more initiative, if less of every other human character, than the upper. And when other meat failed them, they turned to what old habit had hitherto forbidden. So I say I saw it in my last view of the world of Eight Hundred and Two Thousand Seven Hundred and One. It may be as wrong an explanation as mortal wit could invent. It is how the thing shaped itself to me, and as that I give it to you. (323)

Describing the Time Traveller's changing opinion of the future world, Frank McConnell maintains in *The Science Fiction of H. G. Wells* that "The central narrative device of *The Time Machine*, then, is a first-person narrator entertaining a number of alternative explanations for the phenomena he witnesses, coming to the true conclusion about the reality of things only at the end of his tale. This structure . . . provides the novel with a reasonable facsimile of what was being increasingly celebrated as 'scientific method'" (84). Yet the most significant feature of the final interpretation is the Time Traveller's *announced lack of confidence in it*—"It may be as wrong an explanation as mortal wit could invent." He is *not* persuaded that his conclusion is in fact "true"; and his tentative judgment, far from affirming "scientific method," actually signals a new and profound distrust in such processes of interpretation and simultaneously marks a radical change in his behavior.

Prior to this moment, the Time Traveller had indeed been an active "scientific" investigator of the future, trying to talk to the Eloi, travelling through the country and into the Morlocks' underground realm, and exploring the Palace of Green Porcelain. After this moment, the Time Traveller's sole desire is to find his time machine and leave this world, which he quickly does. In visits to other future worlds, he functions not as an investigator but as an observer. True, in the suppressed episode, he does attempt a brief investigation of the kangaroo-like creature to see if it is a human descendant, but the foray is inconclusive, and Wells may have removed this episode precisely because the Time Traveller was violating his newly established character. In all other cases, the Time Traveller makes no effort to probe into or investigate what he sees, but only reports on what he sees. We are surprised to realize that, on the basis of the text, we cannot eliminate some of the fanciful scenarios suggested in the discussed sequels. Perhaps the Eloi and Morlocks did recombine to create a new human race; perhaps humans did survive into the age of the giant crabs—the Time Traveller did not investigate such possibilities. It is as if, having found that all his investigative labors in 802,701 A.D. could only yield a provisional conclusion, the Time Traveller has become deeply suspicious of the efficacy of investigation itself; thus, he is thereafter content to simply observe, and to leave the business of reaching conclusions to others.

Today, while the Western world has not shaken the effects of its Era of Complacency—witness, for example, the continuing popularity of James Bond and the Beatles—literary critics have observed a new attitude in the last two decades, a set of literary and cultural symptoms collectively labelled postmodernism that, if not yet a majority view, may soon become a dominant cultural force. Among other things, postmodernism reflects a deep distrust of all authorities, of all established categories and conventions, and of the very process of conventional interpretation, preferring instead a fascination with surface features. For these reasons, it would seem appropriate for critics in what might emerge as an Era of Doubt to misinterpret *The Time Machine* as a story about epistemology, or rather a story about the failure of epistemology, and to see the Time Traveller as gradually transforming himself into an exponent of postmodernism, finally unsure of his own beliefs and unwilling to trust in any interpretations of what he observes.

Although it may seem reductive to cast *The Time Machine*, with its grand visions of humanity's future, as only an argument about epistemology, such reductiveness is not uncommon in modern science fiction criticism. For example, Carl D. Malmgren's *Worlds Apart: Narratology of Science Fiction* (1991) concludes by making exactly this argument about all science fiction: "SF thus by definition deals with the problems, possibilities, and limits of knowledge; it is the epistemological genre *par excellence*. . . . reading SF entails using, analyzing, critiquing, or subverting scientific paradigms of knowledge and their application to human life" (172).

Have I offered, then, the definitive interpretation of *The Time Machine*? Of course not; it may be as wrong an explanation as mortal wit could invent. Indeed, since the Time Traveller himself is unsure of his interpretation, only presumptuous critics would ever proclaim the certainty of their own viewpoints. But since there is poetic justice in seeing the novel as a fable of failed epistemology—for we then cease to interpret *The Time Machine* at the same moment as the Time Traveller does—it is the stopping point that I will choose, leaving to future eras the task of journeying further through Wells's novel and finding new ways to misinterpret it.

Bibliography

"Arena." *Star Trek*. New York: NBC-TV, January 19, 1967.

Asimov, Isaac. *Earth Is Room Enough*. 1957. New York: Fawcett Crest Books, 1970.

—————. "The Fun They Had." In *Earth Is Room Enough*, by Isaac Asimov, 157-60.

—————. "The Holmes-Ginsbook Device." In *Opus 100*, by Isaac Asimov. 1969. New York: Dell Books, 1970, 270-80.

—————. "Someday." In *Earth Is Room Enough*, by Isaac Asimov, 179-88.

"Balance of Terror." *Star Trek*. New York: NBC-TV, December 15, 1966.

"The Best of Both Worlds." *Star Trek: The Next Generation*. Los Angeles: Syndicated, June 19, 1990 and September 24, 1990.

"Beyond Cyberpunk: Science, Science Fiction, and Information Technology in the 1990s." Panel at the 16th Annual Western Humanities Conference, Riverside, October 1997. Panelists were David Brin, George Slusser, Joshua Stein, and Gary Westfahl.

Billman, Carol. *The Secret of the Stratemeyer Syndicate: Nancy Drew, The Hardy Boys, and the Million Dollar Fiction Factory*. New York: Ungar Publishing Company, 1986.

Blurb to *The Time Machine*, by H. G. Wells [author unidentified, undoubtedly either Hugo Gernsback or T. O'Conor Sloane]. *Amazing Stories* 2 (May 1927): 148.

Blurb to *The Time Machine*, by H. G. Wells [author unidentified]. *Famous Fantastic Mysteries* 11 (August 1950): 10.

Bogart, Shirley, adapter. *The Time Machine*, by H. G. Wells. Great Illustrated Classics. New York: Baronet Books, 1992.

Borst, Ronald V., Keith Burns, and Leith Adams, editors. *Graven Images: The Best of Horror, Fantasy, and Science-Fiction Film Art from the Collection of Ronald V. Borst*. New York: Grove Press, 1992.

Campbell, John W., Jr. *Collected Editorials from Analog*, selected by Harry Harrison. Garden City: Doubleday and Co., 1966.

—————. "Introduction." In *The Astounding Science Fiction Anthology*, edited by John W. Campbell, Jr. New York: Simon & Schuster, 1952, ix-xv.

—————. "Introduction." In *Who Goes There?* Chicago: Shasta Press, 1948, 3-6.

—————. "Non-Escape Literature." In *Collected Editorials from Analog*, by John W. Campbell, Jr., 227-31. Editorial originally published in 1959.

——————. "The Old Navy Game." *Astounding Science-Fiction* 25 (June 1940): 6.
——————. "We *Must* Study Psi." In *Collected Editorials from Analog*, by John W. Campbell, Jr., 217-26. Editorial originally published in 1959.
"The City at the Gate of Forever." *Star Trek*. New York: NBC-TV, April 6, 1967.
Clute, John. "Fabulation." In *The Encyclopedia of Science Fiction*, edited by John Clute and Peter Nicholls. New York: St. Martin's Press, 1993, 399-400.
Crothers, Bosley. Review of *The Time Machine* [film]. *New York Times*, August 18, 1960, 19.
"Day of the Dove." *Star Trek*. New York: NBC-TV, November 1, 1968.
DeRogatis, Jim. "(A) Bum's Note(s)." *Impression* [internet magazine], March 8, 1999.
"The Devil in the Dark." *Star Trek*. New York: NBC-TV, March 9, 1967.
"Discussions" [readers' letters and responses]. *Amazing Stories* 2 (July 1927): 410, 414.
Dixon, Franklin W. [Leslie McFarlane, writing from an outline by Edward Stratemeyer]. *The Great Airport Mystery*. The Hardy Boys #9. New York: Grosset and Dunlap, Publishers, 1930.
——————. *The House on the Cliff*. The Hardy Boys #2. New York: Grosset and Dunlap, Publishers, 1927.
——————. *Hunting for Hidden Gold*. The Hardy Boys #5. New York: Grosset and Dunlap, Publishers, 1928.
——————. *The Missing Chums*. The Hardy Boys #4. New York: Grosset and Dunlap, Publishers, 1928.
——————. *The Mystery of Cabin Island*. The Hardy Boys #8. New York: Grosset and Dunlap, Publishers, 1929.
——————. *The Secret of the Caves*. The Hardy Boys #7. New York: Grosset and Dunlap, Publishers, 1929.
——————. *The Secret of the Old Mill*. The Hardy Boys #3. New York: Grosset and Dunlap, Publishers, 1927.
——————. *The Shore Road Mystery*. The Hardy Boys #6. New York: Grosset and Dunlap, Publishers, 1928.
——————. *The Tower Treasure*. The Hardy Boys #1. New York: Grosset and Dunlap, Publishers, 1927.
Dixon, Franklin W. [true author or authors unknown]. *Night of the Werewolf*. The Hardy Boys #59. New York: Wanderer Books, 1979.
"The Doomsday Machine." *Star Trek*. New York: NBC-TV, October 20, 1967.
Duncan, David. *The Time Machine* [film script]. April 16, 1959. Eaton Collection of Science Fiction and Fantasy Literature, Rivera Library, University of California at Riverside.
Durgnat, Raymond. *Films and Feelings*. Cambridge: M.I.T. Press, 1967.
"Errand of Mercy." *Star Trek*. New York: NBC-TV, March 23, 1967.
"Even Better than the Real Thing" [U2 music video]. Island Records, 1992.
Farber, Jim. "VH1 Blends Music with History." *New York Daily News*, July 29, 1998 [downloaded from web site].
Feiffer, Jules. "Introduction." In *The Great Comic Book Heroes*, compiled, introduced, and annotated by Feiffer. New York: Bonanza Books, 1975, 11-53.
Franklin, H. Bruce. *Future Perfect: American Science Fiction of the Nineteenth Century*. Revised edition. New York: Oxford University Press, 1978.
——————. "*Star Trek* in the Vietnam Era." *Science-Fiction Studies* 21 (March 1994): 24-34.
Friedell, Egon. *The Return of the Time Machine*, translated by Eddy C. Bertin. New York:

DAW Books, 1972. Originally published in Germany in 1946.

Gernsback, Hugo. "A New Sort of Magazine." *Amazing Stories* 1 (April 1926): 3.

——————. *Ralph 124C 41+: A Romance of the Year 2660*. 1925. Second Edition. New York: Frederick Fell, 1950.

——————. "Science Fiction Week." *Science Wonder Stories* 1 (May 1930): 1061.

Gunn, James. *The Joy Makers*. New York: Bantam Books, 1961.

Haining, Peter, editor. *The H. G. Wells Scrapbook*. London: Clarkson N. Potter, 1978.

Hendershot, Cyndy. "The Atomic Scientist, Science Fiction Films, and Paranoia: *The Day the Earth Stood Still*, *This Island Earth*, and *Killers from Space*." *Journal of American Culture* 20:1 (Spring 1997): 31-41.

Hill, Helen, and Violet Maxwell, authors and illustrators. *Charlie and His Coast Guards*. New York: The Macmillan Company, 1925.

——————. *Charlie and His Friends*. New York: The Macmillan Company, 1927.

——————. *Charlie and His Kitten Topsy*. New York: The Macmillan Company, 1922.

——————. *Charlie and His Puppy Bingo*. New York: The Macmillan Company, 1923.

——————. *Charlie and His Surprise House*. New York: The Macmillan Company, 1926.

Hollinger, Veronica. "Cybernetic Deconstructions: Cyberpunk and Postmodernism." In *Storming the Reality Studio*, edited by Larry McCaffery, 203-18.

James, Mertice M., and Marion A. Knight, editors. *Book Review Digest: 1926*. New York: H. W. Wilson Company, 1927.

——————, editors. *Book Review Digest: 1927*. New York: H. W. Wilson Company, 1928.

Jameson, Fredric. *Postmodernism, or, The Cultural Logic of Late Capitalism*. Durham: Duke University Press, 1990.

Jones, Raymond F. *This Island Earth*. Chicago: Shasta Publishers, 1952. Chapters 1-4 previously published as "The Alien Machine," *Thrilling Wonder Stories* 34:2 (June 1949): 74-88; Chapters 5-8 previously published as "The Shroud of Secrecy," *Thrilling Wonder Stories* 35:2 (December 1949): 64-79; Chapters 9-14 previously published as "The Greater Conflict," *Thrilling Wonder Stories* 35:3 (February 1950): 92-113. Text of entire novel also available in *Reel Future*, edited by Forrest J. Ackerman and Jean Stine. New York: Barnes & Noble, 1994, 180-299.

Kaminsky, Stuart. *Murder on the Yellow Brick Road*. New York: St. Martin's Press, 1977.

Keller, David H. "The Revolt of the Pedestrians." *Amazing Stories* 2 (February 1928): 1048-59.

Kern, Gary. "The Triumph of Teen Prop: *Terminator II* and the End of History." In *Nursery Realms*, edited by Gary Westfahl and George Slusser, 48-69.

Kismaric, Carole, and Marvin Heiferman. *The Mysterious Case of Nancy Drew and the Hardy Boys*. New York: Simon & Schuster, 1998.

Kornbluth, C. M. *Not This August* [also published as *Christmas Eve*]. Garden City: Doubleday and Co., 1955.

Kroker, Arthur, and David Cook. "Television and the Triumph of Culture." In *Storming the Reality Studio*, edited by Larry McCaffery, 229-38.

Landon, Brooks. "Bet on It: Cyber/video/punk/performance." In *Storming the Reality Studio*, edited by Larry McCaffery, 239-44.

——————. *Science Fiction after 1900: From the Steam Man to the Stars*. New York: Twayne Publishers, 1997.

"Let This Be Your Last Battlefield." *Star Trek*. New York: NBC-TV, January 10, 1969.

Lewis, C. S. "On Science Fiction." In *Of Other Worlds: Essays and Stories*, by C. S.

Lewis, edited with a preface by Walter Hooper. 1966. New York: Harcourt, Brace, and World, 1967, 56-73.

Lundquist, Lynne, and Gary Westfahl. "Coming of Age in Fantasyland: The Self-Parenting Child in Walt Disney Animated Films." In *Nursery Realms*, edited by Gary Westfahl and George Slusser, 161-70.

McCaffery, Larry. "Introduction: The Desert of the Real." In *Storming the Reality Studio*, edited by Larry McCaffery, 1-16.

McCaffery, Larry, editor. *Storming the Reality Studio: A Casebook of Cyberpunk and Postmodern Fiction*. Durham: Duke University Press, 1991.

McConnell, Frank. *The Science Fiction of H. G. Wells*. New York: Oxford University Press, 1981.

McFarlane, Leslie. *Ghost of the Hardy Boys: An Autobiography*. New York: Methuen/Two Continents, 1976.

Malmgren, Carl D. *Worlds Apart: Narratology of Science Fiction*. Bloomington: Indiana University Press, 1991.

"A Matter of Honor." *Star Trek: The Next Generation*. Los Angeles: Syndicated, February 4, 1989.

Miller, P. Schuyler. "The Reference Library." *Astounding Science Fiction* 52 (October, 1953): 142-51.

Milward, John. "How to Really Clean Up by Airing Dirty Laundry." *The Los Angeles Times*, Sunday Calendar Section, June 27, 1999 [downloaded from web site].

"Money for Nothing" [Dire Straits music video]. Capital Records, 1985.

Murphy, Cullen. "Starting Over." *The Atlantic Monthly* 267 (June 1991): 18-22.

O'Brien, Darcy. *A Way of Life, Like Any Other*. New York: W. W. Norton & Company, 1977.

"The Omega Glory." *Star Trek*. New York: NBC-TV, March 1, 1968.

Packard, Edward. *The Cave of Time*. Choose Your Own Adventure #1. New York: Bantam Books, 1979.

—————. *The Mystery of Chimney Rock*. Choose Your Own Adventure #5. New York: Bantam Books, 1980.

Pal, George, and Joe Morhaim. *The Time Machine II*. New York: Dell Books, 1981.

"Patterns of Force." *Star Trek*. New York: NBC-TV, February 16, 1968.

Pohl, Frederik. *The Way the Future Was: A Memoir*. 1978. New York: Ballantine Books, 1979.

Prager, Arthur. *Rascals at Large, or, The Clue in the Old Nostalgia*. Garden City: Doubleday and Co., 1971.

Priestley, J. B. "Introduction." In *The Time Machine*, by H. G. Wells. New York: Limited Editions Club, 1964, v-ix.

"A Private Little War." *Star Trek*. New York: NBC-TV, February 2, 1968.

Rabkin, Eric S. "Infant Joys: The Pleasures of Disempowerment in Fantasy and Science Fiction." In *Nursery Realms*, edited by Gary Westfahl and George Slusser, 3-19.

Riley, Philip J., editor. *This Island Earth*. Absecon: MagicImage Filmbooks, 1990.

Sale, Richard. *The Oscar*. New York: Simon and Schuster, 1963.

"Shadow of the Gun." *Star Trek*. New York: NBC-TV, October 25, 1968.

Skotak, Robert. "Production Background." In *This Island Earth*, edited by Philip J. Riley, 17-38.

Slusser, George. "Literary MTV." In *Storming the Reality Studio*, edited by Larry McCaffery, 334-42.

Stine, R. L. *The Beast from the East*. Goosebumps #43. New York: Scholastic, Inc., 1996.

————————. *Beware of the Purple Peanut Butter*. Give Yourself Goosebumps #6. New York: Scholastic, Inc., 1996.

————————. *The Werewolf of Fever Swamp*. Goosebumps #14. New York: Scholastic, Inc., 1993.

Stine, R. L., as told to Bob Arthur. *It Came from Ohio!: My Life as a Writer*. New York: Scholastic, Inc., 1997.

Susann, Jacqueline. *Valley of the Dolls*. New York: Random House, 1966.

Suvin, Darko. *Metamorphoses of Science Fiction: On the History and Poetics of a Literary Genre*. New Haven: Yale University Press, 1977.

————————. *Positions and Presuppositions in Science Fiction*. Kent: Kent State University Press, 1988.

"A Taste of Armageddon." *Star Trek*. New York: NBC-TV, February 23, 1967.

This Island Earth. Universal, 1955. Shooting script by Edward G. O'Callaghan and Franklin Coen reprinted in Philip J. Riley, editor, *This Island Earth*, 1-109 (original script pagination, also followed in parenthetical citations in the text; script's page one is actually page 52 of the book).

The Time Machine. Galaxy Films/MGM, 1960.

Trimble, Bjo. *The Star Trek Concordance*. New York: Ballantine, 1976.

"The Trouble with Tribbles." *Star Trek*. New York: NBC-TV, December 29, 1967.

Tryon, Thomas. *Crowned Heads*. New York: Alfred A. Knopf, 1976.

2001: A Space Odyssey. Metro-Goldwyn-Mayer, 1968.

"The Ultimate Computer." *Star Trek*. New York: NBC-TV, March 8, 1968.

Van Loan, Charles E. *Buck Parvin and the Movies: Stories of the Motion Picture Game*. New York: George H. Doran Company, 1915. With nine stories: "The Extra Man and the Milkfed Lion," "The International Cup," "Man-Afraid-of-His-Wardrobe," "Water Stuff," "Buck's Lady Friend," "Desert Stuff," "Author! Author!," "Snow Stuff," and "This Is the Life!"

Vidal, Gore. *Hollywood: A Novel of America in the 1920s*. New York: Random House, 1990.

Wells, H. G. *The H. G. Wells Reader* [editor unknown]. Philadelphia: Courage Books, 1996.

————————. *The Time Machine*. In *Three Prophetic Novels of H. G. Wells*, selected and with an introduction by E. F. Bleiler. New York: Dover Publications, 1960, 263-335.

————————. *The Time Machine*. New York: Bantam Books, 1968. Reprinted with new cover in 1976.

Westfahl, Gary. "The Dark Side of the Moon: Robert A. Heinlein's *Project Moonbase*." *Extrapolation* 36 (Summer 1995): 126-35.

————————. "Extracts from *The Biographical Encyclopedia of Science Fiction Film*." *Foundation: The Review of Science Fiction*, no. 64 (Summer 1995): 45-69.

————————. "The Genre That Evolved: On Science Fiction as Children's Literature." *Foundation: The Review of Science Fiction*, no. 62 (Winter 1994/1995): 70-75.

————————. "Janeways and Thaneways: The Better Half, and Worse Half, of Science-Fiction Television." *Interzone*, no. 140 (February 1999): 31-33.

————————. "'Man against Man, Brain against Brain': The Transformation of Melodrama in Science Fiction." In *Themes in Drama, Volume XIV: Melodrama*, edited by James Redmond. Cambridge: Cambridge University Press, 1992, 193-211.

————————. *The Mechanics of Wonder: The Creation of the Idea of Science Fiction*. Liverpool: Liverpool University Press, 1998.

————————. "Mystery of the Amateur Detectives: Gary Westfahl Writes about the Early

Days of the Hardy Boys." *Million: The Magazine about Popular Fiction*, no. 14
(March/June 1993): 24-32.

———. "Point and Cringe: A Non-Innovative, Non-Interactive Column." *Interzone*,
no. 131 (May 1998): 52-53.

———. "Superladies in Waiting: How the Female Hero Almost Emerges in Science
Fiction." *Foundation: The Review of Science Fiction*, no. 58 (Summer 1993): 42-62.

———. "The True Frontier: Confronting and Avoiding the Realities of Space in
American Science Fiction Films." In *Space and Beyond: The Frontier Theme in Science
Fiction*, edited by Gary Westfahl. Westport: Greenwood Press, 2000, 55-66.

———. "Where No Market Has Gone Before: 'The Science-Fiction Industry' and
the *Star Trek* Industry." *Extrapolation* 37 (Winter 1996): 291-301.

———. "The Words That Could Happen: Science Fiction Neologisms and the
Creation of Future Worlds." *Extrapolation* 34 (Winter 1993): 290-304.

———. "Zen and the Art of Mario Maintenance: Cycles of Death and Rebirth in
Video Games and Children's Subliterature." In *Immortal Engines: Life Extension and
Immortality in Science Fiction and Fantasy*, edited by George Slusser, Gary Westfahl,
and Eric S. Rabkin. Athens: University of Georgia Press, 1996, 211-20.

Westfahl, Gary, and George Slusser, editors. *Nursery Realms: Children in the Worlds of
Science Fiction, Fantasy, and Horror*. Athens: University of Georgia Press, 1999.

Whitfield, Stephen E., and Gene Roddenberry. *The Making of Star Trek*. New York:
Ballantine, 1968.

Index

About the Author

GARY WESTFAHL teaches at the University of California, Riverside. In addition to writing a column for the science fiction magazine *Interzone*, he is the author or coeditor of several books on science fiction and fantasy, including *Cosmic Engineers: A Study of Hard Science Fiction* (1996) and *Space and Beyond: The Frontier Theme in Science Fiction* (2000), both available from Greenwood Press.